EUROPEAN WOMEN

EUROPEAN WOMEN

A Documentary History 1789–1945

Edited by

Eleanor S. Riemer
and
John C. Fout

Schocken Books   ●   New York

First published by Schocken Books 1980

10 9 8 7 6 5 4 3 2 1   80 81 82 83

Copyright © 1980 by Schocken Books Inc.

Library of Congress Cataloging in Publication Data
Main entry under title:

European women.

Bibliography: p.
1. Women—Europe—History—19th century—Sources. 2. Women—
Europe—History—20th century—Sources. 3. Women—Employment—
Europe—History—19th century—Sources. 4. Women—Employment—
Europe—History—20th century—Sources. 5. Women in politics—
Europe—History—19th century—Sources. 6. Women in politics—
Europe—History—20th century—Sources. I. Riemer, Eleanor S.
II. Fout, John C., 1937-
HQ1587.E98   301.41'2'094   79-26373

Manufactured in the United States of America

Document 25 is quoted from Fanni Nurina, *Women in the Soviet Union*.
Reprinted by permission of International Publishers.

Document 49 by Aletta Jacobs is quoted from Norman Haire, ed., *Some More
Medical Views on Birth Control*. Reprinted by permission of E. P. Dutton.

Document 50 is quoted from Rudolf Schlesinger, ed., *The Family in the
U.S.S.R.* Reprinted by permission of Routledge & Kegan Paul Ltd.

Illustrations 1-4 and 7-8 are reproduced by permission of the Economic and
Public Affairs Division, The New York Public Library, Astor, Lenox and
Tilden Foundations. Illustration 6 by permission of the General Research
and Humanities Division, The New York Public Library, Astor, Lenox and
Tilden Foundations. Illustration 5 is from the Gerritsen Collection and is
reproduced by permission of the Kenneth Spencer Research Library of the
University of Kansas.

For Joan Kelly, *donna graziosa*

Contents

Illustrations follow page 114

Acknowledgments   xi

Introduction   xiii

Part One: Women and Work   1

I. Varieties of Occupations for Working-Class Women   3

  1. "Working in the fields is not such hard work as working in the factory." (*England, 1843*)   5

  2. A Temporary Shelter for Unemployed Women (*France, c. 1890*)   8

  3. "A Shop Girl's Day in a Clothing Store" (*France, 1897*)   10

  4. A Woman Doctor's Report on Working Conditions for Women in Russian Factories (*Dr. M. I. Pokzovskaia, Russia, 1914*)   12

II. Attempts to Improve Working Conditions and Organize Women Workers   18

  5. Women Workers Strike (*Amalie Seidl, Austria, 1893*)   20

  6. The "Charter of Reforms" of the Women's Co-operative Guild (*England, 1897*)   23

  7. Organizing a Women's Union (*Italy, 1903*)   26

III. Promoting the Employment of Women   29

  8. Society for Promoting the Employment of Women (*England, 1859–1877*)   30

  9. Program and Statutes of the Women's Educational Association in Leipzig (*Germany, 1866*)   37

  10. Opening the German Civil Service to Women (*Germany, 1878*)   40

  11. Women to Women: Handbooks for Choosing an Occupation (*France, 1891; England, 1897*)   42

  12. A School of Social Work for Women (*Paula Mueller, Germany, 1905*)   47

IV. The Meaning of Work for Women   50

13. "Work in some form or other is the appointed lot of all." (*Anna Jameson, England, 1859*) 50
14. "What Is Work?" (*Jenny Heynrichs, Germany, 1866*) 53
15. The Meaning of Work for the Working-Class Woman (*Germany, 1930*) 55

Part Two: Women's Politics 57

V. Middle-Class Women's Politics: Social Reform, Suffrage, and the First Feminist Movement 59
16. "Declaration of the Rights of Woman and Citizen" (*Olympe de Gouges, France, 1790*) 62
17. "Why I Am a Guardian" (*Dora Downright, England, 1888*) 67
18. "The Prisoner" (*Helen Gordon Liddle, England, 1911*) 71
19. The Making of a Militant (*Emmeline Pankhurst, England, 1912*) 75
20. "The Question of the Vote for Women" (*The French Union for Women's Suffrage, France, 1913*) 79
21. "Call to the Women of All Nations" (*Holland, 1915*) 81
22. "Restatement of Policy After 25 Years" (*International Alliance of Women, Germany, 1929*) 84

VI. Working-Class Women and Socialism 87
23. A Socialist Platform for the Protection of Women Workers (*Louise Kautsky [Austria], International Socialist Workers' Congress, Zurich, 1893*) 91
24. Becoming a Socialist (*Austria, 1890s*) 93
25. Women and Socialism in the Soviet Union: An "Official" View (*Fanni Nurina, U.S.S.R., 1934*) 99

VII. Women and Nazism 104
26. Nazi Women (*Germany, 1933*) 106
27. Women Against the Nazis (*Germany, 1930s*) 110

Part Three: Women and the Family in Modern Society 115

VIII. Childhood 117
 28. Home Education for Girls (*Louise D'Aulnay,
 France, 1867*) 119
 29. Combating Child Abuse (*Pauline Kergomard,
 French Association for Child Rescue,
 France, 1880s*) 122
 30. A Working-Class Childhood (*Adelheid Popp,
 Austria, 1880s*) 126

IX. Single Women 132
 31. "Our Social Life Has Changed": Young Women
 in the Victorian Period (*England, 1820 and
 1889*) 135
 32. "Small—Clean—Alone": The Joys of Living
 Alone (*Louise Otto, Germany, 1881*) 138
 33. A Rural Woman: Childhood, Working as a
 Domestic in Paris, Keeping Her Illegitimate
 Child, *Memoirs (Julliette Sauget, France,
 1886–1920*) 141

X. Married Women 146
 34. The Middle-Class Housewife and the Problem
 of Troublesome Domestics (*England, 1860*) 151
 35. The Good Housewife (*Switzerland, 1895*) 155
 36. Advice to Mothers on the Feeding of Children
 (*England, 1897*) 157
 37. Triple Toil: The Life of the Working Wife and
 Mother (*Germany, 1930*) 161

XI. Changing Attitudes toward Marriage and
 Motherhood 163
 38. A Dissatisfied Mother (*Austria, 1899*) 165
 39. The Manipulation of Motherhood (*Germany,
 1907*) 168
 40. The Renaissance of Motherhood (*Ellen Key,
 Sweden, 1914*) 171
 41. Communism and the Family (*Alexandra
 Kollontai, U.S.S.R., 1918*) 176

Part Four: Woman and Her Body   181
  XII. Health, Nutrition, Pregnancy   183
     42. The Importance of Physical Education for
        Girls (*England, 1859*)   187
     43. A Sex Education Guide for Mother and
        Daughter (*Belgium, 1905*)   190
     44. Maternity (*England, 1915*)   193
     45. Letters from Pregnant Working Women
        (*Germany, 1923*)   199
  XIII. Contraception and Abortion   202
     46. Survey of Abortion and Birth Control Methods
        (*Germany, 1913*)   205
     47. "Letters from Struggling Parents" (*England,
        1919 and 1920*)   210
     48. Widening of the Scope of Human Freedom and
        Choice (*F. W. Stella Browne, England, 1922*) 211
     49. The First Birth Control Clinic (*Aletta Jacobs,
        Holland, 1928*)   214
     50. "I Object": Soviet Citizens on Abortion
        (*U.S.S.R., 1936*)   217
  XIV. Sexuality and Sexual Self-Definition   220
     51. "Men Will Have Their Victims" (*Josephine
        Butler, England, 1871*)   222
     52. Challenges to Victorian Morality: Selections
        from *The Adult* (*England, 1897–1898*)   229
     53. "The Truth About Myself": Autobiography of
        a Lesbian (*Germany, 1901*)   232

     Selected Bibliography   237

     Index   253

Acknowledgments

Women's history is a unique field in many respects, not the least of which is the cooperation, sharing of information and ideas, and mutual support among women in the field. This book is thus the result of the efforts—direct and indirect—of many dedicated women. Several individuals require special acknowledgment for their invaluable assistance: Gerda Lerner, who supported the project in its early stages and offered thought-provoking comments and suggestions; Sandra Weinbaum, who read the completed manuscript and made many useful comments on it; Rose-Ellen Schwartz, who read parts of earlier versions; Ann Ilan Alter, who brought document 28 to our attention and translated it; Anne Darrow Vartanian, who translated many of the French documents and assisted in countless other ways; Estelle Rosenbloom and Mary Champ, who typed the manuscript, often under harried conditions.

I also would like to express my gratitude to the students in my course "Women in European Society" at the State University of New York/College at Old Westbury in the spring of 1978, who were the first students to read the documents and whose comments immeasurably helped the final selection process. I also wish to express my gratitude to the Institute for Research in History and its Women's History Research Group for providing an environment in which scholars can meet and freely exchange ideas. Finally, I would like to thank Lawrence D. Cavanagh, Jr., for his aid, understanding, and kindness.

Eleanor S. Riemer

I would like to thank the many people at Bard College who have been so helpful to me while I was working on this book. First, I am very grateful to my colleagues in the Social Studies Division who approved my research grant from the Kellogg Foundation; the grant allowed me the semester off in the spring of 1978 to develop a new course in women's history and to do research on this book. I would also like especially to thank my colleagues in the history department, Professor Christine Stansell and Professor Mark Lytle, for their help and encouragement. My thanks also to Professor Emeritus William Frauenfelder for his help on some of the

German translations. The library at Bard greatly facilitated my work and I am grateful for all the help given by Ms. Ida Brier. With her expertise in inter-library loan, she managed to locate many obscure books both here and abroad. I would similarly thank many of my students for their enthusiastic help, especially those in my women's history class and Daryl Wiltsie, Scott Lithgow, and Victor Victoria. A special word of thanks to Becky Rice, who asked me to do my first tutorial in women's history with her about five years ago; I hope this book will make up for a terrible tutorial.

Our thanks to the Boston Public Library, the New York Public Library, and the University of Kansas. The Kenneth Spencer Research Library of the University of Kansas is the holder of the (Dr. Aletta H. Jacobs) Gerritsen Collection, one of the best collections on European women available in this country. The collection has been microfilmed by the Microfilming Corporation of America and is now available for general use. While that microfilming was underway in New Jersey, the University of Kansas and the Microfilming Corporation of America generously gave us permission to use the collection there. We are very grateful for that permission and the hospitality of the staff of the Microfilming Corporation.

Finally, my thanks to Mr. Edwin Rodriguez and Mr. Al Lewis for their help in taking the photographs. And, my heartfelt thanks to my friend Israel Rodriguez for his boundless help and support.

John C. Fout

Introduction

Until very recently, history has generally been written by men and about men. Historians have either ignored women entirely or dealt with them only peripherally, inasmuch as their lives touched on men's world and men's concerns. Even recent studies that appear to focus on women too often do not concentrate on women's experiences but on what *men* thought about women, the laws *men* made to govern women, or how *men* have oppressed women. That kind of history still considers women in terms of men's ideas, needs, and actions; and so women remain marginal objects in a world centered on men.

This documentary history takes a different approach. It is a woman-centered history. Its aim is to reveal what women themselves were doing, saying, and thinking, the factors that affected their lives, and the motivations that lay behind their actions. It is based on two convictions: first, that women have a unique history, which has been ignored by historians, and second, that to uncover women's past we must turn to women's own words and deeds. Thus, this history of European women focuses directly on women's experiences, aspirations, and consciousness.

The documents in this volume present the thoughts of women who lived in western and central Europe and Russia between the late eighteenth and the mid-twentieth century. A few were written by famous women, but most are the words of unrenowned, "average" women—factory workers, shop clerks, housewives, mothers. It is a commonly held belief among historians and the general public that this kind of material is difficult, if not impossible, to obtain since it is assumed that these women did not write about themselves and no one else thought to ask them about their lives and record their responses. Indeed, when we began our research for this book, we were not certain we would find sources that would accurately reveal the interests and personal lives of the masses of working women and middle-class housewives. However, we soon discovered that our most formidable problem lay not in finding *enough* sources but rather in *selecting* the best and most representative documents from among the wealth of published material at our disposal. We found enough women's sources to fill several volumes in books, women's magazines, and the numerous periodicals written, edited, and sometimes typeset and printed by women, for women. A particularly rich source of documents was the publications of the hundreds of women's organizations—local, national, and international, middle- and working-class—which existed in the nineteenth and early twentieth centuries. Far from being silent about their lives and ideas, European women, especially from the middle decades of the nineteenth century, poured forth a steady stream of books, pamphlets, journals, and broadsides in which they detailed their concerns, activities, and demands. Luckily for scholars, these sources are widely available in libraries and special collections in Europe and America. Moreover, some nineteenth- and twentieth-century women and men amassed large libraries of works by and about women, and some of these have recently been placed on microfilm or otherwise made available to researchers in American libraries.* If historians until now have not used women's own sources to reconstruct women's past, it is only because they have not looked for them.

We made our selections with several considerations in mind. We chose accounts that are typical of women's experiences and at the same time represent as wide a geographical diversity as possible. In addition, for each topic—women's work, women's politics, women and the family, woman and her body—we chose documents by working-class as well as middle- and, to a lesser extent, upper-class women. Each selection, then, whether a report on working conditions in Russian factories, an account of British feminists' political activities, or the letter of a discontented Austrian housewife, illustrates experiences common to women across Europe. Most of the selections from continental Europe have never before been translated into English.

Many hours were spent discussing how to organize this book. Should we begin with family life and women's sexual and reproductive concerns and then proceed "outward" to women's roles in society at large? Or should we start with the major social

*A particularly valuable source is the Gerritsen Collection, recently published on microfilm by the Microfilm Corporation of America. This is the collection of the Dutch feminist Dr. Aletta Jacobs (see document 49) and her husband, C. V. Gerritsen. The collection of the Hungarian feminist and peace advocate Rosika Schwimmer is at the New York Public Library as the Schwimmer-Lloyd collection. Two important microfilm collections on women's history are *Herstory* (Bell and Howell, Wooster, Mass.) and *History of Women* (Research Publications, Inc., New Haven, Conn.).

and economic changes of the period and women's roles in them? We decided on the latter alternative since we believe it is necessary to understand at the outset the changes brought about by industrialization and modernization and women's responses to them. In many instances the material in different sections of the book overlaps, but this merely reflects the impossibility of sorting out one aspect of women's lives from the others. For example, working-class women's roles and responsibilities as wives and mothers often determined whether or not they worked for wages and the kinds of jobs they held. Many middle-class women became involved in social reform activity because they viewed this as a logical and necessary extension of their moral responsibilities as mothers. Women's desires to limit family size, be better educated, and improve their health and working and living conditions also led middle- and working-class women to organize to achieve reforms. For women, motherhood and wage work, health and unionization, sexuality and politics were all interrelated.

Keeping in mind the difficulties and potential dangers involved in dividing up women's lives and concerns, we organized the book into four parts. Part one, "Women and Work" includes documents that illustrate the kinds of paid work done by working- and middle-class women, their attitudes toward work, and how work related to other aspects of their lives. These documents also discuss how women strove as individuals and through their own associations to improve working conditions and wages, train women for jobs and find employment for them, open new fields to women, and professionalize women's unpaid charitable activities in order to create new, paid occupations.

Part two, "Women's Politics," presents an overview of women's political involvement which goes beyond the struggle for the vote and encompasses most of the organized activities of women in the late eighteenth, nineteenth, and early twentieth centuries. The documents illustrate the development of the middle-class social reform and feminist movements, the history of socialist feminism, and women's roles in and opposition to Nazi totalitarianism.

Part three, "Women and the Family in Modern Society," includes accounts of childhood, single womanhood, marriage, and motherhood, as well as documents that discuss women's changing attitudes toward motherhood and family life in the late nineteenth and first part of the twentieth centuries.

The documents in part four, "Women and Her Body," tell us

about women's health problems, their experiences with pregnancy, contraception and abortion, and their views on sex and sexual relationships.

The parts are divided into chapters, each of which has an introduction that provides an overview of the topics discussed in it, fills in gaps, and clarifies major issues. In addition, every document is preceded by a short introduction that provides further information about its author and discusses the selection's importance in terms of the general trends of the period. Documents in one section which bear on the concerns of another have been carefully cross-referenced.

Several points should be mentioned before proceeding to the documents themselves. As the sources clearly show, there were great similarities in the experiences of women of different nationalities all across western and central Europe, and Russia in many instances. Nevertheless, some of the major changes in women's lives occurred at different moments in different countries as each nation underwent successive stages in industrialization and modernization. For example, England industrialized earlier than the rest of Europe, so many of the alterations in women's lives which accompanied the industrial and urban revolutions occurred earlier there than in other countries. Indeed, while western European nations became increasingly urban and industrial in the nineteenth century, Russia remained largely a peasant society. Yet (allowing for some exceptions in Russia) the patterns of work, political activity, and family life were remarkably similar.

While the processes of industrialization and urbanization profoundly changed the lives of all Europeans during the nineteenth and twentieth centuries, they did not affect people of different classes, or of different sexes within the same class, in the same ways. For example, the shift in the primary workplace from the home to the factory and the workshop which accompanied industrialization affected working-class men and women differently. In the pre-industrial domestic economy all family members —wife, husband, even young children—had worked together as a unit, and married women had combined economically productive labor with their child-care and housekeeping responsibilities. Industrialization removed production from the home and made it difficult or impossible for women to earn wages and care for their children and households. While industrialization created new jobs, most of them were restricted to men and single women. Over the course of the nineteenth and early twentieth centuries, married women increasingly found themselves at home caring for their young children and doing unpaid housework while their husbands and older sons and daughters worked away from home for wages. This was a new situation for married women and one that brought with it profound changes in the relationships between wife and husband and mother and child, as the documents in parts one and three illustrate. But these sources also clearly show that married working-class women never totally ceased performing paid labor. Textile workers generally continued to work in factories after they married and had children. Other married women at or near their homes at jobs that allowed them to take care of their families and households while they earned needed income. These women took in boarders, did laundry, did piecework for garment manufacturers and other sewing operations, and peddled goods in the streets. But opportunities for married women to earn wages in these ways decreased as time went on. Moreover, after the passage of compulsory education laws, children remained at home and were dependent longer, and women's child-care responsibilities increased. At the same time, working- as well as middle-class women were bombarded by propaganda that idealized motherhood and women's domestic roles. By the twentieth century it was widely believed that mothers generally did not and should not work and fathers should be the sole breadwinners for their families. This notion came to be accepted as the natural—and historical—order of things, even though the ideal often conflicted with reality.

Middle-class women, too, faced new situations and challenges in the nineteenth and twentieth centuries. Although some lower-middle-class women continued to work alongside their shopkeeper husbands as they had in the past, most married middle-class women did not, and never expected to have to work for wages. Their lives were centered on caring for their children and homes. But most middle-class women did not lead leisured existences. Indeed, they found that the demands on their time and energy increased as modernization progressed, and middle-class families' standards for cleanliness, food preparation, and physical comfort were upgraded.

Middle-class women's maternal and housewifely roles were

justified in the nineteenth century by a twofold conception of women's nature and capabilities. On the one hand, women were considered passive creatures who were physically and intellectually inferior to men. Thus, women needed protection and direction from their fathers and husbands. On the other hand, women, because they were nonaggressive and sexually passive and were removed from the contamination of the competitive workaday world, were deemed morally superior to men and were to be respected for that. A woman's unique capability and greatest responsibility in life was caring for the moral and spiritual needs of her family.

The contradictions within this ideal and women's attempts to reconcile or dispel them are recurring and major themes in the documents. From the middle of the nineteenth century large numbers of middle-class women consciously and methodically expanded their maternal and moral roles— and thus their sphere of competence—outside their homes to society at large. One way they accomplished this was by transforming middle- and upper-class women's traditional, and often haphazard, charitable work into organized movements for social reform. These women became increasingly interested in the problems of poor women and children. They believed they understood and shared many of the concerns of working-class mothers and considered these women and their children the primary victims of the economic and social dislocations caused by urbanization and the new industrial order.

Through their social welfare and reform work, middle-class women gained a sense of both their own competence and their limitations in a world controlled by men. Many also realized that although women of their class expected to be dependent wives, economic and social realities were such that there was no guarantee women would be supported by men throughout their lives. Many came to believe that their own limited educations and the restrictions placed on them by the law and the ideals of ladylike conduct left women ill-equipped for the roles they might have to— or want to—play in life. Thus, the reform of society and reforms for women became closely identified and often were confronted simultaneously by organized women all over Europe.

This activity formed the basis of the first feminist movement, and feminism was at the heart of middle-class women's politics in the nineteenth and early twentieth centuries, as part two clearly shows. The term "feminism" is vague and difficult to define. One recent study calls feminists "all those in the nineteenth century who supported express efforts to ameliorate the conditions of women through public, *organized* activity, be it for educational, legal, political or social purposes."* This is a broad definition, but perhaps it is the best possible one, since women's activities were so varied and broadly based. Feminist women organized to open up work opportunities to women, improve their educations on all levels, end legal discrimination against women, end the sexual exploitation of women and girls, and improve their health. Some women who called themselves or were called feminists by their contemporaries wanted women to be better educated only so that they would be better wives and mothers. Others sought to enter men's spheres and cooperate, or compete, with men in politics and economic life. Many feminists became convinced that the only way to achieve equality and justice for women and improve society was for women to share direct political power with men. These women made gaining the vote their primary target.

One insight to be gained from the documents is that although middle-class feminists were generally very class-conscious and many were concerned primarily with promoting the interests of women of their own class, large numbers of these women recognized strong bonds among all women. Middle-class feminists could empathize with the physical and emotional problems working-class women faced as wives, mothers, and biological females, and genuinely sought to alleviate the oppression of working-class women in the factory and the home. Indeed, the authors of many of the selections in this book appear to feel that women of different classes often had more in common with one another than they did with the men of their own classes.

Working-class women, too, were politically active and organized to promote their interests as women. They formed their own unions in industries where women were the majority of the work force and, although they were often discouraged from doing so, joined men in their unions. Women's demands as workers were often different from men's. Women wanted to improve working conditions and increase wages, just as men did, but they also wanted to secure reforms that would aid them in meeting all their responsibilities as workers, wives, and mothers. Demands for maternity and child-care leaves and shortened working hours for

*Marilyn Boxer and Jean Quataert, eds., *Socialist Women* (New York, 1978), p. 5.

mothers of small children were important among women workers. Working-class women were also active in socialist political parties and revolutionary undergrounds with men of their own class. Some socialist women developed a feminism that differed in significant ways from that of their middle-class sisters. Instead of seeking reforms within the existing capitalist system, socialist feminists saw the root of women's oppression in capitalism and "envisioned a radically transformed society in which men would exploit neither man nor woman."* Unfortunately, socialist men generally insisted that women's needs had to be subordinated to the "larger" working-class struggle and often were hostile to attempts by women to take control of their own lives. Although socialist parties called for the equality of women in all areas of life, they by and large refused women posts of leadership and authority within their organizations. In the first part of the twentieth century, most male leaders refused to support or were openly hostile to working-class women's demands for birth control information and abortion law reform, as part four demonstrates. In these struggles working-class women often found their allies among middle-class feminists.

This introduction has focused on feminism and women's organized activities for several reasons. First, in the nineteenth and early twentieth centuries women acted collectively to bring about changes in all aspects of their lives—personal, educational, sexual, economic, and political. Indeed, the history of women in this period is to a large extent the history of women organizing to define women's issues and meet women's needs. Second, and perhaps most interesting to contemporary readers, the study of middle- and working-class feminism reveals that many of the goals of the current feminist movement in Europe and America are not new ones for European women. Issues such as equal pay for equal work, women's right to enter the professions, the need for women workers to unionize, the necessity of day-care facilities for children of working mothers and the need for pregnancy and maternity leaves, women's right to determine whether or not to bear children—all these and many, many more were raised by women at one time or another during the past two hundred years. Moreover, women realized that if their needs were to be met, they had to educate one another, raise their consciousness (they used the phrase

*Ibid., p. 6.

in the late nineteenth century), and work together. Obviously women were not successful in finding solutions to all their problems, since many are still with us today. But if women in the last part of the twentieth century are to carve out new paths and directions for themselves, they should know what is and what is not new, what has succeeded, what has failed, and why. Women today need to know their past if they are to determine their future.

Part One
—•—
WOMEN AND WORK

If choice of occupation is what you want, surely it may be said, here it is in abundance. But there is one notable fact which ought not to be overlooked: namely, that whatever mill, yard, factory or workshop you enter, you will find the women in the lowest, the dirtiest, and the unhealthiest departments. The reason is simple. The manager of a business naturally asks who will do the inferior work at the lowest rate, and as women's labor is the cheapest, it falls as a matter of course to their share. It is an undeniable fact that in this country a very large proportion of the hard labor is done by women.

"What Are Women Doing?"
English Woman's Journal,
March, 1861, p. 53.

The economical position of women is one of those subjects on which there exists a "conspiracy of silence." While most people, perhaps, imagine that nearly all women marry and are supported by their husbands, those who know better how women live, or die, have rarely anything to say on the subject. Such social problems as this are certainly painful; they may or may not be insoluble; they must not be ignored....

The truth is, that the facts of society have changed more rapidly than its conventions. Formerly muscles did the business of the world, and the weak were protected by the strong; now brains do the business of the world, and the weak are protected by law. The industrial disabilities of women, unavoidable under an earlier regime, have become cruel under the later. There is neither the old necessity of shelter, nor the old certainty of support.

Josephine E. Butler,
The Education and Employment of Women
(London, 1868), p. 3.

A discussion of women's work in the nineteenth and twentieth centuries must begin with the understanding that during the entire period millions of women worked for pay. While attitudes toward work for women and the kinds of jobs women held varied during the period, women never ceased to be employed in large numbers, and work was always a vital concern for them.

Several other important considerations about women's work must be kept in mind. First, although different countries underwent industrialization at different times, the economic and social changes that accompanied industrialization and modernization were quite similar. Thus the pattern of work for women was essentially the same across Europe. It must be emphasized, however, that middle- and working-class women had vastly different work experiences, and that the patterns of work for married and single women were different. Single women generally benefited more from expanding work opportunities than did married women, who were more restricted because of family responsibilities and who were often victims of intense prejudice against their working. Finally, while this chapter is concerned with the paid labor of women, it must be remembered that the majority of women, whether they worked for wages or not, still worked in their homes without pay. Many middle-class women also worked as unpaid volunteers in the vast network of charitable activities which they organized.

This part is concerned with a number of aspects of women's work. The first chapter (documents 1-4) describes working conditions for working-class women. The second (documents 5-7) describes how these women began to organize themselves to oppose the exploitative conditions under which they labored. The third (documents 8-12) is concerned with the efforts of middle-class women to promote the employment of women of their own class by professionalizing traditional women's work and creating new jobs for women. The fourth chapter (documents 13-15) illustrates the meaning of work for women.

I

Varieties of Occupations for Working-Class Women

The varieties of occupations and the working conditions described in the documents in this chapter clearly reveal the abysmal working conditions under which working-class women labored in the nineteenth and early twentieth centuries. During this period the jobs open to women were those that required the least skills, were the lowest paid, and often involved the heaviest physical labor. Women's wages were habitually 20 to 50 percent lower than men's despite the fact that they worked just as hard or harder. Women had practically no access to the higher-paid, skilled occupations; men, fearing women's competition, reserved those jobs for themselves and barred women from apprenticeships in guilds and unions which would have provided the necessary training. Although new jobs were opened to women by the twentieth century and working conditions would improve, the dismal pattern of women's employment remained the same.

Women were represented in a vast array of occupations including many that have been traditionally thought of as men's. As one mid-nineteenth-century observer noted:

> They are to be found in metal-works, nail-works, rope-works, lead-works—in bleaching-mills, paper-mills, silk-mills and cloth-mills—in glass-houses, potteries, and brick-yards, and at the mouths of coal-pits and stone-quaries, where the "bank-women" are described as working "not like men, but like horses."*

Women obviously held a wide variety of jobs in the nineteenth century, but the majority of nonagricultural women workers were concentrated in three areas: domestic service, the garment industry, and textiles. Of these, the first was a traditional woman's

---

*"What Are Women Doing?," *English Woman's Journal*, March 1861, pp. 52–53.

occupation, and the second, also a traditional occupation, was generally not touched by industrialization. It remained a home industry or evolved into the infamous sweatshops where pay was lower than in factories and work was seasonal (often there was no work in slack periods and twenty-hour days in the heavy season). The textile industry was the only one of the three that was fully industrialized and provided millions of women and children with factory employment. By the twentieth century, working-class women worked at a myriad of new industrial jobs opened up by advancing technology and mass production, but still were generally confined to unskilled positions which were poorly paid.

The textile factories in which women worked were notorious for dangerous machinery, long working hours (in the early period as many as fifteen to eighteen hours), and lack of sanitary facilities for the workers; no toilets, no place to eat or rest, and often little or no time for either. What is more, we have come to realize how dangerous these factories were to health. Workers were subjected to excessive heat and contamination through exposure to chemicals and especially fibers that we now know cause "brown lung" and related diseases which bring on disability and early death. This exposure was prolonged since in the early stages of industrialization children entered the factories as young as five or six. To stop workers from rebelling against the low wages and the inhuman working conditions, factory owners maintained a brutal system of control which included punishments in the form of instant dismissal, transfer to the worst jobs, and a series of fines for the slightest infractions of factory discipline. Women, of course, shared many of the above disabilities with male workers. Women, however, also were sexually abused and exploited in factories owned and run by men. This was condoned within a system in which even the government inspectors were men, and women faced punishments or dismissal if they resisted. Finally, it was not until the late nineteenth century that women began to receive limited maternity benefits and protection.

Women's work in agriculture was equally hard. Married rural women had the responsibility for their households and the care of their families, and in addition were responsible for a garden plot or a small number of farm animals which provided much needed income for families where husbands' wages were never sufficient. Married women often also have a third burden, working as day laborers, especially at harvest time. Young unmarried women, as a rule, did not remain at home, since their families could not afford to support them. They went off to work for larger landowners as domestic servants and farm helpers or, if such employment was not available, went to work in local factories. Once married, they could not continue their "live-in" agricultural life. Rural women who worked in factories usually gave up that work, too, after the birth of one or two children. Prejudice against employing married women, the double burden of family responsibilities and long working hours in the factories, and the limited mobility of married women combined to force women to give up factory work. They then turned to home industry or agricultural employment, which was generally available only on a seasonal basis.

Document 1

The accounts of the three women below were given as testimony before special assistant Poor Law Commissioners, government officials making a parliamentary inquiry into conditions of agricultural labor. Although these women found agricultural labor hard, they readily preferred it to working in factories. They could bring nursing infants into the fields and leave earlier than the men to attend to household chores. The poverty of these women is readily apparent; wages were so low that everyone except the very youngest children had to work. There was never enough food, and the women and children were even less well fed than men; what little meat they had was usually reserved for their husbands. Since the testimony was given to the government officials responsible for the disbursement of money to the poor, these women were anxious to present themselves as hard-working, "worthy" poor.

"Working in the fields is not such hard work as working in the factory.".
England, 1843

Mrs. Smart, Calne, Wiltshire
I went out leasing (gleaning) this autumn for three weeks, and was very lucky: I got six bushels of corn. I got up at two o'clock in the morning, and got home at seven at night. My other girls, aged

Reports of Special Assistant Poor Law Commissioners on the Employment of Women and Children in Agriculture (London, 1843), pp. 65-68.

10, 15, and 18, went with me. We leased in the neighbourhood, and sometimes as far as seven miles off.

I have had 13 children, and have brought seven up. I have been accustomed to work in the fields at hay-time and harvest. Sometimes I have had my mother, and sometimes my sister, to take care of the children, or I could not have gone out. I have gone to work at seven in the morning till six in the evening; in harvest sometimes much later, but it depends on circumstances. Women with a family cannot be ready so soon as the men, and must be home earlier, and therefore they don't work so many hours. In making hay I have been strained with the work: I have felt it sometimes for weeks; so bad sometimes I could not get out of my chair. In leasing, in bringing home the corn, I have hurt my head, and have been made deaf by it. Often, out of the hay-fields, myself and my children have come home with our things quite wet through: I have gone to bed for an hour for my things to get a little dry, but have had to put them on again when quite wet. My health is very good now.

I generally had 10d. a-day, sometimes as much as 1s. a-day. My husband earns 15s. a-week, but his employment is not regular. Our boys are brought up to their father's work.

We pay 7£ a-year rent for our cottage and large garden. There are three rooms in the cottage; two bed-rooms, in which we have three beds; and we find great difficulty in sleeping our family. When we wash our sheets, we mush have them dry again by night. In the garden we raise plenty of potatoes. We have about a shilling's worth of meat a-week; a pig's milt sometimes; a pound or three-quarters of a pound of suet. Seven gallons of bread a-week; sometimes a little pudding on a Sunday. I can cook a little. I was, before I married, housemaid, and afterwards cook in a family.

Mrs. Britton, Calne, Wiltshire

I am 41 years old; I have lived at Calne all my life. I went to school till I was eight years old, when I went out to look after children. At ten years old I went to work at a factory in Calne, where I was till I was 26. I have been married 15 years. My husband is an agricultural labourer. I have seven children, all boys. The oldest is fourteen, The youngest three-quarters of a year old. My husband is a good workman, and does most of his work by the lump, and earns from 9s. to 10s. a-week pretty constantly, but finds his own tools,—his wheelbarrow, which cost 1£, pickaxe, which cost 3s., and scoop, which cost 3s.

I have worked in the fields, and when I went out I left the children in the care of the oldest boy, and frequently carried the baby with me, as I could not go home to nurse it. I have worked at hay-making and at harvest, and at other times in weeding and keeping the ground clean. I generally work from half-past seven till five, or half-past. When at work in the spring I have received 10d. a day, but that is higher than the wages of women in general; 8d. or 9d. is more common. My master always paid 10d. When working I never had any beer, and I never felt the want of it. I never felt that my health was hurt by the work. Hay-making is hard work, very fatiguing, but it never hurt me. Working in the fields is not such hard work as working in the factory. I am always better when I can get out to work in the fields. I intend to do so next year if I can. Last year I could not go out, owing to the birth of the baby. My eldest boy gets a little to do; but don't earn more than 9d. a-week; he has not enough to do. My husband has 40 lugs of land, for which he pays 10s. a-year. We grow potatoes and a few cabbages, but not enough for our family; for that we should like to have forty lugs more. We have to buy potatoes. One of the children is a cripple, and the [Poor Law] guardians allow us two gallons of bread a-week for him. We buy two gallons more, according as the money is. Nine people can't do with less than four gallons of bread a-week. We could eat much more bread if we could get it; sometimes we can afford only one gallon a-week. We very rarely buy butcher's fresh meat, certainly not oftener than once a-week, and not more than sixpenny worth. I like my husband to have a bit of meat, now he has left off drinking. I buy ½ lb. butter a-week, 1 oz. tea, ½ lb. sugar. The rest of our food is potatoes, with a little fat. The rent of our cottage is 1s.6d. a-week; there are two rooms in it. We all sleep in one room, under the tiles. Sometimes we receive private assistance, especially in clothing. Formerly my husband was in the habit of drinking, and everything went bad. He used to beat me. I have often gone to bed, I and my children, without supper, and have had no breakfast the next morning, and frequently no firing. My husband attended a lecture on teetotalism one evening about two years ago, and I have reason to bless that evening. My husband has never touched a drop of drink since. He has been better in health, getting stouter, and has behaved like a good husband to me ever since. I have been much more comfortable, and the children happier. He works better than he did. He can mow better, and that is hard work, and he does not mind being laughed at by the other men for not drinking. I send my eldest boy to Sunday school; them that are younger go to the day school. My eldest boy never complains of work hurting him. My husband now goes regularly to church: formerly he could hardly be got there.

Mary Hunt, Studley, Wiltshire

I am in my fiftieth year. I have had 12 children, and, if it please God, I shall very soon have my 13th. I was left early without father and mother, with a crippled brother, whom I had to help to support. I began to work in the fields at 16. I had to work very hard, and got a good deal of lump-work. I have earned as much as 2s.6d. a-day at digging, but I was always considered as a very hard worker. I married at 22, and had to put up with a good deal with a young family; and have often had only salt and potatoes for days together. I was always better when out at work in the fields; and as for hard work I never was hurt by it. I have carried half a sack of peas to Chippenham, four miles, when I have been large in the family way. I have known what it is to work hard.

I think it a much better thing for mothers to be at home with their children; they are much better taken care of, and other things go on better. I have always left my children to themselves, and, God be praised! nothing has ever happened to them, though I have thought it dangerous. I have many a time come home, and have thought it a mercy to find nothing has happened to them. It would be much better if mothers could be at home, but they must work. Bad accidents often happen. I always hold to it to put children out early, and to bring them up to work; they do better. Families are better altogether when children go out regularly; the children are better than when kept at home getting into all sorts of mischief.

Document 2

In an age when there was no unemployment insurance or old-age pensions, unemployed single women, abandoned wives, and widows who did not have relatives to support them had to fall back on meager public assistance or private charitable organizations. Conditions in public workhouses were wretched, since the intention was to make staying in them as unpleasant as possible to keep the poor out and taxes low. Middle- as well as working-class women—governesses, servants too old to work, widows left with children and without resources—could end up in the workhouse. Women, and especially prostitutes, were subjected to the worst treatment of all. The prostitutes, generally working-class women who engaged in prostitution at those times when they could not find other work, resorted to the public workhouse when unable to support themselves on the street. What follows are the regulations of a temporary shelter run by Protestant women in Paris. Conditions in this private shelter were undoubtedly better than any public workhouse. (See also documents 17 and 19.)

A Temporary Shelter for Unemployed Women
France, c. 1890

Regulations
Temporary Shelter for Women
48 rue de la Villette, Paris

This house was founded to take in homeless Protestant women and to provide them with temporary employment.

Children under 10 years of age can be admitted to the house with their mother.

We admit only women recommended by persons known to us; they must be supplied with an admission card, or a note addressed specially to the directress of the shelter.

The admission card entitles one to a week's stay in the house (if there is room). Each card can be renewed three times; but the stay in the house may not be prolonged beyond four weeks; work in the house is compulsory.

We shall attempt as much as possible to adapt the work to the strength and knowledge of each resident.

Work consists of housecleaning, laundry, general housekeeping and work done for the profit of the house.

Any resident who shows ill will or laziness in the work of the shelter cannot continue in residence and will be dismissed by the directress at a moment's notice, the admission card notwithstanding.

"Asile temporaire de jour et de nuit pour femmes ouvrières sans travail et domestiques sans place," rapport présenté par Mme. Seignobos, déléguée, *Actes du Congres International des oeuvres Institutions féminines* (Paris, 1890), pp. 163–65.

Regulations

The daily schedule is as follows: in the morning, after each resident has helped put the rooms in order, the sewing begins. In the summer, the sewing is done from 7 o'clock in the morning to 7 o'clock at night. Bedtime is set at 9 o'clock at night, the prescribed time for closing the doors.

The house does not accept new admissions on Sundays between noon and 4 o'clock during religious services.

The time needed to find a job will be granted to the resident, but they should never go out without the permission of the directress. We rely on the discretion of the residents not to take advantage of leaving the premises, and if possible, to take care of their business by letter.

The directress has the duty and responsibility to check the baggage of each departing resident.

Order and silence are required in the workroom, as well as in the dormitories. Work must be done carefully and regularly, and with entire obedience to the orders of the directress, who has complete authority. Tolerance and peace must reign among all the residents. Any person who causes disorder or trouble or who is guilty of rudeness or any infraction harmful to the good order of the house, will be dismissed immediately by the directress, whenever this occurs.

Document 3

The following article, written by a Parisian shop girl, was printed in a French feminist journal, *The Woman of the Future (La femme de l'avenir)*. It is a particularly moving personal account describing the long working hours and the heavy physical labor that shop clerks endured. While sales work was considered more respectable and cleaner than factory work, it was hardly "genteel." Shop girls were young single women and, as this document illustrates, had little personal life. Some shop owners provided housing for their female employees. While this benefited many young workers, especially new immigrants from the countryside, it also made it difficult for young women to leave their jobs or protest against their low wages and working conditions. If a worker quit or was dismissed, she had to leave the owner's housing immediately. (See document 6.) Most shop girls had to give up their jobs if they married.

In the first half of the nineteenth century most sales clerks were men. In the latter part of the century this field came to be dominated by women and, as in other instances where this happened, it lost status. Nevertheless, more and more jobs were opened in this sector and an increasing number of working women moved into sales work. For efforts to improve working conditions in retail stores, see document 6. (See also part three, chapter IX.)

"A Shop Girl's Day in a Clothing Store"
France, 1897

In the clothing business there are two seasons very different from one another: one is the heavy season and the other the slow. The heavy season causes terrible fatigue as you can judge from this account.

Arriving at 8:15 in the morning, going down to the racks, repeated trips to the stockroom to bring down the merchandise which is likely to be sold during the day (about two thousand garments are sold in a day).

The storeroom is on the sixth floor and the saleswomen carry the clothes down on their arms or balance them against their hips.

After many climbs to the top of the store, after dusting the shelves, comes the best moment of the day: three-quarters of an hour of peace and quiet. There is nothing to say about the food; it is good and adequate.

After lunch quickly back to work. Trips to the front desk, more trips to the racks, more treks to the stockroom, loaded down like pack horses.

Finally, our preliminary physical labors are over; there follows the hubbub of hordes of shoppers.

There is a customer who wants an item that we've been looking for unsuccessfully for a long time and we find it as soon as she leaves.

It's a continual hustle and bustle; we leave one customer for another without forgetting to write down all the information that the manager is liable to ask for whenever it suits him.

Forgetfulness, understandable in such a crowd, is severely punished.

After countless try-ons, the garments are in complete disorder,

"Une journée de vendeuse dans un magasin de nouveautés," *La femme de l'avenir* 1, no. 2 (December 15, 1897), p. 2.

the racks are bare and the clothes lay piled in a heap. If at this moment a customer asks for a jacket, it is absolutely impossible to find the right size unless by some lucky miracle it is at our fingertips.

Finally, the sales are completed; then comes the straightening up, the most tiresome work of the day. We have to put away this formless mass of rags which now lies in a heap on the floor.

At this moment, the dinner bell rings; the second peaceful moments pass too quickly.

Barely rested, we have to climb back up to the shelves, then go back to the display cases, then up to the front desk coming back loaded with garments to put them in their proper places.

At nine o'clock or sometimes at ten o'clock we are free; we return home limping, irritated, exhausted to the point of tears, only to begin again the next day. One day follows the next and they are all the same.

Besides the hard tasks to which we are all subjected, there are others set aside as punishments. These are the errands. We leave in the morning supplied with about fifty cards to bring to the wholesalers. These are orders and complaints for which we must bring back replies.

It is sometimes one o'clock in the afternoon when we return exhausted and terribly hungry after climbing forty flights of stairs. We must run all these errands on foot since we receive no carfare. Sometimes, in order not to be late, we must pay for a bus, or even a taxi.

As for the slow season, it is the best for the saleswomen, because the work is steady and not beyond their strength.

Earnings are on the average of one franc a day and the commission varies between three and twelve francs.

In the slow season, commission earnings are reduced by one half.

Compulsory vacations, involuntary layoffs because of illness or fatigue, and penalties are all factors contributing to the lowering of wages.

Document 4

Although this document describes factory life in Russia shortly before the first world war, it epitomizes women's work in factories all across Europe as each country went through the early stages of industrialization. In western Europe by the 1890s there were some female factory inspectors, and legislation had eliminated some of the worst abuses of factory life, but this was generally not true in Russia before the revolution. (It should be reiterated that even in the West, "improvement" was only relative.) Hard physical labor, wages lower than men's, unhealthy working conditions, long hours, and sexual exploitation were common experiences for Russian women as they were for their European sisters. This report by a woman doctor notes the existence of Russian women's organizations which, like the numerous middle- and working-class womens' organizations in the West, were concerned with women's issues and sought to stop the exploitation of women workers. It also makes it abundantly clear that millions of Russian women worked at hard physical labor in the prerevolutionary era. (See documents 15, 24, 30, 37, 45.)

A Woman Doctor's Report on Working Conditions for Women in Russian Factories
Dr. M. I. Pokzovskaia, Russia, 1914

Reliable information regarding labour conditions as they affect women in Russia is as yet difficult to obtain. There are no official reports or investigations available. The male factory inspectors who could conduct a systematic and detailed investigation into the labour conditions in connection with women factory workers are not sufficiently interested in the matter, and there are no women factory inspectors. The facts quoted in this paper are collected from two prominent labour papers, and from various official and private sources.

The Factory Inspectors' Report for 1911 states that 2,051,198 persons came under the inspection of the department, of which number 1,412,921 were male and 638,277 were female workers. Only factories proper come under the provisions of factory inspection: all workshops, stores and business premises, wholesale depots, and offices, as well as domestic employment, are outside the provisions of such inspection. It is, therefore, reasonable to state that the real number of women engaged as wage earners in Russia is to be counted by millions. From 1901 to 1910 the proportion of female workers to male workers increased 5.1 per

Translated in condensed form from an article by Dr. M. I. Pokzovskaia in the *Woman's Messenger* of July–August and September, 1913, printed in *Jus suffragii*, January 1, 1914, pp. 56–57, and February 1, 1914, pp. 68–69.

cent, the proportion seems, however, to have remained stationary from 1910 onwards. Textile industries absorb the largest number of women workers. Towards the end of 1911 the number of female workers engaged in the manufacture of textiles was 452,924—52.1 per cent of the whole number of workers engaged in such industries. . . .

There is also a large increase of woman labour in the bookbinding, the cardboard, shoe, rubber, and brick-making industries, also in the earthenware and china works. In the year in which the report was published women also began to be employed in printing and stamping works. In 1911 in the province of Kostroma the number of women employed in factories and works, for the first time exceeded the number of men so employed. It is of interest to notice that in some of the works which employ women the latter are made to do the heaviest and hardest physical work which is habitually considered to be men's work. For instance, in several wood depots and saw mills . . . women carry tree trunks and boards to and from the rafts, etc. According to the official report the number of young girls between 14 and 16 years of age who are employed in factories, has, between 1901 and 1911, increased by 53 per cent. In the textile industries alone 50,770 girls were employed in 1911. There were besides 12,501 female children under 14 employed in textile manufactures. In the province of Moscow children of both sexes are employed chiefly in the cotton and silk mills and in the glass factories. . . .

Earnings

The Imperial Commission which sat between 1902 and 1905 with the object of establishing a minimum wage standard in connection with the War Department, established a minimum wage of 21 rbls. for men and 17 rbls. for women per month. . . . The average pay of the female factory worker is below even the above established minimum standard, and, furthermore, since 1902 the cost of living has considerably increased.

Some working women's budgets were brought before the First National Congress of Russian Women by Mrs. Frossina in 1908. One woman cotton operative, 23 years of age, six years employed at the factory, well educated, a member of a trade union, earns 300 rbls. a year. Of this sum, 25 rbls. is sent to her people at her home village; rent of a corner in a room, 42 rbls. a year; food, 132–144 rbls. a year; clothes, boots, underclothing, 43–44 rbls. a year; public baths and laundry (which she does herself) 9.16 rbls.; newspapers, journals, 1.40 rbls.; unforeseen expenses, 20 rbls.; savings, 30 rbls. a year; the remaining 10 rbls. are spent on amusements, union fees, tramways, etc. This is the budget of a worker in the best-paid (textile) industry. Another budget is that of a mother and daughter, and is illustrative of the life of women workers in one of the worst-paid industries. The mother has worked in the factory for 37 years, and she receives 0.75 rbls. a day. The daughter has been employed for seven years, and she receives 0.55 rbls. a day. On an average, and allowing for intervals in employment, they *earn together* 324 rbls. a year. Of these earnings 10 rbls. is sent to a son banished on account of political agitation. The rent of a small room is 54 rbls. a year; lighting and house expenses amount to an additional 2.15 rbls.; boots, clothing, and laundry, 80.40 rbls. as, it is pathetically stated, the daughter likes to dress nicely; the food for both amounts to 131.63 rbls...; it consists chiefly of tea and bread with a meat stew on Sundays and a bottle of milk as a special treat twice a month. Generally speaking, the Russian working woman considers herself comfortably off if she receives 20 rbls. a month. A large number, however, according to the Factory Inspectors' Report, at least half, earn considerably less, and in order to make ends meet they have to rent a corner of a room, share a bed with a fellow-worker, systematically underfed, go without necessary decent clothing, and without recreation, or any intellectual food. Thus they live not temporarily, but permanently, without any hope for improvement in their lot.

The matter of fines which are exacted from factory workers by their employers is a very serious one. Fines are imposed for: late arrival, work which is not found to be up to standard, for laughter, even for indisposition. At a certain well-known calendar factory in St. Petersburg the women workers receive 0.45 rbls. a day, and the fines have been known to amount to 0.50 rbls. a day. At a weaving factory, also in St. Petersburg, women operatives may earn as much as 1.25 rbls. a day, but owing to deductions for various fines the earnings often sink to as low as 0.25 rbls. a day. If a worker is feeling unwell and sits down, a fine is incurred.... If an article is dropped, the fine is [levied and]...if the worker fails to "stand to attention" at the entrance of employer or foreman and until he leaves the room, she is fined.... At a well-known chocolate factory

in Moscow the fine for laughing is 0.75 rbls. and if a worker is 15
minutes late she is dismissed for one week. At another old-
established and famous chocolate factory in case of sudden illness a
woman employee is instantly discharged. In a certain cartridge
factory the workers are searched before leaving, and those who
persist in having pockets are fined. . . .
    In the majority of factories where women are employed the
working day is from 10 to 11½ hours, after deducting the dinner and
breakfast intervals. On Saturday, in many factories the work
sometimes lasts 16 and 18 hours per day. The workers are forced to
work overtime on pain of instant dismissal or of transference to
inferior employment, and in the case of children actual physical
force is used to make them continue in their places. Dining and
lunch rooms are rarely provided, and in many places no definite
time is allowed for meals. In one well-known factory one hour is
allowed for meals, but there is no place where the workers can eat
their food except in the work-rooms or in the lavatories.
    The position of women workers on the tobacco plantations is
the worst. According to a report published by the Sevastopol
branch of the Women's Protective Union, young girls are
sometimes kept at work during 22 hours in the day. Owing to the
difficulties of carrying on the process of breaking the tobacco
leaves in the daytime, the girl-workers are driven into the
plantations at 4 A.M., where they work until 9 A.M. After that they
are engaged in the processes of weighing and tying the packets of
tobacco, which work is continued through practically the whole
day, with the exception of short intervals for meals. At the same
time the women workers are continually exposed to brutal and
degrading treatment and assault. Not infrequently their earnings
are not paid to them.
    It happens sometimes, as on April 25th, 1913, at a cotton
spinning factory in St. Petersburg, that the workers strike as a
protest against the dismissal of old workers and their replacement
by girls between 14 and 16 years of age. The result of the strike was
a wholesale dismissal of all the women, whose places were filled by
young girls. Not infrequently the women strike on account of the
rude treatment which they receive from the foreman, actual bodily
ill-treatment not being unknown. Such strikes rarely accomplish
anything.
    The worst aspect of woman's factory labour is, however, the

moral danger to which women are exposed from those in power over them.

Immoral proposals from foremen and from their assistants are of general occurrence, and women who resist are persecuted in every possible way, and sometimes actually violated. In a large tobacco factory in St. Petersburg the women workers who were asking for raised pay were cynically informed that they could augment their income by prostitution.

All these hard conditions in connection with factory life have the result of driving a certain number of women workers into tolerated houses of prostitution or into the streets. This is directly encouraged by the management of some factories.

The Factory Inspectors' Report for 1911 does not mention, in enumerating the nature of various complaints received from workers, any complaints of a moral nature on the part of women factory workers. This may partly be accounted for by the fact that the women shrink from mentioning these facts to male inspectors, partly on account of the attitude of the inspectors themselves, of whom many consider it perfectly natural that the factory management should, in regard to its female employees, assume the part of the quondam owner of serfs. Women factory inspectors would render invaluable service in protecting women workers from moral exploitation and danger. In February, 1913, a Bill to allow women to act as factory inspectors was introduced in the Imp.[erial] Duma. On April 24th it was debated and favourably received. It was, therefore, a matter of general surprise when the Secretary of the Board of Trade, on behalf of the Government, declared that at a Cabinet Council the Minister of the Department of Trade and Labour had declared that female inspectors would be entirely superfluous, since the male inspectors were carrying out the work of inspecting factories entirely satisfactorily in every way. The Cabinet Council thereupon negatived the proposal of allowing women to act as factory inspectors.

II

Attempts to Improve Working Conditions and Organize Women Workers

The history of women since the late eighteenth century is to a large extent the history of women forming associations to meet their own needs and promote their special interests. These associations were established by women of all classes and addressed a wide variety of issues. Working-class women fought exploitation in the workshops and factories by forming protective societies. Although before the 1870s, many circumstances prevented women from forming their own unions or joining men's unions, there were random efforts at organization. Women struck for better working conditions and higher pay and became increasingly aware of the possibilities these actions offered them. From the 1870s onward, there was a dramatic and steady increase in the number of women participating in union activity all across Europe. This participation was both in women's own unions, which sprang up first in industries in which women workers predominated, and in mixed unions, in which women joined their male co-workers. The mixed unions, however, were dominated by men who were often hostile to women, while other unions completely barred women from membership. Nevertheless women's unionization proceeded apace.

In England, for example, the first women's trade union, that of women employed in bookbinding, was founded in September 1874. Also established in that year were the Society of Dressmakers, Milliners and Mantlemakers and the Society of Upholstresses. In 1900, according to the *Trade Unions Thirteenth Report*,* there were 122,047 women trade union members in Great Britain. Of these, 8,974 were members of unions composed exclusively of women. In all, women were members of 138 different unions and comprised 37 percent of the total membership. In Germany,

*Trade Unions Thirteenth Report—1900 Board of Trade, by the Commissioner of Labor (London, 1901), p. xxi, and Clementina Black, "The Women's Trade Union and Provident League," *The Women's Gazette*, November 3, 1888, p. 6.

according to one report, there were 256,668 women in unions by 1911.† These included bakers and confectioners, artificial-flower makers, brewery workers and millers, bookbinders, printer's assistants, clerks, factory workers, butchers, barbers and hairdressers, gardeners, hotel and restaurant workers, municipal workers, glaziers, shop assistants, woodworkers, fur workers, cooperative storekeepers, leather workers, lithographers, painters, metalworkers, porcelain workers, saddlers and portfolio makers, tailors, boot and shoe operatives, stone workers, tobacco workers, upholsterers, textile workers, transport workers, home workers, sick attendants, and workers in foodstuff trades.

Women were somewhat slower than men to unionize, for a number of reasons. One important factor was that women were largely confined to unskilled jobs, and were thus easily replaced and vulnerable to employer pressures. Another obvious consideration was that married women workers had two and sometimes three occupations: their work for wages, their unpaid housework if they had children, and child-care responsibilities (see document 37). Women simply had less time than men to participate in union activities. What is more, women were less well educated than men and had less experience in public life. The fact that many women did not work in factories but in home industries and scattered workshops meant that they were not easily organized into unions. The hostility of men who viewed women as competitors for their jobs also served to limit women's participation in many unions. Finally, in some countries women were legally barred from political activities. Since most unions were associated with socialist political parties, these restrictions discouraged women from joining unions.

Another form of association which sought to improve the lot of workers was the cooperative. The cooperative movement sought to provide cheap goods and services and better wages and working conditions for workers. There were producer cooperatives (farm cooperatives for example), cooperative stores, cooperative laundries, etc. The cooperative movement proved very beneficial to women, especially married women, both as workers and as consumers.

†*Special Report submitted to the Fourth Convention of the National Women's Trade Union League of America*, submitted by the Women Workers' Secretariat of the General Commission of Trade Unions of Germany (Berlin, 1913), pp. 4–6.

Document 5

The textile industry was a major employer of European women in the nineteenth century. Some textile factories employed only women, while in many others women were the majority of the work force. The textile industry was one of the few which employed large numbers of married as well as single women, so women worked in textile factories for most of their lives. Amalia Seidl's experiences in an Austrian textile factory in the late 1890s were similar to those of textile factory workers across Europe. Low wages, miserable working conditions, and attempts to organize led her and her co-workers to strike. Out of that strike and the solidarity that evolved from it, emerged a women's union. Amalia Seidl was typical of many early union activists whose union activity led them into wider political involvements. (See documents 15, 24, 30, 37, and 45.)

Women Workers Strike

Amalie Seidl, Austria, 1893

About twenty years ago, conditions in the Viennese textile industry were considerably worse than they are now, which doesn't mean that women workers today have cause for satisfaction. In 1892, when at the age of 16 I began working in a textile factory, the work day was from 6 in the morning to 7 in the evening. The workers were not organized and had to be satisfied with wages of Kronen 1 to Kr. 1.50 a day. One cannot imagine how low the living standard was for women workers. In 1893, I worked in a factory that employed about 300 men and women workers of whom a majority did not earn more than Kr. 7 a week. One of the demands of the subsequent strike was a weekly wage of Kr. 8. As packer in the warehouse, I was paid the splendid wage of Kr. 10 and belonged to the ranks of the best-paid women workers. Although we were in no way organized, I succeeded in making my colleagues understand the importance of a May Day celebration, and we were successful in getting the first of May off. The following day, the one and only topic of conversation in the factory was the events of that May Day. I tried to convince the workers during the rest period

Amalie Seidl, "Der erste Arbeiterinnenstreik in Wien," in *Gedenkbuch 20 Jahre österreichische Arbeiterinnenbewegung*, ed. by Adelheid Popp (Wien, 1912), pp. 66–69.

in the factory's large hall that with an appropriate organization, we could improve our working conditions. No one noticed in the course of my speech, which was intently listened to, that the head of the factory had also listened, perhaps for several minutes. It goes without saying that a punishment followed at once, namely, my dismissal. I learned upon returning to the warehouse that my working papers were ready for me at the office. Since I had worked overtime, I hadn't left the factory at the same time as the others, who, by the way, must have heard about my dismissal. When I reached the street where my parents lived, I saw to my astonishment that the police were stationed at the front door and the door itself was locked. The rather spacious court yard was crowded with women workers from the factory waiting for me and shouting that they wouldn't take my dismissal lying down. I addressed them from a stump telling them that this was all very nice, but if they really wanted to go on strike, they should demand more than just my reinstatement. What we should demand, we didn't really know, but strike we would. We agreed in the end that I should show up at the factory the next day (May 3); by then they would have reached a consensus about demands and also would have agreed on the colleagues who were to transmit the demands of the women workers to the administration. I was to wait by the windows for news of the outcome. All this was carried out; the demands for a reduction of working hours from 12 to 10 and my reinstatement were rejected. Because of the great heat in the work rooms, the women stood about half dressed and went barefoot, but at a moment's notice, they all left the factory, their clothes on their arms and carrying the baskets with the meager midday meal or their containers of coffee. They got dressed on the grounds of a nearby inn while I rushed to comrade Dworschak (Popp)* to bring her the news of the strike. The first meeting was promptly held in the afternoon on the Meidling meadowlands. The work force of three other factories also joined us, and after a few days about 700 women were on strike. It caused a sensation, this being the first women's strike [in Vienna], and the bourgeois press took notice of it, complaining that now women workers also were being "incited." There were exceptions. The correspondent of an English bourgeois daily wrote that "the strikers who used the 14 days mainly for recreation in the open air looked considerably

*See document 30.

better at the end of the strike than before." No wonder! They could hardly be expected to look blooming with a work day of 12 and 13 hours in rooms where the temperature sometimes rose to 54°C. [126°F.] or in the bleachery with its stench of chlorine, or in the dye shop where "lovely" fumes made breathing a torture. Thanks to the solidarity of the labor movement, we were so well supported that we received only a little less money than what we got in the factory. There was no question that the strikers would not give in; they were going to stand firm. After holding out for 14 days, they had their way. The demands were met: a ten-hour work day, a weekly minimum wage of Kr. 8, May 1 to be a holiday, and also my reinstatement in the Heller factory from which I had been dismissed. A great number of women joined the organization but only to turn their backs on it as soon as I left the factory. Also the *Women Workers' Newspaper (Arbeiterinnen-Zeitung)* was widely read for a while.

I naturally had to do a lot of speaking during the strike (as well as I was able to at that time) and as a result was drawn into the workers' movement. I had been a member of the Workers' Educational Club VI as early as the fall of 1892 and had attended a women's meeting where I heard comrade Anna Boschek speak. The fact that such a young woman dared to speak in public made a great impression on me and aroused my desire to be able to do the same; but I lacked the courage. I gave it a try nevertheless at a big meeting of the dyers in a hall in Rudolfsheim on the first of May 1893. Then came the strike and I had to speak. In the course of some meetings in the summer and fall of 1893, I was indicted for different violations of the penal code and sentenced to three weeks in prison which I served in February 1894 in the state penitentiary. I still remember how pleasantly surprised I was when I entered "the cell." It was a large, well-lighted, friendly room which I had to share with 12 to 17 convicts. Since the Viennese state penitentiary at that time had no facilities for "political females" I didn't get a single cell, nor did I know that I could have asked for one; besides, I probably wouldn't have dared. But prison life was bearable, for I was in no way spoiled at home. And I fared a lot better than during the time when I had been a servant girl with a monthly wage of Kr. 6.

But a "subversive person" I must have been! My defense counsel, Dr. Ornstein, had to intervene because the police, despite my living with my parents, wanted to deport me to my father's home town, a Bohemian village. After my discharge I had to sign an affidavit at police headquarters which gave the police the right to remove me from Vienna, should I be convicted again. Since that time, conditions in Austria have changed to the extent that we enjoy today much greater freedom of speech. Hence, I suffered no further punishment, although such a prospect would have deterred me in no way. I have spoken in hundreds of meetings without getting into conflict with the law. I am also active in the party, to the extent that my family situation permits. Now that my children have less need of me, I have been especially interested in the [socialist] cooperative movement which, like the trade unions and political movements, is necessary for the rise and ultimate victory of the working class.

Document 6

The Women's Co-operative Guild was founded in Britain in 1883 as an auxiliary of the Co-operative Societies, organizations of men and women which established and ran cooperatives. The Guild organized married women into consumer cooperative societies and lobbied to improve the wages and working conditions of workers and the health, legal, and political rights of women whether they were wage earners or not (see document 44). In 1897 the Guild sought to improve the working conditions of saleswomen in cooperative stores and in so doing to set an example for ordinary stores to follow. The Guild also vigorously supported the Shop Assistants' Trade Union in its efforts to win improvements for its members. The Guild's "Charter of Reforms" of 1897 is reproduced here. It should be noted that the program would just begin to alleviate the harsh working conditions under which shop women lived and labored.

The "Charter of Reforms" of the Women's Co-operative Guild
England, 1897

There are certain harmful conditions of employment often

Lilian Harris, *The Treatment of Women Employés in the Co-operative Movement* (Manchester, 1897), pp. 11–13.

found in ordinary shops, from which the co-operative stores with which we are concerned are almost entirely free.

1. Very late hours, which mean a day of fourteen or fifteen hours work to the employés, are almost unknown. One store keeps open till 11, and one till 10.30 o'clock one day in the week, and in sixteen the hour of closing on the late night is 10 o'clock. But most of the others close at 9 o'clock on their late night, and a good many never keep open later than 8.30 o'clock.

A short day once a week is also found in all these stores, and in nearly every case it is a real half-holiday, the store being closed at noon, or in some cases at 1 o'clock in the morning. A few stores do not shut till 1.30 or 2 o'clock, and there is an instance where the name of half-holiday cannot be given to the short day, as the store keeps open till 5 o'clock.

2. One of the great evils that shop assistants suffer from in ordinary shops, especially where they "live in," is the short time allowed for meals and rest. We hear of half-an-hour for dinner and a quarter-of-an-hour for tea being the whole time in a day of thirteen or fourteen hours, which a girl has, not only for meals, but for rest also. And even this time is often shortened if customers happen to come in at meal times. In the report of the labour commissioners, evidence is given showing how bad this is for the girls, who have not time to eat a proper meal in the middle of the day, and are too worn-out to eat it at night; whose health is injured by "bolting" their food, and who suffer from illnesses brought on by the long hours of standing.

Guild members who deal only at their stores can feel satisfied that the girls who serve them are not suffering in this way. "Living in" is unknown, and the general custom is for the employés to go home for their dinner. As a rule, an hour is allowed for dinner, and half-an-hour for tea, and sometimes a longer time is given. Seats are provided for shop assistants in about half the stores.

3. Another custom occasionally found in shops is that no notice of leaving should be given on either side, with the result that girls have sometimes been turned away late at night in a place where they had no friends and nowhere to go. None of our 104 stores are guilty of such a custom, and a week or a fortnight's notice or pay must be given on either side. Sometimes the length of notice is a month, but a week is the most usual term.

4. Lastly, *fines* are practically unknown in co-operative stores.

Only two societies report any system, and in one it is stated that they are never enforced. In societies where bonus is given, it is sometimes withheld if not deserved, and cashiers are obliged to make up deficiencies in cash. . . .

Limited Hours and a Minimum Wage

There can be no doubt that the first requisite is a *limit to the weekly hours* and a *minimum living wage*. As regards the former, the eventual aim of all workers, men and women alike, is *the forty-eight hours week*. And it will hardly be questioned that any sum under 15s. a week must mean pinching and privation, with no chance of providing for old age to the woman who is dependent on it, and who very probably has others to support as well as herself.

It may seem a dream to some to look forward to all women earning not less than 15s. a week, or working not more than forty-eight hours a week; but we find each of these conditions carried out to some extent in two districts—the short hours in the North, and good wages in Lancashire.

What Shop-Assistants Ask For

But it will doubtless take some time before this goal can be attained, and in the meantime it is necessary to take gradual steps towards it. By so doing co-operators will not only be helping their own employés, but will strengthen the hands of the Shop Assistants' Trade Union, which is seeking to improve the conditions of all shop-assistants. In the bill they have introduced into Parliament we see what the shop-assistants themselves declare is necessary. The chief points are:

1. A limit of the daily hours of work by closing all shops at stated times.
2. A limit to the time shop-assistants can be kept after closing hours.
3. Regular hours for meals.
4. Improved sanitary arrangements in shops, and where assistants "live in," in the sleeping accommodation.
5. Seats for women employés.

It would of course make it even easier for co-operative stores to shorten their hours if such a bill affecting all shop assistants were passed, and it is to the direct money interest of co-operators to support it.

Our Charter of Reforms

But co-operators can begin without waiting for the outside
world; and the standard below which it seems to me no co-
operative store should fall may be summed up as follows:

1. Early closing of stores, so that no employé should work
   more than fifty-two hours a week.
2. No woman over eighteen to be paid less than 10s. a week.
3. The abolition of overtime.
4. Good sanitary accommodation for women, separate from
   that for men.
5. Cloak rooms and lavatories in new buildings, and dining
   rooms where desirable.
6. Proper arrangements for keeping the sanitary accommodation, cloak rooms, dining rooms, etc., clean and in
   good order at the expense of the store, and not of the
   workers.
7. The amount of wages offered to be stated in all
   advertisements of situations.
8. Sick pay.
9. One week's holiday in addition to all general and bank
   holidays.
10. No holiday without pay.
11. Early shopping, so that shop assistants may be able to
    leave when the store closes.

Document 7

During the nineteenth century most governments enacted
various kinds of "protective" legislation for women and child
workers. These laws limited the hours women and children could
work, set a minimum age for child labor, and prohibited the
employment of women and children in some "dangerous"
occupations. Unfortunately, these protective laws often worked to
the detriment of the women they were supposed to aid. In the
absence of a minimum hourly wage, limits on the number of hours
women could work resulted in lower earnings. Furthermore, the
restrictions completely closed certain occupations to women, and
in other cases employers refused to hire women, who were
prohibited from working at night or overtime.

The Italian working women who wrote the letter which follows were victims of this kind of protection. When the Italian Parliament limited the number of hours women could work, they could not earn enough to support themselves. They then turned to unionization to alleviate their plight and wrote to English women unionists for advice and help. That they sought the aid of English women is striking evidence of women's efforts to aid one another, the international character of women's organizations, and consciousness among women of their common experiences and needs (see documents 23 and 39).

Organizing a Women's Union
Italy, 1903

Chamber of Labor
Union of Tailoresses, Dressmakers and Allied Trades
Turin, Corso Siccardi 12

Respected Madam,
    The financial, physical and hygienic conditions in which the woman worker, and the tailoress in particular, finds herself, are so deplorable and depressing that they have aroused a feeling of indignation even among persons opposed to all civil and humanitarian progress, and have induced favorable consideration for a law to regulate the labor of women and children. Such a law, protective of an oppressed class, was recently approved by the clerical and middle-class Parliament of Italy, having been carried through by the valiant efforts of the numerically small Socialist party. But although some small improvement in the matter of the duration of hours of work has been thus secured, we nonetheless feel ourselves morally helpless in face of the economic conditions which exist. No one of us can by twelve hours of work (the maximum permitted by the law referred to) earn a living while wages remain at their present absurd rate. We are thus compelled to work "double," supplementing our labor in the workshop by labor at home, if we wish to gain an honest livlihood. These things being so, and we being touched to the heart by the enchanting

This document has been slightly edited for clarity from a poor English translation which appeared in an English Trade Union magazine, *The Women's Trade Union Review*, no. 58, July 1905, p. 42.

words "brotherhood" and "solidarity," we, on the 22nd of November, 1903, formed ourselves into a union; and, knowing the importance that the economic conditions of our fellow working women beyond the Alps are superior to our own, we look towards you in longing, the cry of our oppressed soul vibrates thrillingly in your ear; may this, our fervent appeal to your uprightness, your knowledge, not be made in vain! We trust in your exquisite kindness you will make known to us what are the wages earned by our comrades "over there." What is the length of their working day, and what are the top prices given for complete models, dresses, and suits of clothes? Our union will base its aspirations on the evidence of your conditions; it will know how to fight and win. With the hymn of our victory will mingle the effulgent glory of your wise example.

Thanking you heartily in anticipation and pledging ourselves in all cases to fellowship, we greet you fraternally.

The Committee

In view of the difficulty of the work upon which our union is about to enter, we shall be most grateful to you for a speedy reply.

III

Promoting the Employment of Women

The 1850s and 1860s saw the beginning of a virtual revolution in attitudes toward work among middle-class women. Women reacted against the nineteenth-century ideal of the "perfect lady"—the "angel in the house," a wife whose passivity, domesticity, and economic dependence were a comfort to her husband and a symbol of his middle-class status. To have a wife who did not have to work was visible testimony to a middle-class man's success. However, the realities of nineteenth-century economic life and women's own needs and desires were often contrary to this ideal. By midcentury it was apparent that many middle-class women could or would not live their lives in that way.

Many women never married at all, and those who did were not necessarily assured of sufficient support either during their married lives or in widowhood. In England the census of 1861 reported a total female adult population of 5,782,983, and of these, 3,436,729—single women, wives, and widows— worked for their own subsistence. Moreover, the number of single women and widows supporting themselves had increased from 2 million in 1851 to 2.5 million in 1861. "This is not an accident," Josephine Butler proclaimed; "it is a new order of things."* Among those women employed outside the home was a sizable number from the middle class; women who had been brought up to be ornamental ladies, but found they had to provide their own support. However, most were unable to find employment that would allow them to preserve their middle-class status.

For these women the problem was twofold: lack of education and lack of opportunity. Because of their limited education and the prejudice against women working, few occupations aside from

---

*Josephine E. Butler, *The Education and Employment of Women* (London, 1868), p. 4. (See document 51.)

governess were open to them (see document 28). But there were not enough positions as governess to meet the needs of those who had to work and, what is more, many middle-class women found this occupation—with its servantlike aspects—distasteful and unrewarding.

Women who were cognizant of the problems resolved that they themselves had to take action if women's needs were to be met. Women had to be better educated, both for traditional women's occupations and to be able to compete for jobs with men. Furthermore, it soon became apparent that new types of work had to be provided for women. Individual women began by writing essays and books in which they tried to make women and men aware of the need for women to work and the benefits of work for women themselves and society as a whole (see documents 13 and 14). Women's periodicals were founded which spoke specifically to these issues. Yet women realized that discussion was not enough; they had to organize if they were to bring about change. Thus during the latter half of the nineteenth century they founded organizations all across Europe to help women find employment.

At first, many of the organizations saw their goal as finding whatever jobs they could for women who had to earn their livelihood. However, their members quickly realized the complexities of women's problems and began to address themselves to a wide variety of goals and issues. Hundreds of organizations appeared; some dealt with specific issues such as the legal status of women, opening university education to women, or finding women employment in specific fields. Others correctly perceived that the important concerns were all interrelated and addressed several simultaneously. Thus, not only work but numerous other women's issues were consciously raised and addressed by formal organizations and in journals and magazines written and edited by women for women. This process was the birth of the modern middle-class feminist movement (see part two, chapter V).

Document 8

In England the struggle to change attitudes toward work for middle-class women and to secure employment for them was led by the *English Woman's Journal* and its outgrowth, the Society for Promoting the Employment of Women. The *Journal* was founded in 1858 by a group of women which included Bessie Rayner Parkes, who was one of its editors until 1867 and is the author of the second selection reproduced here. One early issue of the *Journal* referred to itself as the publication of the "working portion of our sex... from the seamstress to the artist and literary woman—who have their bread to earn."* The feminist editors of the *Journal* recognized the complex interrelationships among women's issues and published articles on a wide variety of topics. Although the Journal and the Society were primarily concerned with middle- and upper-middle-class women, they sometimes addressed the needs of lower-middle-class and working-class women as well. Like women engaged in similar endeavors all over Europe (a women's employment bureau opened in Germany in the 1860s, for example), these English women were astonished and overwhelmed by the numbers of women who sought work. They were also dismayed by the women's inadequate preparation to support themselves. These feminists attempted to solve these problems in several ways: by operating an employment register, by organizing classes to provide women with technical education, and by campaigns to persuade employers to hire women.

Some of the most significant practical efforts of the Society were classes that trained women to be secretaries and bookkeepers, occupations which until then were exclusively held by men. As the third selection below shows, the Society then sought out employers who would hire those women. Ironically, their very success in promoting clerical work as a "sedentary occupation," naturally suited to women's nature, helped to create the stereotype of the female secretary. Thus, although white-collar jobs were opened to women and white-collar work became a major area of employment for women, they were relegated to the worst-paid and lowest-status positions, from which there was no opportunity to advance. The concentration of women in clerical work was so great that by the twentieth century a "pink-collar ghetto" had emerged.

---

*"Association for Promoting the Employment of Women," *English Woman's Journal*, September 1860, p. 54.

Society for Promoting the Employment of Women
England, 1859-1877

Yet, what is it we working women ask? What is it we are made to think and feel through every fibre of the frame with which it has pleased God to endow us as well as men, and for the maintenance of which in health, ease, and comfort, we, with men, have equal rights?

It is work we ask, room to work, encouragement to work, an open field with a fair day's wages for a fair day's work; it is injustice we feel, the unjustice of men, who arrogate to themselves all profitable employments and professions, however unsuited to the vigorous manhood they boast, and thus, usurping women's work, drive women to the lowest depths of penury and suffering.

We are sick to our hearts of being told "women cannot do this; women must not do that; they are not strong enough for this, and that, and the other" while we know and see every hour of our lives that these arguments are but shams; that some of the hardest and coarsest work done in this weary world is done by women, while, in consequence of usurped and underpaid labor, they are habitually consigned to an amount of physical endurance and privation from which the hardiest man would shrink appalled.

"A Year's Experience in Woman's Work"

In November, 1859, the *English Woman's Journal* had already been dealing with the various questions of woman's industry for not quite two years. The Society for Promoting the Employment of Women was as yet inchoate, but maturing its plans. A Reading-room for ladies, and a Register for noting applications for the more intellectual and responsible departments of female labor, had just been brought into existence. Such was the beginning of our present organization, a year ago. Last winter every department received a great accession of funds and of activity. The Journal greatly increased in circulation; the Society was absorbed into one created

"Association for Promoting the Employment of Women," *English Woman's Journal*, September 1860, p. 55.

"A Year's Experience in Woman's Work," *English Woman's Journal*, October 1861, pp. 112-17.

by and dependent on this Association, with a committee of twelve ladies and twelve gentlemen, which immediately began to consider the formation of model industrial classes; the Reading-room was removed to large and excellent premises in a central situation; and, as a natural consequence of these improvements, to which a wide publicity was given by the press, the Register was literally deluged with applicants. . . .

When first this Register was opened, it was merely intended to act in a limited way among the ladies at that time subscribing to the *English Woman's Journal*, who, in those days of its infancy, numbered a few hundreds. Many of these ladies were actively concerned in charity; and had founded, or supported, or visited, industrial schools, and small hospitals, homes for invalids, and refuges of different kinds—institutions, in fact, requiring female officers. We thought that by opening a register which should act merely among our subscribers, we might occasionally find opportunities of putting the right woman into the right place; that Mrs. A. might recommend an excellent matron or school teacher, and Mrs. B. hear of her through our simple plan, combining an entry in a register book and an advertisement in the Journal for the current month. If in this way we get two really good and well-trained officials placed in a month, it would compensate for the little extra trouble. Being thus, as it were, a plan private to the circulation of the Journal, it was not otherwise advertised, nor was any publicity then sought for it. But when the whole question started into life, the advertisements put forth by the Society appear to have aroused the attention of women in all parts of the country; and as the Society and the Journal now had contiguous offices in the same house, no practical distinction could be made, and the secretaries of either were literally deluged with applications for employment. We had no sooner explained to the ladies who came on Thursday that the formation by the Society of model classes or businesses for a select number did not imply an ability on our part to find remunerative work for indiscriminate applicants, than the same task had to be gone over again on Friday. Indeed, I remember one Friday, in the month of March, when twenty women applied at our counter for work whereby they could gain a livlihood—all of them more or less educated—all of them with some claim to the title of lady.

Although not professing personally to enter into these applica-

tions, the replies to which devolved on the secretaries, I was very
constantly in the office of the Journal when they were made, and
entered into conversation with the ladies; in many cases, indeed,
they came with notes of introduction to me or to my co-editor, and
I had to ask them what kind of work they wanted, and, indeed, a
more important question, for what kind of work they were fitted.
In this way we may certainly lay claim to have heard more of
women's wants during the last year than any other people in the
kingdom; and that, just because the demands were so indefinite—
the ladies did not want to be governesses, they wanted to be
something else, and we were to advise them. In this way I have
conversed with ladies of all ages and conditions: with young girls
of seventeen finding it necessary to start in life; with single women
who found teaching unendurable as life advanced; with married
ladies whose husbands were invalided or not forthcoming; with
widows who had children to support; with tradesmen's daughters,
and with people of condition fallen into low estate.

To find them work through the Journal Register was a sheer
impossibility. Not only were they far more numerous than one had
ever contemplated; but they were of a different class. I had hoped to
hear of and to supply a few well-trained picked women to places of
trust among our subscribers; but here were literally hundreds of
women neither well-trained nor picked; outnumbering any demand by ninety-nine percent. . . .

Since, therefore, we possessed but small power to aid numbers
through the medium of our own organization, it remained to be
seen whether we could form a link between our Register and,
firstly, the semi-mechanical occupations to which women have
acquired, or might acquire, a title; and, secondly, the benevolent
institutions of the country; so as to supply workers to the one, and
matron and female officials to the other.

To this end we adopted an idea struck out by a friend, and
printed long slips for distribution, containing, besides the address
of the Victoria Press and Law-Copying Class (in case any vacancy
might occur, or more hands be wanted), the addresses of the two
chief offices of the Electric Telegraph in London, in both of which
women are largely employed; and also the addresses of the two
chief institutions for training and employing nurses; also of Mrs.
Lushington's cooking school, etc., intending to add to the list
whenever we heard of any new institutions which would be

regarded as centres of women's work. At the bottom of this list we notified that we ourselves kept a limited register for really competent matrons, clerks, and secretaries.

Now, in regard to what I have termed semi-mechanical occupations, I will dismiss them with a few remarks, to which I earnestly request your consideration. I am in this paper considering the needs of educated women—of women who have been born and bred ladies; it is a real distinction from which, even in America, the most earnest democrats cannot escape, and which in England, however much the strict edges of the lines of demarcation between class and class may be rubbing off, still exists in full force. Looking at it from one point of view, we are sometimes tempted to regret the false notions of gentility which prevent women working bravely at whatever comes nearest to hand; but, in considering a whole class at large, an honest observer must feel that there is something noble, something beyond a mere effort after "gentility," in the struggle to preserve the habits, the dress, and the countless moral and material associations of the rank to which they were born. A good and refined education is a very valuable thing; and if educated women are to work at all for money, and I see no escape for a certain number being obliged in our country to do so, that education ought to secure them something more than a mere pittance. . . .

But for older and for highly educated women—for those to whom the keeping up of a social position has become a moral necessity, and for those who have others dependent on them—we surely ought to seek some employment which will secure them a fair income and not consign them to simple trades, which, let them be ever so extended over numbers, cannot be parallel to the professions which gentlemen require, or to the commercial enterprise which they carry on on a large scale.

Now there is work which really clever and energetic women are wanted to perform, and which people are everywhere beginning to say they ought to perform; all work involving moral superintendence over women, and physical care of the sick and infirm of both sexes. Mrs. Jameson* dwelt constantly of late years on this whole subject, in her writings and in her private conversations; and Miss Nightingale has begun to organize the training of women for the

*See document 13.

latter purpose, and nurses are also educated at several institutions under lay or Church influence. But as to placing educated women to act as officials in charitable, industrial, penal, or reformatory establishments, I really think I may say that nothing is done or doing. We keep reiterating the need of them in each and all; but I do not see that we are nearer the realization of our wish than we were five years ago.

Now, why is this? I can supply one part of the answer from our own experience of the last year; because the women who from natural ability might be disposed and competent to undertake such posts with advantage to themselves and others, do not ask for them, have little idea of the kind of work, and little desire for it, and would probably fail in doing it if they tried; because they have had no training.

Although I have seen many highly educated and refined women in want of employment during the last year, I have not seen half a dozen who were competent, by their own conviction, to take the responsibility of management on a large scale; the matronship of female emigrant ships, the control of a wild troop of reformatory girls, the overseership of female factory operatives, or the female wards of a workhouse.

"Letter to Business Men"

Permit me to ask your favourable consideration of the following statement which I am instructed by the Committee of this Society to lay before you.

For upwards of 18 years this Society has been giving thorough and systematic training on Book-keeping in all its branches to girls; for whom, when they have passed an examination satisfactorily, it makes it its business to find situations. A large number of young women have been trained and placed out by us. These women have become a support instead of a burden to their families and we can produce testimonials which vouch for the good results of our work.

Hitherto the situations which we have been able to obtain for

Form Letter to Businessmen, Society for Promoting the Employment of Women, c. 1877.

our Students have been chiefly in shops: very few, however competent, have succeeded in finding work in the offices of Accountants, Warehousemen, Bankers, Merchants, or Insurance Companies.

Women as a rule are quick workers; the salaries paid to them when *thoroughly trained to office work,* average from 20/- to 30/- weekly; and, a sedentary occupation being suitable to them, they can perfectly well work for long hours when necessary. The employment of men and women in the same establishment is found to improve the moral tone of both; mutual respect is engendered and the work does not suffer. This is the actual experience of many shops, and of offices, both under government and otherwise.

It is unnecessary to point out here the advantages which would accrue to the community if *more* of our surplus women became breadwinners instead of mere consumers, and I would ask you to help our efforts to obtain for women clerks work, which they are quite capable of performing, whenever an opening may occur in your own office or elsewhere.

This Society is most careful in the recommendation of candidates, and all enquiries are promptly attended to.

[signed]
GERTRUDE J. KING,
Secretary.

Document 9

The formation of the Women's Educational Association of Leipzig, Germany, was another example of women organizing to educate other women for work. The Association, which was middle-class and very class-conscious, combined traditional middle-class education with new technical training that enabled women to obtain employment. The Association's program and statutes, reproduced in part here, are typical of those of many women's associations formed in the last half of the nineteenth century. It is interesting to note that this women's organization was democratic in nature while Germany as a whole had an authoritarian political system.

Program and Statutes of the Women's Educational Association in Leipzig

Germany, 1866

Program

1. The Association recognizes as its primary task the education and advancement of the female sex, especially for those with no opportunity for continuing education and mental recreation.

2. For this purpose, evening programs of instructive lectures, readings and declamatory and musical presentations will be offered by qualified ladies.

3. Girls who have been confirmed will receive instruction in a Sunday School.

4. The Association will support the Co-operative of the Workers' Educational Committee and reserves the right to establish similar useful enterprises within the limits of its financial resources.

5. The Women's Educational Association of Leipzig contributed substantially to the founding of the General German Women's Association and considers itself a branch thereof.

Statutes

1. The Association shall set up its own Educational Committee specifically charged with the following: organizing lectures, readings, musical and declamatory programs, as well as offering such intellectual attractions that will contribute to the continuing education of women. The Committee shall consist of 5 members.

2. A minimum of 25 such evening programs shall be offered annually for the general female public without distinction of class. Non-members shall pay an entrance fee.

3. Any respectable, independent female person without distinction of class may become a member of the Association. Upon admission, members shall pay dues of 5 Neugroschen, and make a contribution monthly of 5 Neugroschen. Larger amounts are gratefully received.

4. Each member upon admission commits herself to stay with the Association for at least three months and fulfill the assumed obligations during that period.

5. Each member upon admission shall be given a membership

"Vereinsnachrichten," *Neue Bahnen: Organ des Allgemeinen Deutschen Frauenvereins*, vol. 1, no. 6 (1866), p. 47, and no. 7 (1866), pp. 55–56.

card made out in her name and receive two entrance tickets to all lectures. These tickets will show the corresponding number of the member. These numbered tickets may be passed on to other female persons, even to those of the servant class. The member in question, however, shall be responsible for the respectability of strangers who make use of the tickets.

6. A default of duties of more than two months can result in the dismissal from the Association. Excepted from this rule are members who are sick or away on a trip, if the Administration is so informed. Members who have withdrawn from the Association and apply for readmission will be considered as new members. Intent to resign can be given at any time; however, the members in question have to inform the Administration in writing and return their membership cards. As long as such a declaration is not given, such members will be held liable to meet their obligation to the Association.

7. The Association in support of its program and within the limits of its financial resources shall set up a library in the fields of literature, art and music for gratuitous use by its members. The library shall be under the supervision of the Education Committee.

8. The Sunday School shall give confirmed girls a practical preparation for life, i.e., through instruction in needlework and dressmaking, in arithmetic, French, German, singing and as soon as it is feasible, also in bookkeeping. At the same time, the school shall exert an elevating and refining influence on the development of mind, heart and moral behavior. The precise rules of the Sunday School will be spelled out in its statutes.

9. The cooperative has a double purpose; first, to make available to its members first-class goods at inexpensive prices; second, to set up for each member a savings account from the dividends accruing from the amount of purchases made and from the weekly dues and the interest thereof.

P.S. With a sufficient number of members, the cooperative shall extend its activities to include raw materials of industry.

10. The business of the Association shall be managed by a board consisting of nine ladies, i.e., a first and second president, a secretary, a treasurer and five advisory committee members. The board shall appoint eight supervisors who by twos shall look after maintenance of order at lectures and in general assemblies. The education Committee shall be formed by volunteers approved by the board.

11. The election of board members shall be held by ballot during the annual general assembly and is valid for one year. The board can be reelected. Upon resignation or death of a board member, the election by ballot of a new member shall be held at the next general assembly. At board meetings as well as in general assemblies, resolutions shall be passed by a simple majority vote.

Document 10

During the last three decades of the nineteenth century, women entered the civil service in many European countries. This was made possible by several developments. New civil service jobs were created by technological innovations such as the development of the telegraph, the telephone, and the typewriter, and by the expansion of government functions. Moreover, feminist efforts to secure employment for women were more easily realized in these new occupations, which had not yet become male preserve.. Communications and public transportation were government-owned in Germany, as they were all over Europe, and government jobs in these areas offered important opportunities to middle-class women. Yet, as the document below illustrates, the gains made by women were often illusory, since men quickly sought to limit competition from women. The complicity and blatant prejudice of the German government was typical of the situation everywhere. The case of the German Civil Service was just one example of the institutionalization of lower salaries and inferior working conditions for women.

Opening the German Civil Service to Women
Germany, 1878

Berlin. In October 1873, at the suggestion of her Royal Highness, the Crown Princess, the administration of the Telegraph Center decided to employ ladies in its service. The main idea was to open up a respectable branch of business to ladies of the upper middle class, the daughters of officials and officers. At that time, the administration announced that the ladies, after first passing an examination, were to be employed for a four-week

"Briefe," *Neue Bahnen: Organ des Allgemeinen Deutschen Frauenvereins*, vol. 13, no. 3 (1878), pp. 21–22.

probation period; later, however, they could expect permanent employment with pension rights and housing benefits, just the same as male employees. As to the salary scale, the ladies would draw a yearly remuneration of 750 Marks, payable in monthly installments of Mk. 62.50. In addition, they were promised that they would receive, like the male employees, a special bonus of about Mk. 9 per month for the telegrams processed. After the first year of service the first thirty ladies employed would receive a raise in salary from Mk. 750 to Mk. 900, and after the second year from Mk. 900 to Mk. 1050; those in line after the first thirty ladies would move up into the second salary category. Finally, after three years, they could expect permanent employment and receive housing benefits and pension rights. The work schedule and the work itself is the same as for men, except for night service, for which up to April of this year they were paid extra; now they receive a fixed remuneration. As far as performance is concerned, the ladies have given no cause for reproach. On the contrary, the officials of the Telegraph Service have repeatedly acknowledged that their performance is altogether equal to that of the men. This is confirmed by the fact that the demanding service of the Stock Exchange is also in the hands of ladies.

While the experiment to engage ladies as telegraph employees can be regarded as a complete success, the initial benevolence and the favorable disposition toward them in the upper circles of the Telegraph Service has turned into ill-will. There is little doubt that the Telegraph Administration is intent on making the situation as difficult as possible for the ladies in order to force them to voluntarily resign.

FIRST: Despite the fact that many of the ladies already have more than three years service behind them, only fifteen have been granted the maximum salary after the second year; and when two left the service, no one was moved up to the top salary class. Hence, only thirteen ladies now draw the maximum salary of Mk. 1050.

SECOND: Prospective female applicants are not called, even when there is a vacancy. Hence, the ladies are slowly eliminated from the Service.

THIRD: The monthly bonus has been discontinued for all employees; hence for the ladies also; the promise made for compensation seven months ago has not been kept as of today.

FOURTH: Up to the present, and after four years, not a single lady in Prussia has been permanently employed, hence, they are not entitled to housing benefits and pensions. On the contrary, by withdrawing the bonus, the ladies have suffered a monthly loss of Mk. 3 and are now forced more than ever before to supplement their income by taking parttime jobs.

FIFTH: More recently, the ladies off-handedly were given notice that they would no longer draw a yearly salary or compensation, but beginning in October, they would be employed on a day-to-day basis with a daily remuneration of Mk. 2.50. This amounts to saying that they are put in the class of unskilled labor, that they will never have the prospect of permanent employment, will receive no housing benefits, and have no pension rights, in short, that all their expectations are voided. At same time, they can expect to be dismissed from one day to another. It is doubtful that they will receive their daily wages in case of sickness. At any rate, taking them away or granting them is entirely within the power of the authorities.

SIXTH: Every male employee automatically has the right to a two-week summer vacation. Not so the ladies. If a lady takes a leave of absence on the basis of a medical certificate, she is obliged to pay her substitute the daily remuneration, arbitrarily fixed at a high rate. Last year, it amounted to Mk. 0.75 per day, this year Mk. 1.50.

SEVENTH: In such manner, the service is made almost unbearable for the ladies. Unprofessional deportment is rebuked; conversational exchange prohibited. Formerly, every third Sunday was free, now only every seventh, but who knows how long this will last, for everything is determined by arbitrary decrees.

Document 11

These two selections are "how-to" guides for women seeking work. Many such guides were published as books and as features in women's magazines in the late nineteenth century. The second selection is from *Our Sisters,* a popular magazine for middle-class women. While the major part of each issue was devoted to articles such as "Frocks and Frivolities" and "The Home Gardener," there was also a regular column entitled "What to Do with Our Daughters, or the Remunerative Employments of Women." The magazine thus tried to reconcile two images of women, the old myth of the delicate lady and the new reality of the working woman. At the same time it gave advice on how to become a pharmacist: it assured its readers that to be one a woman did not have to be "strong-minded," a quality a Victorian lady was taught to avoid. The first selection is from a French book by Mme. A. Paquet-Mille, which was less class-conscious, more positive, and more feminist than *Our Sisters*. This guide discussed all kinds of employment opportunities for women: traditional women's occupations, male-dominated occupations, and new occupations created by technological advances and the expansion of service industries.

Women to Women:
Handbooks for Choosing an Occupation
France, 1891; England, 1897

Mme. Paquet-Mille's *New Practical Guide for Girls in the Choice of a Profession*

Foreword

Since society has resolutely adopted the path of reform, there is much discussion of the means by which the moral and material condition of women can be improved. The question of woman's independence is taken up on all sides and from every point of view; the quest for this independence is undeniably honorable, when its only aim is to extend the sphere of woman's activities.

The French woman, whose enthusiasm is tempered by reason and intelligence, has understood that she will attain her true social freedom only by knowledge and work. The flexibility of her fine and solid mind allows her to engage in all the careers opened up by progress; she knows that life's demands have increased with the passage of time; she eagerly prepares herself for the active role she must fulfill. . . .

To be sure, one must recognize that the best plan for a woman's life is one that enables her to develop her abilities for the exclusive well-being of those around her. . . . But how few of them are thus privileged! How many of them, on the contrary, are forced by circumstances to seek their livelihood by their own work. . . .

Thus we offer this book to families seeking a career for their children.

A. Paquet-Mille, *Nouveau guide pratique des jeunes filles dans le choix d'une profession* (Paris, 1891), pp. ix–xiii, 14, 265.

The scope is vast, for we have made a point of being as complete as possible; but we have sought to include only information pertaining to each profession, without being sidetracked by long discussions and personal evaluations; for the choice of an occupation must be carefully made by our readers, who will apply it to their own ways of life and aptitudes.

This guide is in two parts, Paris and the Provinces, but each part contains details which can be profitably consulted by all interested readers.

To facilitate the use of this book, we have divided these parts into chapters composed of professional work, office work, and manual work, and in setting up these chapters we have adopted a methodical plan which gives all relevant information at a glance: the nature of the work, apprenticeship, wages and layoffs.

This small encyclopedia, whose only merit is its truthfulness, will demonstrate by the number of careers pursued by women, that the manlike education of our sex is not a dangerous utopia. It can, on the contrary, contribute to the nation's progress and prosperity by utilizing the diversity of feminine abilities....

Dentists

Many women practice the profession of dentistry. This has been for a long time a free profession, requiring no diploma. This is still the case, but Parlement is considering a proposal by Dr. David, a deputy and founding director of the School of Dentistry of Paris, to regulate this profession.

The School of Dentistry was founded in 1884 and accepts students of both sexes, to whom after two years of practical and theoretical training, it awards the dentist's diploma of the Ecole de Paris.

Admitted on an equal footing with their male colleagues, several women have been graduated and are presently practicing with varying degrees of success. Here again is a sedentary profession requiring intelligence, education, and manual dexterity, which fortunately replace physical strength, which will no longer be needed in the future of dentistry....

Chemical Products

Casting and boxing of dyes, pencil leads, cleaning pastes for copper and marble, et cetera; this is the work of an industry which primarily employs women. As one can see, this work is neither very complicated nor tiring!

Apprenticeship: It takes about two months to master the different operations. The beginner makes about 1 Fr. per day, then 1 Fr. 50 and ends up being paid by the piece, as are the others. *Wages:* Vary from 3 Fr. and 3 Fr. 50 per day for experienced workers. The real working day is 11 hours. When by chance there is a notable drop in orders, there is a reduction in the number of work hours, but the workers are never completely laid off.

Women as Chemists [Pharmacists]

The Pharmaceutical Society, in opening up its ranks to women, has provided them with an eminently suitable calling. There is no lack of persons of both sexes who still loudly proclaim that a woman doctor is a thing unsexed. These persons could scarcely bring their arguments to bear against Pharmacy, and maintain that there is anything essentially unfeminine in the making up of drugs and pills. The calling of a chemist does not necessitate the possession on the part of a woman of all those faculties and qualities generally summed up as "strong-mindedness." In the peaceful seclusion of a drug shop, a woman chemist, unlike a doctor or a nurse, is not brought face to face with those stern realities: disease, pain, deformity, death. True, she works in with the doctor and the nurse, and her share in the healing of the sick is responsible enough; but for all that, her life work involves no such wear and tear, no such physical and mental strain, no such constant demands upon her endurance, patience, and staying power. Should her services be required for an operation to which some chemists devote attention, namely, tooth drawing, and should she not feel equal to the occasion, she need only refer the sufferer from toothache either to a dentist or a male colleague around the corner!

Women Chemists in Infirmaries and Hospitals

Having duly qualified herself, a woman stands a good chance of getting employment at infirmaries and hospitals, where there is an increasing demand for female dispensers and assistants. Many doctors prefer to send their own medicines to their patients, and

"What to Do with Our Daughters, or Remunerative Employment of Women— Women as Chemists," *Our Sisters*, February 1897, pp. 85-86.

these usually employ a dispenser to make up their prescriptions. The work in this case is done in the doctor's surgery, and is an occupation well suited to women. In country places there are a good many openings of this kind, and there are already a fair number of instances in which a woman fills the post of doctor's dispenser. In this case she receives a fixed salary and runs no risk. On the other hand, if she is possessed of sufficient capital to do so, to open a shop often proves a paying concern. The world is so constituted that different classes of people are more or less bound to profit by each other's misfortunes. And the invalid, or the invalid's relatives, paying the bill for medicines supplied, are sometimes tempted to think that the chemists' business must be a profitable one.

How to Qualify

In order to register as an apprentice or student, the candidate must first pass a preliminary examination held four times a year in various large towns throughout the kingdom. The fee is two guineas, and the subjects comprise English grammar and composition, Latin grammar and translation, and arithmetic. If the candidate can produce a certificate, that he or she has passed one of a list of given examinations held by the different Universities, the Boards of Examiners are empowered to accept this certificate in lieu of the preliminary, provided always that Latin, English, and arithmetic were included in that examination.

Minor and Major Examinations

After having been registered as having passed the preliminary examination, the candidate will proceed to work up for the minor and major examinations. For the minor, the candidate must not be under twenty-one, and must produce a certificate of having been engaged for three years either as apprentice, student, or otherwise employed in translating or dispensing prescriptions. Candidates in going up for this examination are advised to have attended at least 60 lectures in chemistry, 45 lectures and demonstrations in materia medica, and to have worked 18 hours a week at practical chemistry. The fee for the minor examination is five guineas, that of the major three guineas. The subjects for the minor are: Chemistry and Physics, Botany, Materia Medica, Prescriptions, Practical Dispensing, and Pharmacy. In the major examination, the knowledge required in Chemistry and Physics, Botany and Materia Medica is much fuller. Students are also examined in the Pharmacy Act, 1868, dealing with the sale of poisons.

Document 12

A major change in middle-class women's work in the nineteenth and twentieth centuries was the gradual transformation of their traditional charitable work from unpaid, volunteer activities to paid, professional social work occupations. The nineteenth-century "lady" was expected to engage in some form of charitable activity. But for many women this was more than just a duty; it provided an escape from the boredom of home life and it gave them the opportunity to go out into the world (see documents 17, 19, 29, and 51). Charitable work gave these women a sense of purpose and accomplishment. Although thousands of women performed vital functions for society as volunteers, amateur "lady bountifuls" were often ineffectual because they were generally not properly trained. Women themselves came to realize that the conduct of charitable work had to be improved. Moreover, many understood that the professionalization of this work would provide needed paid careers for middle-class women. Thus they did not view becoming a professional social worker as a radical departure from acceptable women's roles. Rather they believed it was an extension of their concerns and duties as wives and mothers.

The following document is the sophisticated curriculum of a school established to train women to become social workers. The school was run by the German Evangelical Women's Federation which was associated with the Inner Mission, a social welfare organization of the German Protestant Church. Even conservative women's groups such as this one saw the need for providing work for women.

A School of Social Work for Women
Paula Mueller, Germany, 1905

There is an increasing urgency for women to contribute to the solution of the problems of our times. Women have come to recognize the practice of social work as their right. But in order to be able to fulfill this duty and to carry out such a responsibility, one needs training. In the past the view was held that voluntary participation in the Inner Mission Society, in social welfare work, served a good purpose. Now the demand is even greater and [social

Martin Hennig, ed., *Quellen zur Geschichte der Inneren Mission* (Hamburg, 1912), pp. 599-601.

work] requires a basic course of instruction which is also conducive to character building. All activity in the area of social work had a more or less private character in earlier times. Today it requires a knowledge of economic conditions and social relationships and thus has become a part of the social sciences. The solution of the "social question" requires the common work of man and woman. The duties which are imperative for women grow from year to year and require a new division of labor as well as basic education. Only through these can we succeed in creating women's social [work] occupations which will not only obviate social misery but also will open up a satisfying field of activity for educated women.

In October 1905, the German-Evangelical Women's Federation established a Christian-social training school.

The school pursues a twofold objective. It serves not only young women who wish to study Christian charity and social rescue work for a year, but also women who would like to perform social work as a profession, whether in a paid or unpaid capacity.

The course spans the period from the middle of October to the 30th of September, with the exception of a 14-day Christmas vacation. The women who are seeking a professional education are obligated to take the complete course. They then will have the right to receive a certificate, on the basis of which they will be able to procure an appropriate position (directress or assistant in institutions of the Inner Mission Society and institutions of public charity: young people's welfare, care of the poor, police assistants, association secretaries, etc.) through the headquarters of the employment office.... Those women just seeking to continue their education are obligated to continue the course until the 30th of June.

The course consists of two parts, one theoretical, one practical, which alternate and supplement each other.

The theoretical part spans the period from the middle of October until the 31st of January. The students are expected to study for the classroom meetings. The instruction is divided between the following subjects:

[Subject]	Class Hours —Weekly
1. Introduction to the Social Spirit of the Bible	3
2. Christian Charity and the Inner Mission	2½

[Subject]	Class Hours —Weekly
3. Women's Social Work	2½
4. The "Social Question" and Political Economy	4
5. Sociology	1
6. Pedagogy	2½
7. Hygiene	1
8. Bookkeeping for the home	1
	17½

The months of February, March, April, July, August, and September are reserved so students can actually practice [social work] at the institutions of the Diaconate [a Protestant nursing order] and public charity. In a great number of these institutions the individual student is taken on for three months and instructed in pertinent work. There are the institutions of the city of Hannover: the home for cripples, Magdalene Asylum, a children's hospital, city hospital, various nursing homes, the children's convalescent home of Herrenhausen, the day-nursery of the Linden velvet weavers, and the public assistance house of the Hannoverian local branch. The out-of-town institutions: hospitals in Kassel, Lüneburg, Celle, and Verden, a maternity home in Bremen, the child-welfare institution in Altencelle, and the women workers' home and infants' home of the Kassel local branch. The students' wishes regarding a choice of specialization will be respected if possible. Naturally the students are subject to the rules of the house during their practical apprenticeship, which they spend in the institution.

The months of May and June serve in addition as a period for special introduction to different areas of social work, building on the three months of theoretical instruction. That is accomplished through theoretical instruction and lectures, and goes hand in hand, as much as possible, with practical work in private and communal charitable organizations, in community service, in welfare offices, in association polyclinics, private clinics, day nurseries, etc. There will also be an opportunity given to the students in the first three months of the course to take part in surveys and lectures of various kinds. The students, stimulated by the work they themselves produce in their reports and critiques, will be well qualified to fully comprehend the material presented to them and express their own ideas about it.

IV

The Meaning of Work
for Women

The revolution in women's work which began in the 1850s was not limited to practical attempts to enable women to be self-supporting. From midcentury, middle-class women were postulating and widely discussing in print both the need for women to work and the meaning of work for women. Many argued that work outside the home was a liberating and rewarding experience for women, one that allowed them to fully develop their intellectual and human potentials. They insisted that work was just as important for women as for men and called for a recognition of women's *right* to work.

One premise of this new outlook was that women who did not have the opportunity to work were destined to lead unfulfilled lives. Of course, the kind of work that the authors of documents 13 and 14 discuss, occupations which would allow women to use their intelligence and be independent, were available to only a few middle-class women. These occupations were and remained generally reserved for men. The professions were the most rewarding fields, but despite all efforts to open them to women, relatively few found employment there. Women were also effectively barred from most executive decision-making positions in business. Thus, the new "meaning of work" did not apply to most of the jobs women held throughout the period despite the high hopes of some idealists. The majority of women worked in factories or workshops, in clerical jobs, or in retail stores where the regimentation, repetition, and physical burdens were hardly liberating, creative, or fulfilling.

Document 13

Anna Jameson (1794–1860) was a professional art critic and art historian who, although married, had to support herself, her parents, and her younger sisters by her writing. She was a tremendously influential figure for English feminists; her arguments for women's work and her philosophy of work were widely disseminated in the *English Woman's Journal* and by the Society for Promoting the Employment of Women, among others. Jameson insisted that work was a moral necessity for women and called for the public recognition of women's right and duty to work. One of her most influential arguments was that work outside the home, such as caring for the sick and overseeing workhouses and schools, was not distinct from women's traditional role. She insisted instead that it was an extension, indeed, the culmination, of women's domestic concerns and duties. For Jameson meaningful work was found not only in paid employment but also in unpaid charitable work by which women contributed to the betterment of society. Thus Anna Jameson and the middle-class feminists she influenced were eager to see women educated and properly trained in social work professions.

"Work in some form or other is the appointed lot of all."

Anna Jameson, England, 1859

The great mistake seems to have been that, in all our legislation, it is taken for granted that woman is always protected, always under tutelage, always within the precincts of a home; finding there her work, her interests, her duties, and her happiness: but is this true? We know that it is altogether false. There are thousands and thousands of women who have no protection, no guide, no help, no home; who are absolutely driven by circumstance and necessity, if not by impulse and inclination, to carry out into the larger community the sympathies, the domestic instincts, the active administrative capabilities with which God has endowed them; but these instincts, sympathies, capabilities, require first to be properly developed, then properly trained, and then directed into large and useful channels, according to the individual tendencies. We require in our country the recognition—the public recognition, by law as well as by opinion—of the woman's

Anna Jameson, "The Communion of Labor," in *Sisters of Charity, Catholic and Protestant and the Communion of Labor* (Boston, 1859), pp. 31–32, 150–51, 165, 169–70.

privilege to share in the communion of labor at her own free choice, and the foundation of institutions which shall train her to do her work well....

The questions as yet unsettled seem to be these:

Whether a more enlarged sphere of social work may not be allowed to woman in perfect accordance with the truest feminine instincts? Whether there be not a possibility of her sharing practically in the responsibilities of social as well as domestic life? Whether she might not be better prepared to meet and exercise such higher responsibilities? And whether such a communion of labor might not lead to the more humane ordering of many of our public institutions, to a purer standard of morals, to a better mutual comprehension and a finer harmony between men and women, when thus called upon to work together, and (in combining what is best in the two natures) becoming what God intended them to be, the supplement to each other?...

I return to the so-called "rights and wrongs of women" only to dismiss them at once from our thoughts and our subject. Morally a woman has a right to the free and entire development of every faculty which God has given her to be improved and used to His honor. Socially she has a right to the protection of equal laws; the right to labor with her hands the thing that is good; to select the kind of labor which is in harmony with her condition and her powers; to exist, if need be, by her labor, or to profit others by it if she choose. These are her rights, not more nor less than the rights of the man. Let us, therefore, put aside all futile and unreal distinctions....

Work in some form or other is the appointed lot of all, divinely appointed; and, given as equal the religious responsibilities of the two sexes, might we not, in distributing the work to be done in this world, combine and use in more equal proportion the working faculties of men and women, and so find a remedy for many of those mistakes which have vitiated some of our noblest educational and charitable institutions? Is it not possible that in the apportioning of the work we may have too far sundered what in God's creation never can be sundered without pain and mischief, the masculine and the feminine influences?—lost the true balance between the element of power and the element of love? and trusted too much to mere mechanical means for carrying out high religious and moral purposes?

Document 14

Jenny Heynrichs was co-editor of *New Paths [Neue Bahnen]*, the Journal of the All-German Women's Association. *New Paths*, like the *English Woman's Journal*, sought to help women find work. Heynrichs, like Anna Jameson, believed work was a joyful and creative experience as well as an economic necessity for those women who did not marry. Heynrichs and other middle-class feminists who shared her views insisted that they were not proposing any changes in the political or economic systems, just women's increased participation in the world of work.

"What Is Work?"
Jenny Heynrichs, Germany, 1866

Work, liberating and liberated work, is the slogan of our association, the banner around which we gather. It may seem superfluous, therefore, to raise once more the question "What is work?" in the pages of our magazine; one should assume that no one could have any further doubt about the importance of our association with this word. . . .

Work, be it intellectual or physical, is always the lively and vigorous union of our intellectual and physical powers for a definite, clearly articulated purpose. Work is creativity accompanied by the comforting realization that one is bringing forth something really good and necessary, with the conviction that a sudden, arbitrary cessation would cause a sensitive void, produce a loss. The worker, wherever he may be employed, feels himself to be a link in a chain that holds society together, a link which, should it drop out, would have to be replaced at once by another. He knows that such a replacement could be found at once, that no man is irreplaceable. Yet there is something very inspiring in the knowledge that through his dropping out a replacement is required; that one does not disappear without vacating a place, as if one never had it. This knowledge makes one feel content, fit, strong; it ennobles the lowest kind of work. This knowledge is given to all men and if they lack it, they have only themselves to

Jenny Heynrichs, "Was ist Arbeit?," *Neue Bahnen: Organ des Allgemeinen Deutschen Frauenvereins*, vol. 1, no. 2, 1866, pp. 9–10.

blame, not society. But thousands of women are lacking that knowledge because they are brought up for only one vocation— marriage.

Who could deny that the vocation of wife and mother is the highest, most sacred and most fulfilling that can fall to the lot of women. Who could deny that the work involved in this calling makes her a most praiseworthy and useful member of society. But who could fail to perceive that, given our established social conditions and the way they have come about through progressive development, a great many young women remain unmarried, unprovided for and dissatisfied.

Most of our young women, not only those from the well-to-do and aristocratic families, but also those from families of modest and limited means, are taught a variety of things. They embroider and crochet, sing and play the piano, draw, read French and English, possibly lend a hand in the household while attending balls and going promenading, all this with the expectation of a suitor who is to provide them with a home and their own domain. But the years go by, the hoped-for savior does not arrive, and the home, the parental house that has sheltered them falls into ruin with the death of the father. They are left behind, uncared for as the sad saying goes. Thrown back on their own resources and taking stock of the many things they have learned, they discover with dismay that while keeping occupied they have whiled away their lives and are unable to do any kind of work.

Work is the practical application of that which one thoroughly understands, for which one has prepared oneself and has chosen as the business of one's life. And this kind of work is only open in a very few fields to our women and many among them have not grasped yet that this alone is what is meant by work. The goal of our endeavors is to open to women the blessings of the world. We do not want a break up of the social order, no political conquests, only a breakthrough for work. In this manner, we think we can deliver the world from the insufferable old maids, at odds with themselves and others, from the women who through poverty and misery have fallen victim to vice, from luxury which like a cancer erodes the happiness of family life. We think we can restore to marriage meaning and sanctity and the right to noble love. May God help us in this task.

Document 15

For working-class women like the factory worker of 1930 whose short autobiography appears below, work was neither joyful nor creative. To this woman, work was meaningless. Her job was boring and repetitious; it offered no financial or spiritual rewards and provided no satisfaction. Indeed, she believed that the severe regimentation of factory life destroyed her vitality and intelligence. It was not her paid work but rather her free moments away from her job which gave meaning to her life. Her only pleasures came from her free time on Sunday and her political activities. But she had little time even for these because, despite the securing of the eight-hour day and other reforms of the factory system, her job consumed most of her time and drained her energy and enthusiasm. (See documents 30, 37, 44, and 45.)

The Meaning of Work for the Working-Class Woman
Germany, 1930

The alarm clock utters a shrill cry at 5:30. Still very drowsy, I get out of bed, put some cold water in a basin and subject myself to a sponge bath from head to foot; only then do I feel refreshed—as if reborn. By the time I've gotten dressed and combed my hair, it is already 6:00. Then for another quarter of an hour I sit and have breakfast. At 6:15 I get up to go to work; it is not far, five minutes away, but in spite of that I always go a little early since I don't want to get tired out so early in the morning. I leave seven or eight minutes for myself to rest and think.

At 6:30 the sirens signals the beginning of work. For eight hours, or with seasonal work for nine or ten hours, I stand on a wide plank and remove stains; that is, I remove all the stains from clothes which are to be taken for cleaning. This is not so simple as one might think; one has to watch that the material is not damaged through brushing and that the colors don't fade from the acidity. For a trifling bit of damage I resign myself to a severe morality sermon.

Many, many clothes pass through my hands, some of them I like

Mein Arbeitstag—Mein Wochenende: 150 Berichte von Textilarbeiterinnen, ed. by Deutscher Textilarbeiter-Verband, (Berlin, 1930), pp. 15–16.

and often I would like to get one or the other for myself, but that is not possible; my salary is so low I can't afford such expensive clothes. My hourly wage amounts to 49 Pfennige and that, with the wages of my mother, who also works, must pay for the entire household: rent, coal, lights, everything, since my father provides for nothing. As a result, clothing comes last for me.

I cannot call my work boring. Change comes with the variation of the pieces. But my colleagues at work are not ones whom I would choose for myself. They hold to the old ways and are crazy; they cater to the bosses, and hold firmly to the church, attested to by the fact that they go to prayer with lists of petitions to God which they've collected. Also they are not organized [into a union] and are not to be won over.

So I stand on my plank and think and brood about how I can bring my colleagues to worker consciousness, how I can win them over so they will stand with us and fight for better salaries, for better living conditions and for the liberation of the working class.

So I meditate and I think, until in the middle of these thoughts the siren sounds as proof that my work in the factory has ended; exhausted, I go home, and then begins the work at home—cleaning, washing dishes, cooking supper. I am seldom finished before 8:00 in the evening. Once a week I go out for a couple of hours to a party or a young socialist gathering in order that my mind may not become stunted. And after a nights' sleep, the next day begins like the last one.

Only Sunday is a different day for me. I get up early and go by bicycle to a meeting point from which the young socialists ride out onto the heath and collect new strength from nature. I spend beautiful, lovely hours there which serve only enough to get me through another working week—that in turn provides my livelihood and, unfortunately, profit for the capitalists.

H.H.B., 26 years old.

Part Two
WOMEN'S POLITICS

Men in this country obtained parliamentary representation in and through local government. They used the power they had, and they obtained more extended power. We urge women to follow their example— to take an interest in the local affairs in which they have a legal right to be represented, to make their votes felt as a power which must be recognised by all who would govern such affairs, and to be ready to fill personally such offices as they are liable to be nominated for, and to seek those positions to which they are eligible for election.

> Miss Becker,
> The Rights and Duties of Women in Local Government
> *(Manchester, 1879), p. 5.*

It has also been asserted that we should have limited our programme to a mere protest against war and that claims for woman suffrage were out of place on the programme of a peace conference. Those of us who have convened this Congress however have never called it a peace congress, but an international Congress of women to protest against war, and to discuss ways and means whereby war shall become an impossibility in the future. We consider that the introduction of woman suffrage in all countries is one of the most powerful means to prevent war in the future.... But to accomplish this we need political power. Not until women can bring direct influence to bear upon Governments, not until in the parliaments the voice of the women is heard mingling with that of the men, shall we have the power to prevent recurrence of such catastrophes.

> *"Address of Welcome,"* Dr. Aletta H. Jacobs,
> *Women's International League for Peace and Freedom,*
> First Congress, the Hague, 1915 *Report*
> *(Amsterdam: International Women's Committee
> of Permanent Peace, 1915), pp. 7–8.*

Part two is based on a new definition of women's politics which rejects the notion that women's political activities in the nineteenth and early twentieth centuries consisted largely of the struggle for suffrage. Rather the documents demonstrate that throughout the period covered by this book women of all classes engaged in a wide variety of political activities which reflected their concerns and goals as women. Although they did not sit in male parliaments or have the national franchise, middle-class European women took direct political action through social welfare work and in participation in local governments, as members of school boards, poor-law guardians, and factory and prison inspectors. Increasingly politicized by their social welfare activities, middle-class women founded local, national, and international social reform and suffrage associations through which they acted on issues they deemed important to themselves and society at large. The struggle for the vote was a part, and for many the capstone, of women's politics. Working-class women, who suffered under class as well as sex oppression, turned in large numbers to socialist movements which spoke to their needs for more fundamental changes in the economic and social order. Within socialist parties, unions and international associations they worked to further their interests as women. Thus, women participated in "politics" on many levels and acted collectively to better society and improve their own lives.

The first chapter of this part (documents 16–22) discusses various aspects of middle-class women's politics and the development of the first feminist movement in the nineteenth and early twentieth centuries. The next chapter (documents 22–25) describes working-class women's roles in socialism, and the third (documents 26–27) discusses women and Nazism and presents the views of pro-Nazi and anti-Nazi women in the 1930s.

V

Middle-Class Women's Politics: Social Reform, Suffrage, and the First Feminist Movement

From the late eighteenth century middle- and upper-class women, who were prohibited from participating in men's political institutions, sought and found other avenues to effect changes in politics and society. Some middle-class French women turned to revolutionary activity in 1789 and the years that followed. They demonstrated, issued petitions of grievances, fought, and also founded their own political clubs and women's newspapers which developed and promoted women's concerns. From the earliest days of the French Revolution women called for equality of education, equal inheritance rights, equality in marriage, and political rights for women. French women failed to win the equality they sought, but the feminist themes developed during the revolutionary struggle were not forgotten and they became the basis of more moderate middle-class feminist activity all over Europe in the next century.

In the early part of the nineteenth century, middle- and upper-class European women tried to effect political and social change in essentially two ways: by engaging in social welfare and social reform activities and by publishing books and articles devoted to the discussion of the amelioration of society's ills. Specifically feminist demands were generally related to the improvement of women's legal rights and middle-class women's education. The latter was stimulated in part by the activity of French women during the revolution and by Mary Wollstonecraft's *Vindication of the Rights of Women* (1792) and subsequent works in which women demanded to be better educated. Attempts at communication among women were made with the founding of periodicals written by and for women, but all the early publications were short-lived.

Women also engaged in organized social welfare activities, most of which were continuations of upper-class women's traditional charitable work—the care of the poor, aged, and infirm. But both upper- and new middle-class women became increasingly concerned with helping poor women and prostitutes, and with the welfare of children. At first, they viewed their activities merely as extensions of women's maternal and domestic roles and duties. But social welfare work proved to be more than that. It gave these women, who otherwise led highly circumscribed lives, a sense of purpose, accomplishment, and power. For many of these women, this was accompanied by the realization that they too were subordinated and oppressed by men and man-made laws. That consciousness, and women's belief that they could end their oppression and eliminate a host of social problems, led to the development of European-wide middle-class feminist movement beginning in the middle decades of the nineteenth century.

From that time onward women attempted to enter existing political institutions when and wherever they could. Although women could not sit in parliaments, propertied women could in many instances hold local offices. Women gradually secured and expanded these rights and were able to become poor-law guardians, factory inspectors, and members of local school boards. Their activities in these offices allowed them to directly aid poor women and children and to attempt to influence policy. The heart of middle-class women's politics, however, was the founding of women's organizations to address specific issues and the development of an extensive communications network among women. During the last forty years of the nineteenth century, a whole network of local, national, and then international women's associations were founded. Sometimes acting as pressure groups, sometimes acting directly by founding their own institutions, these associations worked to, among other things, improve women's employment opportunites and education (see documents 8–9), end state-regulated prostitution and white slavery (see document 51), aid abandoned children and unwed mothers (see document 29), and change marriage, divorce, and family laws that denied rights to women. Women organized a vocal international movement for temperance which encouraged abstinence not just for its own sake, but because of the deleterious effects of men's alcoholism on children and family life. In the late nineteenth century women organized an international women's peace movement which branded war the ultimate expression of male politics. Often the issues, membership, and leadership of these organizations over-lapped, since large numbers of women recognized that many of these concerns were interrelated and needed to be addressed simultaneously.

Women's organizations carefully developed the means of com-municating their goals and activities. They held public meetings, encouraged press coverage, and published their agendas and proceedings. Many also published journals, periodicals, and other literature which kept members and nonmembers informed of the organizations' activities and of the successes or failures of sister organizations in other places, and which promoted the discussion of issues and strategies. By the end of the nineteenth century politically active women all across Europe were in constant communication with one another. They read each other's books and periodicals, visited one another, shared their experiences and problems, and helped one another found new organizations and make existing ones more effective.

Organized women achieved successes in many areas, especially in improving women's work and educational opportunities and removing some of the most offensive legal restrictions. But by the twentieth century women had not been able to achieve many of the moderate, partial reforms the majority wanted, let alone the total social and economic equality some feminists sought. From the middle of the nineteenth century increasing numbers of activist women had come to the conclusion that the social reforms for which women worked and women's equality could not be achieved until women shared political power with men on an equal basis. Prosuffragists did not claim that women and men were the same. Rather, they insisted that women were very different from men and that because of women's unique talents, interests, and moral values, they would bring a new and higher standard of morality to government and the political process. They insisted that women had to obtain the right to vote, not merely as an end in itself, but also in order to achieve real equality and accomplish all those social reform goals which women's politics ardently sought.

Not all women or women's organizations supported full equality for women or the right to vote as a means to achieve it. Nevertheless, it was the issue of the franchise—a vivid symbol of women's inequality—that attracted large numbers of women to feminism. By the turn of the twentieth century, perhaps to the detriment of other aspects of the women's movement, the drive for the vote came to be the dominant issue in women's politics. Millions of women of all classes who had never before been politically active, as well as those already concerned with social reform and other women's issues, now became involved in the international drive for political equality and the right to participate in government on all levels. It was not a short nor easy struggle; although the vote was won in many countries by the end of the 1920s, this was not the case everywhere. Women in Switzerland did not receive the national franchise until 1971.

After the 1920s, when the struggle for the vote was substantially won, the organized international middle-class women's movement lost most of its vigor. While many national and international organizations founded to win the vote expanded their areas of concern and continued to function, their drive and the number of women involved in them diminished sharply. The reasons for the demise of the first feminist movement are not easily stated. Certainly the Depression, the rise of fascism, and World War II produced setbacks and caused many women to redirect their energies away from women's issues. Some organizations failed to define new and effective strategies in the face of changed circumstances. Most damaging was the weakening and disappearance of lines of communication among women which feminists had carefully developed and which had been responsible for much of organized women's success. This loss of communication not only made effective activity more difficult, but, even more important, meant that the knowledge of women's past concerns and activities was not passed on to the next generation of women. Many of the social, economic, and political questions raised by the first feminist movement—including questions of family relationships and women's sexuality which emerged in the early twentieth century—were not taken up again on a large scale until they were recast into the second feminist movement in the 1960s.

Document 16

Olympe de Gouges (1748–1793) was a playwright and an early supporter of the French Revolution. Like other women, she soon realized that the liberty, equality, and fraternity espoused by male revolutionaries was meant for men only. In 1790 she published

"The Declaration of the Rights of Women," which is reproduced here. It was modeled on the "Declaration of the Rights of Man and the Citizen" of 1789. In her manifesto, she calls for reforms which became the major demands of the middle-class feminists during the revolution and after—political rights for women, reform of marriage laws, government employment for women, equal property rights, and better education. In 1793 Olympe de Gouges openly opposed Robespierre and the Jacobins. She went to the guillotine in November 1793.

"Declaration of the Rights of Woman and Citizen"
Olympe de Gouges, France, 1790

The mothers, daughters, sisters, representatives of the nation, ask to constitute a National Assembly. Considering that ignorance, forgetfulness or contempt of the rights of women are the sole causes of public miseries, and of corruption of governments, they have resolved to set forth in a solemn declaration, the natural, unalterable and sacred rights of woman, so that this declaration, being ever present to all members of the social body, may unceasingly remind them of their rights and their duties; in order that the acts of women's power, as well as those of men, may be judged constantly against the aim of all political institutions, and thereby be more respected for it, in order that the complaints of women citizens, based henceforth on simple and indisputable principles, may always take the direction of maintaining the Constitution, good morals and the welfare of all.

In consequence, the sex superior in beauty and in courage in maternal suffering recognizes and declares, in the presence of and under the auspices of the Supreme Being, the following rights of woman and of the woman citizen:

Article I
Woman is born free and remains equal to man in rights. Social distinctions can be based only on common utility.

Article II
The aim of every political association is the preservation of the natural and imprescriptible rights of man and woman. These

Olympe de Gouges, *Les droits de la femme* (1790) in Bibliothèque Nationale (Lb[39] 9989), p. 24.

rights are liberty, prosperity, security and above all, resistance to oppression.

Article III

The source of all sovereignty resides essentially in the Nation, which is nothing but the joining together of Man and Woman; no body, no individual, can exercise authority that does not emanate expressly from it.

Article IV

Liberty and justice consist in giving back to others all that belongs to them; thus the only limits on the exercise of woman's natural rights are the perpetual tyranny by which man opposes her; these limits must be reformed by the laws of nature and of reason.

Article V

The laws of nature and reason forbid all actions that are harmful to society; all that is not forbidden by these wise and divine laws cannot be prevented, and no one can be constrained to do what they do not prescribe.

Article VI

Law must be the expression of the general will: all citizens, men and women alike, must personally or through their representatives concur in its formation; it must be the same for all; all citizens, men and women alike, being equal before it, must be equally eligible for all high offices, positions and public employments, according to their abilities, and without distinctions other than their virtues and talents.

Article VII

No woman can be an exception: she will be accused, apprehended and detained in cases determined by law; women, like men, will obey this rigorous rule.

Article VIII

The law must establish only those penalties which are strictly and clearly necessary, and no woman can be punished by virtue of a law established and promulgated prior to the offense, and legally applied to women.

Article IX

When a woman is declared guilty, full severity is exercised by the law.

Article X

No one ought to be disturbed for one's opinions, however fundamental they are; since a woman has the right to mount the scaffold, she must also have the right to address the House, provided her interventions do not disturb the public order as it has been established by law.

Article XI

The free communication of ideas and opinions is one of the most precious rights of woman, since this freedom ensures the legitimacy of fathers toward their children. Every woman citizen can therefore say freely: I am the mother of a child that belongs to you, without being forced to conceal the truth because of a barbaric prejudice; except to be answerable for abuses of this liberty as determined by law.

Article XII

The guarantee of the rights of woman and ot the woman citizen is a necessary benefit; this guarantee must be instituted for the advantage of all, and not for the personal benefit of those to whom it is entrusted.

Article XIII

For the upkeep of public forces and for administrative expenses, the contributions of woman and man are equal; a woman shares in all the labors required by law, in the painful tasks; she must therefore have an equal share in the distribution of offices, employments, trusts, dignities and work.

Article XIV

Women and men citizens have the right to ascertain by themselves or through their representatives the necessity of public taxes. Women citizens will not only assume an equal part in providing the wealth but also in the public administration and in determining the quota, the assessment, the collection and the duration of the impost.

Article XV

The mass of women, joined together to contribute their taxes with those of men, have the right to demand from every public official an accounting of his administration.

Article XVI

Any society in which the guarantee of rights is not assured, nor the separation of powers determined, has no Constitution; the Constitution is null if the majority of the individuals of whom the nation is comprised have not participated in its drafting.

Article XVII

Ownership of property is for both sexes, mutually and separately; it is for each a sacred and inviolable right; no one can be deprived of it as a true patrimony from nature, unless a public necessity, legally established, evidently demands it, and with the condition of a just and prior indemnity.

Afterword

Woman, wake up! The alarm bell of reason is making itself heard throughout the universe; recognize your rights. The powerful empire of nature is no longer beset by prejudices, fanaticism, superstition and lies. The torch of truth has dispelled all clouds of stupidity and usurpation. The enslaved man multiplied his forces but has had to resort to yours to break his chains. Once free he became unjust to his female companion. O women! women, when will you stop being blind? What advantages have you received from the Revolution? A more pronounced scorn, a more marked contempt? During the centuries of corruption, your only power was over the weaknesses of men. Your empire is destroyed, what then is left to you? The conviction that men are unjust. The claiming of your patrimony based on the wise laws of nature. The good word of the Lawgiver of the Marriage at Cana? Are you afraid that our French lawmakers, correctors of this morality, so long tied up with the politics which is no longer in style will say to you: "Women, what is there in common between you and us?"— Everything, you would have to reply. If they persisted in their weakness, in putting forth this inconsistency which is a contradiction of their principles, you should courageously oppose these hale pretentions of superiority with the force of reason; unite under the banner of philosophy, unfold all the energy of your character and you will soon see these proud men, your servile adorers, crawling at your feet, but proud to share with you the treasures of the Supreme Being. Whatever the obstacles that oppose us may be, it is in your power to free us, you have only to will it. . . . Since it is now a question of national education, let us see if our wise lawmakers will think wisely about the education of women.

Document 17

By the last decades of the nineteenth century, women in many countries had succeeded in obtaining the right to vote in local elections and to hold some local offices. In England women who paid local taxes were eligible to vote for or seek the office of Poor Law Guardian, an official who oversaw the workhouses and the disbursement of money to the poor. Dora Downright, the author of the selection below, was the first woman in her community to be elected a Guardian (1887). She found her work personally rewarding and, like many women who held similar offices, viewed it as an opportunity to help women and children who previously had to depend on unsympathetic or hostile men.

Feminists urged women to take advantage of opportunities to participate in local government. They believed that this would aid poor women and children and would give middle-class women a direct voice in local affairs. They also hoped that women's success in local office holding would be a powerful argument for granting them the national franchise. By the early twentieth century thousands of women held positions in local governments all over Europe. At the turn of the century approximately 900 women were Poor Law Guardians in England, and by 1910, 18,000 women in Germany held local welfare offices. In these and other countries, women served on school boards, as inspectors of factories and schools (see document 4), and on municipal councils.

"Why I Am a Guardian"
Dora Downright, England, 1888

A woman Poor Law Guardian!! "Women would much better stay in their own homes and look after their concerns," you may

Dora Downright, "Why I Am a Guardian," pamphlet reprinted in London from the *Alliance News* (March 3, 1888), pp. 1–4.

say. I own I thought so, too, once, and was very much surprised last year when some one asked me if I wouldn't consent to stand as a Poor Law Guardian for our Union, which is a good many miles away from London; and still more astonished on finding that the same idea must have struck a good many people—enough, at least, to make them vote for me. I don't know how the gentlemen at the Board liked it; I think there were rather long faces pulled at first. A friend said to me before the election (there is always some friend to say uncomfortable things), "Mrs. Downright, I hear that Mr. Boosey" (he had been a Guardian ten years, and was the owner of the four most thriving public-houses in the neighbourhood) "Mr. Boosey means to resign if you get elected." "All right," said I; "you could not tell me anything which makes me wish to be elected so much." And I was elected; but Mr. Boosey did not retire—he liked the place and the influence it gave him too much for that—and I never met anything but kindness from the Chairman and my fellow-members of the Board.

After the first meeting of the Board, we got into harness and set to work. They appointed me on the House- and School-visiting committees. I had no idea whether I should find anything wrong, or if I did, what was the way to set it right; But by dint of asking questions, and going into all the small details, as I would have done in my own nursery or kitchen, I soon found something to do. "Ladies are so inquisitive," said the Master. "They never will take anything for granted." But I never could, and never did, as sure as my name is Dora Downright.

At first it hardly seemed worth while to be a Guardian; the details that were to be looked after were so very small and trifling, it seemed foolish to refer them to a Board at all. The Master and Matron seemed to have settled everything themselves. The work-house, it was true, was ill-arranged and ill-ventilated, but these were matters, they said, clearly beyond a woman's understanding. The cooking was wasteful and careless, and the washing so badly done that the clothes looked nearly as black after the process as before. I spoke about these two or three times, but the Matron was a rather "personable" looking woman, who wore an amber necklace on Board days, and I hope I mean no disrespect to our Board by saying that there was not a single man on it whom she could not twist round her fingers. But I was able to be of a little use even here. The winter after my election was bitterly cold, and, at my request, the Board allowed some warmer underclothing for the poor old women, and some thicker flannel in the outfits of the little girls, who, poor little drudges, left school to be apprenticed for domestic service as small maids-of-all-work....

There was other work that naturally fell to my share. "If you knew, ma'am, what we has to suffer, you wouldn't mind being a Poor Law Guardian for our sakes" had been said to me more than once upon my election by the respectable labourers' wives, and I did not realise what they meant, but I soon found out. It constantly happens in the rural districts, where the workhouse infirmary is the only hospital attainable within many miles, that women who are not paupers go there when their hour of trial comes near, and one may fancy what the feelings of a respectable married woman must be when for the first time she has to come before a Board of gentlemen, and be questioned why she wants to be admitted as an inmate. But if married women are made to suffer thus, how much less regard is paid to the class which is generally supposed, but I think erroneously, to have no feelings at all? I remember my first case of this kind. She was a young, pale, pretty thing, not much more than a child, and her story was the usual one—drink! A day or two of pleasure, an evening of intoxication, and she was ruined, body and soul, unless God in His mercy sent her some friend to help her. And who should help her if not a woman who had daughters just about her age? As the poor young thing came into the Board-room, accompanied by the beadle, and looking ready to sink to the ground with shame, I saw a glance of curiosity, quite as insulting as compassionate, go round the table. "Mr. Chairman," said I, before they began to question her, "will the Board let me hear this young creature's story, and I will send in my report." It had never been done before, but a minute's reflection showed them that this was the only right and proper manner to deal with such a case, and she was told to sit down in another room and wait for me. I needn't go into her case: it is far too common, alas! to need recapitulation here. I visited her several times during her illness, and when after some weeks I was able to send her home to her parents, a hard-working couple in a distant county, who had consented to receive her back, she was actuated by a sincere desire to do right, and keep straight for the future, and was strengthened against temptation by the total abstainer's pledge. It did seem really worth while to have been chosen a Guardian, if only for the sake of this poor young thing. There have been only too many, alas! of similar cases since, and they are always now referred to me.

But the real struggle was yet to come. We had not been in the habit in our district of keeping very strict accounts—they would generally be made to look well enough at the end of the year. But there were some items of expenditure that struck even my eyes, inexperienced as I was in public business; namely, the large amount spent on beer, spirits and wine, in the Infirmary and the House. Ours was not a large workhouse, like the monster London buildings, but our bill for spirits was for 800 pints, for wine 520 pints, and for nearly 4,000 pints of malt liquor. In all, we paid £250 a year for these items alone, which I thought a great deal, and I had already pointed this out, but was told the medical officer ordered it. I thought with a sigh of the doctors in our politer circles whose prescriptions have so much to do with the subsequent growth of intemperate habits. I wrote to the London Society for returning Women as Guardians, Notting Hill Square, London, and found that the lady Guardians in one of the London Unions had been able to reduce the Infirmary bill for wine and spirits by £200, even though they increased the bill for milk by £80. Encouraged by this, I suggested some reduction, but was out-voted. They could not accept quite all Mrs. Downright's views, said the Chairman.

About Christmas came our battle-royal. It was during the preparations for the paupers' Christmas dinner, and every man was to have, besides beef and pudding, a pint of porter, and every woman half-a-pint. I spoke very earnestly in my seat at the Board. I could not see what right we had to spend the ratepayer's money in drink, which was not only unnecessary, but distinctly bad for the paupers; but I spoke quite in vain. The chairman thought I might be right about the women! He did not mind if they were given tea instead; but I could not admit that it was any more proper for the men to have porter than the women. I could not get more than two or three of the Board to take view. "The poor creatures looked forward to their porter," they said; "it was a shame they should not be merry on Christmas Day." So porter won the day.

But that day of the festivity carried the point. It was not to be expected, while the paupers were "merry" upstairs, that the Master and Matron were not equally merry downstairs, and by night the Master was quite overcome with liquor. He had been so before, God knows, often enough, and the poor people knew it to be their cost, but nobody had dared to complain, and we Guardians had never suspected it. But that night he lost his temper and beat one of the poor little pauper lads so terribly, locking him up afterwards in a freezing outhouse, that the child was found quite senseless and cold the next day, and for weeks the doctor thought he would not get over it. This brutal and unprovoked cruelty on the Master's part could not be overlooked, and the Board instituted an inquiry. We questioned witnesses, examined into facts, and sifted evidence, and soon found more than enough to show how unworthy this man had been of our confidence, and what an escape the poor creatures in the workhouse had when he was removed. We have got the right sort of Master now; a kind-hearted and honest man with good credentials of character behind him, and, I am thankful to say, an inch of blue ribbon in his botton-hole.

I don't think I ever felt prouder than when at the first meeting of the Board after the drunken Master was dismissed, the chairman turned to me and said, "Mrs. Downright, you must let me congratulate you. If it had not been for your watchfulness in the first instance, and your perseverance in searching out the case, we should never have got rid of that fellow. You are like other ladies— you always go straight to the point, and you never know when you are beaten, and so you always win; I think we may feel proud of our Lady Guardian."

So after all, I have resolved that if the electors will vote for me again, I shall go on being a Guardian, though it does cost time and trouble. There is plenty for women and mothers to do at these Boards that no man will grudge their doing, and no man do as well as they. There is Christ's own work to be done, in saving the "little ones" who would otherwise perish, and I wish other ladies would feel this strongly as I do. There would be no lack of Women Guardians then.

Document 18

The call for the vote for women was heard as early as the 1830s in England, but sustained agitation for the franchise did not begin until later in the century. In the last part of the nineteenth century suffrage associations were founded in Britain and every nation of Europe, and many, though not all women's social reform organizations included gaining the franchise among their goals by the century's end. Under the leadership of American suffragists two major international organizations were established: the Interna-

tional Council of Women (ICW, founded in 1888) and the
International Woman Suffrage Alliance (IASW, later called the
International Alliance of Women; the IAW, was founded in 1902).
These international associations brought organized women of all
nations together in the struggle for suffrage and other reforms.
Most of the national and especially the international organizations were moderate or even conservative in their approach and
tactics. They worked through propaganda, petitions, and mass
meetings to influence men to grant women the right to vote. But
since these methods failed to win the vote, some women came to
the conclusion that more radical action was necessary. In England,
the first and largest militant group, the Women's Social and
Political Union (WSPU) was founded in 1903 by Emmeline
Pankhurst and her two daughters (see document 19). The militant
women waged a campaign that included disruption of parliamentary meetings, rock throwing, bombing, and arson (directed at
property, not human life). Although members of the moderate
women's suffrage movement disapproved of their tactics, the
militants' actions and their courage in the face of arrest and
physical violence kept the struggle for the vote in the headlines and
aroused support for women's suffrage—all of which helped swell
the rank of the moderate organizations.

Militant women deliberately courted arrest in Britain and, once
imprisoned, went on hunger strikes. The government responded
with forced feedings. The document below is one woman's account
of that experience.

"The Prisoner"
Helen Gordon Liddle, England, 1911

The time has come, water is brought her, and the prisoner gets
up—too quickly—her head swims—the floor and walls envelop
her, and nearly pulling over the washstand, she falls helpless across
the bed. She must be more careful—move more slowly—her head
aches and she feels thoroughly unstrung. After her morning
ablutions she sits up in bed again, ready for the doctors and their
crew when they may arrive—she has a whole hour to wait—she is
glad to lie down—to stay quite still, for she is hardly able to bear
the ordeal that is coming.

Helen Gordon Liddle, *The Prisoner* (Letchworth, 1911), pp. 48-51.

The daylight is here—the wardress and nurses are in the kitchen having breakfast, and she is very lonely here. Now she hears a hated step—heavy and dogged—a step that detests opposition—and the prisoner knows she must oppose it.

Presently four wardresses appear—her gate is unlocked—her bed moved into the middle of the cell—she is laid flat upon it—two wardresses take her feet, one each her arms. The prisoner resists but does not make a scene—that is past now—the stage of resistance that she keeps is reserved for the doctors.

They wait—the long minutes will never pass—the prisoner shivers nervously—the nurse comes in with a large basin of food. She has evidently found the doctor in a bad temper—she says as much, and they nod over it together. One wardress wonders if she will be able to stand it this morning—she says she has been ill after each time the prisoner has been fed and evidently dreads the coming brutality.

Now the step is coming from the doctor's room, and they both enter the cell.

Oh, if only this hour could be borne alone—how full the cell is—seven people to one prisoner—a woman. What power the woman has! The short, thickset man moves behind her, and with a quick, rough movement drags her head back—well she remembers the first day when he dragged her back by the hair—as a menace, surely—and we live in a civilized country.

The prisoner is at her weakest this morning—her physical powers are at their lowest ebb—her mouth, which has been so tortured, is ulcerated, and shrinking from the slightest touch.

In his right hand the man holds an instrument they call a gag, partly covered with india rubber, which part the prisoner never feels, and the moment of battle has come.

The prisoner refuses to unclose her teeth—the last defense against the food she out of principle, refuses to take—the doctor has his "duty" to perform—his dignity also to maintain before five women and a tall junior doctor. His temper is short—has already been ruffled. So he sets about his job in a butcherly fashion—there is no skill required for this job—only brutality. He puts his great fingers along her teeth—feels a gap at the back, rams the tool blindly and with evident intention to hurt her, and cause the helpless woman to wince—along the shrinking flesh—how long will it take before superior strength triumphs? Tears start in the prisoner's eyes—uncontrollable tears—tears she would give any-thing to control.

It is still dark in the cell and the man strains at her mouth blindly, without result. "Can you see?" asks the junior doctor. "No," blusters the other, "better bring a light." But he does not wait until the taper is brought—ah—at last he has forced the tool in, and with leverage the jaw opens.

He has still to hold it for twenty minutes or so while the food is being poured or pushed or choked down her throat—unluckily the gag has been forced in so carelessly that it has caught in the cheek, between it and the sharp teeth below.

The pain is maddening—she strains at her hands—her feet are in a vice—her head is held—she tries to speak—her jaw is forced to its widest. They pour the food down—it is a mince of meat and brown bread and milk—too dry—too stiff—they hold her nose [so] that she cannot breathe, and so she must breathe with her mouth and swallow at the same time, the doctors helping it in with hot hands that have handled a pipe and heaven knows how many patients—scraping their fingers clean on her teeth from the horrible mess.

It would seem they were not doctors, for they force it down so heedlessly that the prisoner chokes and gasps for breath, the tears pouring from her eyes. The young doctor is called away—the pain is too much for her—she moves her head—the doctor gives another twist, and the nurse, to get it over sooner, pours the food quicker.

The limit is reached, and for the first time the prisoner gives way—great sobs of pain and breathlessness come faster and faster—she cannot bear it—she tries to call out "Stop!" with that tortured wide-open mouth—and with one wrench she frees her hands and seizes the gag.

The doctor says to the officers—"She says it is hot." "No," they cry—the horror of the scene upon them—"she said stop."

He waits, gloomily with irritation, and in a moment free from the restraint of his fellow physician, without a word he drags her head back and she is held down again.

A short quick thrust and her mouth is gagged again—the prisoner tries to control herself—her sobs increase—her breathless-ness also—there is nothing but the pain and the relentless forcing of food down her throat—her choking despair, and the bitter draught of tonic and digestive medicine which is also poured down her throat.

At last it is over, and she is left sick and shaken with the whole scene. She sits up—tearing at the now filthy cloth surrounding her neck, and with a shudder of revolting disgust throws it from her. The officers, too, are silent—she who had dreaded it has left the cell at once, looking white as death—now another goes hurriedly away with white face—the prisoner is dressed—her bed is made, and the day begins—oh, how wretched she is.

Document 19

Emmeline Pankhurst (1858–1928), founder of the militant WSPU, was active in politics for most of her life. One of her earliest childhood memories was of helping her mother collect money for the newly emancipated slaves in the United States. She went to her first suffrage meeting with her mother at the age of fourteen. In 1879 she married Dr. Richard Pankhurst, who drafted the first bill for the enfranchisement of women (The Women's Disabilities Removal Bill), which was introduced into the House of Commons in 1870. While her daughters Christabel and Sylvia (who later joined their mother in the suffrage struggle) were still infants, Emmeline Pankhurst became deeply involved in the fight for the vote, serving on the executive committee of the Manchester Women's Suffrage Society. In 1894 she became a Poor Law Guardian because she believed that that kind of service would prove women's fitness for the national franchise. But Pankhurst's experiences among poor women made her see the franchise in a new light. Henceforth, she believed the vote for women was not just a right, but a "desperate necessity."

Mrs. Pankhurst made the following speech in 1912 at the trial for her involvement in a demonstration during which windows were smashed in London and Westminster. From the prisoner's dock, she clearly explained how and why she became a militant.

The Making of a Militant
Emmeline Pankhurst, England, 1912

To Revolt Against Injustice

Now, gentlemen, I want to tell you a few of the things that led me, in 1903, when the Women's Social and Political Union was founded, to decide that the time had come when we had reached a situation, which, I think, I can best describe in the words of the

E. Pankhurst et al., *Suffrage Speeches from the Dock* (London, 1912), pp. 30–33.

Chancellor of the Exchequer, Mr. Lloyd George, when he was addressing an audience in Wales a little while ago. He said: "There comes a time in the life of a people suffering from an intolerable injustice when the only way to maintain one's self-respect is to revolt against that injustice." That time came for me, and I am thankful to say it very soon came for a large number of other women as well; that number of women is constantly increasing. There is always something which I may describe as the last straw of the camel's back, which leads one to make up one's mind, especially when the making up of one's mind may involve the loss of friends, loss of position, loss of money—which is the least of all things, I think—and the loss of personal liberty.

I have told you that I have been a Poor Law Guardian. While I was a Poor Law Guardian I had a great deal of experience which I did not possess before of the condition of my own sex. I found that when dealing with the old people in the workhouse—and there is no work more congenial to women than this work of a Poor Law Guardian—when I found that I was dealing with the poor of my own sex, the aged poor, I found that the kind of old women who came into the workhouse were in many ways superior to the kind of old men who came into the workhouse. One could not help noticing it. They were more industrious; in fact, it was quite touching to see their industry, to see their patience, and to see the way old women over sixty or seventy years of age did most of the work of the workhouse, most of the sewing, most of the real work which kept the place clean, and which supplied the inmates with clothes. I found that the old men were different. One could not get so much work out of them. They liked to stop in the oakum-picking room, because there they were allowed to smoke; but as to real work, very little was done by these old men. I am not speaking in a prejudiced way; I am speaking from actual experience as a Poor Law Guardian. Any Poor Law Guardian could bear me out.

I began to make inquiries about these old women. I found that the majority of them were not women who had been dissolute, not women who had been criminal during their lives, but women who had lived perfectly respectable lives, either as wives and mothers, or as single women earning their own living. A great many were domestic servants, or had been, who had not married, who had lost their employment, and had reached a time of life when it was impossible to get more employment. It was through no fault of their own, but simply because they had never earned enough to save, and anyone who knows anything about the wages of women knows it is impossible to earn enough to save, except in very rare instances. These women, simply because they had lived too long, were obliged to go into the workhouse. Some were married women; many of them, I found, were widows of skilled artisans who had pensions from their unions. But the pensions had died with them. These women, who had given up the power of working for themselves, and had devoted themselves to working for their husbands and children, were left penniless; there was nothing for them but to go into the workhouse. Many of them were widows of men who had served their country, women who had devoted themselves to their husbands; when the men died the pensions died, and so these women were in the workhouse. And also I found younger women—always women, doing the bulk of the work. I found there were pregnant women in that workhouse, scrubbing corridors, doing the hardest kind of work, almost, until their babies came into the world. I found many of these women were unmarried women—very, very young, mere girls. That led me to ask myself, "How is it that these women, coming into the workhouse as they do, staying a few weeks, and going out again—how is it they occupy this position?" I found these young girls, my lord, going out of the workhouse over and over again with an infant two weeks old in their arms, without hope, without home, without money, without anywhere to go. And then, as I shall tell you later on, some awful tragedy happened—simply because of the hopeless position in which they were placed; and then there were the little children—and this is the last example I am going to give out of my experience.

Sympathy—Not Deeds

For many years we Poor Law Guardians, especially the women, tried to get an Act of Parliament passed dealing with little children. We wanted an amendment of the Act of Parliament which deals with little children who are boarded out—I do not mean by the Union, but by their parents, the parent almost always being the mother. It is from that class—young servant girls—which thoughtless people always say working girls ought to be; it is from that class more than any other that these cases of illegitimacy come. These poor little servant girls, who only get out perhaps in the evening, whose minds are not very cultivated, and who find all the sentiment of their lives in novelettes, fall an easy prey to those who have designs against them. These are the people by whom the babies are put out to nurse, and the mothers have to pay for their keep. I found, as other Guardians found, when we examined that Act, that it was a very imperfect one. The children were very ill-protected. We found that if some man who had ruined the girl would pay down a lump sum of £20 when that child was boarded out, the inspectors, whom the Guardians had to appoint, had no power to enter the house where the child was to see that it was being properly cared for. We found, too, that so long as a baby-farmer took one child at a time the women inspectors, whom we made a point of appointing, could not perform their object. We tried to get the law amended. For years, as the Attorney-General knows, efforts were made to amend that Act, to reach all these illegitimate children, to make it impossible for some rich scoundrel to escape from any future liability with regard to the young child if this lump sum were paid down. Over and over again we tried, but we always failed because those who cared most were women. We could go and see heads of departments, we could tell them precisely about these things, we could talk to them and get all their sympathy. In fact, in this movement on the part of the women, we have been given a surfeit of sympathy. Sympathy? Yes, they all sympathised with us, but when it came to the women asking them to do something, either to give us power to amend the law for ourselves or to get them to do it for us, it has always stopped short at sympathy. I am not going to weary you with trying to show you the inside of my mind, trying to show you what brought me to the state of mind I was in, in 1903; but by 1903—I was at that time a member of the Manchester Education Committee—I had to come to the conclusion that the old method of getting the vote had failed—had absolutely failed—that it was impossible to get anything done; that some new means, some new methods, must be found. Well, there is another defendant, who is not here to-day, and I want to say as a woman well on in life, that perhaps, if I had not had that daughter who is not here to-day, I might never have found the courage to take the decision which I took in the course of the years 1903, 1904, and 1905.

Document 20

This document is an excerpt from a prosuffrage pamphlet written in 1913 by the French Women's Suffrage Association *(Union Française pour le Suffrage des Femmes).* Despite the hard campaign fought by French women, they did not obtain the franchise until 1946. (Women in Finland obtained the vote in 1906; those in Norway in 1913; Russia, 1917; Great Britain, 1918; Germany, Austria, and the Netherlands, 1919; Italy, 1945; Greece, 1949.)

Most of the views expressed in the document were held by suffragists all over Europe and America. These women recognized that even though women had made gains in education, work, and legal rights, they still lacked equality. They were convinced that women could not achieve equality without the power of the vote.

"The Question of the Vote for Women"
The French Union for Women's Suffrage, France, 1913

Some Arguments in Favor of the Vote for Women

We are going to try to prove that the vote for women is a just, possible and desirable reform.

It is just that a woman vote.

A woman is subject to the law, pays direct and indirect taxes just as a man does; in a country of universal suffrage, laws ought to be established by all the taxpayers, men and women.

A woman possesses her own property; she can inherit, make a will; she has an interest in having her say in the laws relating to property.

A woman has responsibility in the family; she ought to be consulted about the laws establishing her rights and duties with respect to her husband, her children, her parents.

Women work—and in ever greater numbers; a statistic of 1896 established that at that date 6,400,000 French women were gainfully employed, that the proportion of female workers was 42 per cent of the women over thirteen years of age, and that the

Rapport sur la question du vote des femmes, report presented to the Besançon Municipal Council by the Franc-Comtois Group of the Union Française pour le Suffrage des Femmes, (Besançon, March 1913), pp. 6-9.

number of women workers was 35 per cent of the total number of workers, both male and female.

If she is in business, she, like any businessman, has interests to protect; it would be unjust for her not to be represented in the Chambers of Commerce, and in the regulatory bodies and courts dealing with commercial matters. Many questions pertaining to business can be decided only by the Municipal Councils and regulatory bodies.

If a woman is a worker or a domestic, she ought to participate as a man does in voting on unionization laws, laws covering workers' retirement, social security, the limitation and regulation of work hours, weekly days off, labor contracts, etc.

If she is a civil servant (postal employee, schoolteacher, professor), should she not have the right to give her opinions on the questions of her salary, of her service, of vacations, of the special rules to which she is subject? If she is a doctor, lawyer, writer, artist, she must fight to make her rights recognized. And the others, who do not yet work but who will have to work in view of the increasing costs of the necessities of life, will also have to fight to assure that new careers will be open to them as well as to men.

Certainly many beneficial reforms have been made on behalf of women, in the name of justice, by a legislature composed of men. But in order for them to correspond to the real rights of women it is necessary that the latter participate in their establishment.

A woman is from this day on capable of voting.

Her education has improved considerably; the elementary school curriculum for boys and girls is the same, and in coeducational schools girls profit from the instruction at least as much as boys; higher education is available to young women, secondary education is as serious in girls' secondary schools as it is in boys' secondary schools.

Woman's importance in the family is greater and greater, her moral authority and economic power are increasing; new legislation on marriage and divorce and on paternity suits tend to make her independent and allow her to develop her personality.

Finally, her special characteristics of order, economy, patience and resourcefulness will be as useful to society as the characteristics of man and will favor the establishment of laws too often overlooked until now.

The women's vote will assure the establishment of important social laws.

All women will want:

To fight against alcoholism, from which they suffer much more than men;

To establish laws of health and welfare;

To obtain the regulation of female and child labor;

To defend young women against prostitution;

Finally, to prevent wars and to submit conflicts among nations to courts of arbitration.

We will see, by studying what has been accomplished by the women's vote in countries where women have obtained it, that it is legitimate to expect that all these urgent reforms will be realized in France too when French women vote.

Document 21

Peace was a major issue in international women's politics in the late nineteenth and twentieth centuries. Organizations dedicated to promoting peace were established, and international associations of women took up the cause of peace along with suffrage, women's legal rights, child welfare, and other women's issues. The first standing committee established by the International Council of Women was the Committee for Peace and International Relations.

In the midst of World War I, women who had long been active in the struggle for suffrage and other aspects of the women's movement held a conference for peace at the Hague, in neutral Holland. The call to the conference was issued by Dr. Aletta Jacobs of the Netherlands (see document 49), and the meeting was attended by women from warring as well as neutral nations. Both the Call and the Resolutions of the Conference are reproduced here.

"Call to the Women of All Nations"
Holland, 1915

From many countries appeals have come asking us to call together an International Women's Congress to discuss what the

"International Congress of Women," printed in *Jus suffragii*, March 1, 1915, pp. 245–46.

women of the world can do and ought to do in the dreadful times in which we are now living.

We women of the Netherlands, living in a neutral country, accessible to the women of all other nations, therefore take upon ourselves the responsibility of calling together such an International Congress of Women. We feel strongly that at a time when there is so much hatred among nations, we women must show that we can retain our solidarity and that we are able to maintain a mutual friendship.

Women are waiting to be called together. The world is looking to them for their contribution towards the solution of the great problems of to-day.

Women, whatever your nationality, whatever your party, your presence will be of great importance.

The greater the number of those who take part in the Congress, the stronger will be the impression its proceedings will make.

Your presence will testify that you, too, wish to record your protest against this horrible war, and that you desire to assist in preventing a recurrence of it in the future.

Let our call to you not be in vain!

Some Principles of a Peace Settlement
1. Plea for Definition of Terms of Peace

Considering that the people in each of the countries now at war believe themselves to be fighting not as aggressors, but in self-defence and for their national existence, this International Congress of Women urges the Governments of the belligerent countries publicly to define the terms on which they are willing to make peace, and for this purpose immediately to call a truce.

2. Arbitration and Conciliation

This International Congress of Women, believing that war is the negation of all progress and civilisation, declares its conviction that future international disputes should be referred to arbitration or conciliation, and demands that in future these methods shall be adopted by the Governments of all nations.

3. International Pressure

This International Congress of Women urges the Powers to come to an agreement to unite in bringing pressure to bear upon any country which resorts to arms without having referred its case to arbitration or conciliation.

4. Democratic Control of Foreign Policy

War is brought about not by the peoples of the world, who do not desire it, but by groups of individuals representing particular interests.

This International Congress of Women demands, therefore, that foreign politics shall be subject to democratic control, and at the same time declares that it can only recognise as democratic a system which includes the equal representation of men and women.

5. Transference of Territory

That there should be no transference of territory without the consent of the men and women in it.

6. Protest

War, the ultima ratio of the statesmanship of men, we women declare to be a madness, possible only to a people intoxicated with a false idea; for it destroys everything the constructive powers of humanity have taken centuries to build up.

7. Women's Responsibility

This International Congress of Women is convinced that one of the strongest forces for the prevention of war will be the combined influence of the women of all countries, and that therefore upon women as well as men rests the responsibility for the outbreak of future wars. But as women can only make their influence effective if they have equal political rights with men, this Congress declares that it is the duty of the women of all countries to work with all their force for their political enfranchisement.

8. Women's Sufferings in War

This International Congress of Women protests against the assertion that war means the protection of women. Not forgetting their sufferings as wives, mothers, and sisters, it emphasises the fact that the moral and physical sufferings of many women are beyond description, and are often of such a nature that by the tacit consent of men the least possible is reported. Women raise their voices in commiseration with those women wounded in their deepest sense of womanhood and powerless to defend themselves.

9. Women Delegates to Conference of Powers

Believing that it is essential for the future peace of the world that representatives of the people should take part in the conference of the Powers after the war, this International Women's Congress urges that among the representatives women delegates should be included.

10. Woman Suffrage Resolution

This International Women's Congress urges that, in the interests of civilisation, the conference of the Powers after the war should pass a resolution affirming the need in all countries of extending the Parliamentary franchise to women.

11. Promotion of International Good Feeling

This International Women's Congress, which is in itself an evidence of the serious desire of women to bring together mankind in the work of building up our common civilisation, considers that every means should be used for promoting mutual understanding and goodwill between the nations, and for resisting any tendency towards a spirit of hatred and revenge.

12. Education of Children

Realising that for the prevention of the possibility of a future war every individual should be convinced of the inadmissibility of deciding disputes by force of arms, this International Congress of Women urges the necessity of so directing the education of children as to turn their thoughts and desires towards the maintenance of peace, and to give them a moral education so as to enable them to act on this conviction whatever may happen.

Document 22

In the 1920s, after the vote had been won in many nations, the international associations which had been formed during the suffrage struggle reassessed their positions and tried to develop new goals and directions. To emphasize its expanded functions, the International Alliance of Women changed its name in 1923 to the International Alliance of Women for Suffrage and Equal Citizenship (IAWSEC).

The policy statement below was issued by the IAWSEC at the conference in Berlin in 1929 which marked the organization's twenty-fifth anniversary. Many of the issues raised in this restatement of policy had been in the forefront of middle-class feminism for three-quarters of a century. Others were relatively new or at least received greater emphasis at that time. The Conference set up committees and passed new resolutions on a number of issues, including a resolution to end the international traffic in opium and one to work in individual nations to secure the hiring and training of women police to deal with women and children who were victims of crime.

"Restatement of Policy After 25 Years"
International Alliance of Women, Germany, 1929

Restatement of Policy

The Eleventh Congress of the International Alliance of Women for Suffrage and Equal Citizenship reaffirms its steadfast belief in the principles which have guided its programme and work for 25 years and restates them as follows:

1. Woman Suffrage

The Congress instructs the Board of the Alliance to inform all unenfranchised self-governing States of the fact that women are now enfranchised on equal terms with men in 25 nations with unquestioned advantage to the men, the women and the nations concerned, and to urge the enfranchisement of women in these States in order that "government by the people" may everywhere include all the people.

2. Peace and the League of Nations

The Congress declares that it is the duty of the women of all nations to work for friendly international relations, to demand the substitution of judicial methods for those of force, and to promote the conception of human solidarity as superior to racial or national solidarity; That the entrance of women into political life is necessary to promote the cause of peace; That this peace should be based on a League of Nations, which, leaving each nation its autonomy and its liberty of action, establishes a lasting harmony between peoples.

3. Economic Rights

The Congress, realising that economic necessities and the desire and right of women to work and to secure for themselves the means of life, has made them important and irreplicable factors in

"Restatement of Policy after 25 Years" (International Alliance of Women for Suffrage and Equal Citizenship), *Report of the Eleventh Congress* (Berlin, 1929), pp. 308–309.

production, demands: That all avenues of work should be open to women and that education for professions and trades should be available for women on the same terms as for men; That all professions and posts in the public service should be open to men and women, with equal opportunities for advancement; That women should receive the same pay as men for the same work; That the right to work of all women be recognised and no obstacles placed in the way of married women who desire to work.

4. Moral Rights

The Congress declares:

That the same high moral standard based on respect for human personality and inspired by responsibility towards the race, should be recognised both for men and women, and that the laws and their administration should be based on this principle.

The Congress therefore demands that traffic in women should be suppressed and that regulation of prostitution and all measures of exception taken against women in general, or against any group of women, should be abolished.

In view of the declaration of principles voted by the Congress and considering that Traffic in Women and procuration in general are the consequences of a double moral standard between the sexes, the Congress appeals to women throughout the world to base all their work on these principles.

5. Legal Rights

The Congress demands that the married woman should have the same right to retain or change her nationality as a man has; That on marriage a woman should have full personal and civil rights, including the right to the use and disposal of her property; That she should not be under the tutelage of her husband and should have the same rights over her children as the father.

VI

Working-Class Women and Socialism

Working-class women, too, sought to take control of their lives, bring about changes in society and politics, and end their oppression. Many of these women joined working-class men in political organizations, unions, and revolutionary activity, but the social and economic positions of men and women within the working class were different and their goals at times conflicted.

Large numbers of women joined socialist political parties and socialist labor unions in the late nineteenth and early twentieth centuries. These organizations addressed women's needs as workers and, in theory at least, espoused the equality of women. But the parties and unions were dominated by men who stressed the solidarity of the working class as they defined it. Until pressed by feminists, male leaderships generally ignored women's issues and the development of special programs for women workers. In their early stages, most parties and unions did not make a real effort to recruit women. Marxist males habitually referred to women as the most politically "backward" segment of the proletariat. But most male leaders were eventually persuaded that if they were to achieve their goals, women had to be brought into the struggle along with men, and to accomplish that women's needs had to be met. Thus many socialist parties established women's departments. Within their divisions, women worked to recruit other women to party membership, conducted classes that raised workers' consciousness, and provided women with the basic education they often lacked. They also helped one another with personal problems. Socialist women's newspapers facilitated communication between party organizations, unions, and women workers. By the beginning of World War I women comprised 16.9 percent of the membership of the German socialist party (SPD), a total of about 175,000 women. In France they formed 2.3 percent of the membership (about 1,000 women), and about 15 percent of the membership of the revolu-

tionary underground in czarist Russia. Women socialists founded their own branch of the Second International (the association that guided the international socialist movement) and held international conferences in 1907 and 1910.*
Women increasingly joined in men's labor unions, and especially in industries in which women predominated, socialist women founded their own women's unions. In a report to the First International Conference of Socialist Women in Stuttgart, Germany, in 1907, a German delegate, Ottilie Baader, reported that by 1905 there were 74,411 women in socialist unions in her country. By 1907 the figure had risen to 100,000. In Austria, according to another report, there were 42,000 women in mixed (male and female) socialist unions at the end of 1906.†
Feminist socialists insisted that women's problems as females, wives, and mothers as well as workers had to be recognized. Women as a group were the most oppressed segment of the working class. Their wages were lower and their working conditions were often worse than men's (see part one, chapter I). Moreover, in addition to wage earning, women workers bore the burdens of housework and child care (see part three, chapters X and XI). Working-class women realized that while higher wages and working conditions might go a long way toward easing men's lives, these reforms would only begin to alleviate women's oppression. Thus they worked for shorter working hours and protective legislation for women workers, especially pregnancy and maternity leaves and for child-care facilities and free maternity and health care. In the 1920s and 1930s socialist women campaigned in many countries for access to birth control information and the legalization of abortion (see part four, chapter XIII). Although the struggle for abortion in Germany in the 1930s was led by the Communist party, women were not successful in gaining support from male-dominated socialist and communist parties elsewhere. Male leaders often insisted that the promotion of birth control was an attempt to reduce the size (and revolutionary potential) of the working class. Others insisted that birth control

*Marilyn Boxer and Jean Quataert, eds., *Socialist Women* (New York, 1978), p. 2.

†*Reports to the First International Conference of Socialist Women* (Stuttgart, 1907), pp. 7, 15.

was a personal matter, and as such should be subordinated to the interests of party work and the class struggle. Some male leaders believed that the limitation of family size was a palliative that would divert women from revolutionary goals and activity. Some socialist parties officially opposed birth control while their female members widely practiced it. Thus working-class advocates of birth control often turned to middle-class women for allies in their struggle to reduce the size of their families and control their own bodies.*

The insensitivity of many socialist men to women's issues and their failure to allow women in positions of leadership and real power resulted from several factors. First, although socialist ideology proclaimed the equality of women, working-class men, like upper- and middle-class men, retained patriarchal attitudes toward women and family life which made equality impossible in practice. Furthermore, Marxists believed that capitalism was the cause of the oppression of both working-class men and women. Only the establishment of a socialist state would eliminate the basis of women's oppression and allow them to achieve full equality. Thus, socialist male leadership believed that gaining reforms for women within the capitalist system, especially through a separate women's movement, could never end women's oppression. If women were to achieve true liberation, working-class women had to join with working-class men to restructure society, and women's goals had to be subordinated to the "larger" socialist struggle.

In prerevolutionary Russia† Marxists adhered to Engels's belief that the bourgeois family based on male supremacy and women's economic dependence had to be destroyed. They considered women's unpaid housework "unproductive" and insisted that women had to be free to engage in productive, paid labor. Alexandra Kollontai, the most influential of the Marxist feminists (see document 41) insisted that the end of women's subordination to men and their complete liberation would be attained only when women became economically independent. That, in turn, was not

*Sheila Rowbotham, *A New World for Women: Stella Browne, Socialist Feminist* (London, 1977), pp. 41–59.

†This discussion is largely based on Bernice Glazer Rosenthal, "Love on a Tractor: Women in the Russian Revolution and After," in *Becoming Visible*, ed. by Renate Bridenthal and Claudia Koonz (Boston, 1977), pp. 372–85.

possible until women were freed from the burdens of child care and housework. Kollontai maintained that the state had to assume the responsibility of caring for children and had to provide services that would free women from household tasks. Kollontai pressed for, and the Bolsheviks grudgingly adopted on the eve of the revolution, a program that called for the establishment of communal kitchens, dining halls, laundries, and child-care facilities. The Bolsheviks' program also included provisions for protective legislation for women workers and reforms of marriage and divorce laws which would eliminate inequalities between men and women within marriage. Given all these reforms, it was assumed that women would soon achieve full equality.

After the revolution of 1917 many of the reforms working-class women had sought, and working- and middle-class women in the West continued to seek, were instituted (see part three, chapters X and XI, and part four, chapters XII and XIII). Legislation established equal pay for equal work, the right of women to retain their own earnings, the right of a wife to retain her own name and establish her own residence. Divorce was made easier and alimony was eliminated in most instances since women were expected to work. Paid maternity leaves were established, and legislation to protect women workers from hazardous and unhealthy working conditions was enacted. In 1920 abortion was legalized (see document 50). Immediately after the revolution, programs for the establishment of nurseries and child-care centers and other communal facilities were begun and efforts were made to bring women into party membership and government offices.

However, the disastrous effects of the revolution and the civil war on the economy precluded implementation of many of the programs that would have aided women. Moreover, the leadership of the Communist party and the government remained in the hands of men, who established goals and priorities. The Zhenotdel (Women's Bureau) was established in 1917 to deal with women's issues, and Alexandra Kollontai was its head. But the Bureau faced stiff opposition and was disbanded in 1929. Under Stalin there was an increased effort to bring women into the labor force. But the economic planners gave high priority to the development of heavy industry and military needs and low priority to consumer goods and communal facilities which would have aided working women. Protective legislation was often ignored, and maternity leaves and child-care facilities were cut back in budget cuts. Abortion, which was made legal in 1920, was again made illegal in 1936, and divorce was made more difficult (see document 50). Labor-saving devices for the household, which would have eased the lives of women, since they were still expected to do the housework, were not manufactured. Although some efforts were made to educate women and train them for jobs and political activity, most still worked in the lowest-skilled, lowest-paid, and most arduous jobs, and they were still expected to be traditional housekeepers and mothers as well. Thus by World War II, working-class women had made some progress in their socialist state, but the goals of socialist feminists were far from being realized.

Document 23

The question of protective legislation for women workers was a controversial issue in women's politics in the late nineteenth and early twentieth centuries. Many male-led socialist parties initially opposed special legislation for women, claiming all workers' needs were identical. As this document indicates, socialist women insisted that the special problems of women workers as wives and mothers had to be recognized and that socialists had to fight for legislation to ease their oppression.

Middle-class women were divided over the issue of protective legislation. Contrary to what the socialists claimed, some middle-class women's organizations campaigned tirelessly for protective reforms, for a variety of reasons (see document 39). Others opposed protective legislation because they believed (as did many socialists) that regulation could sometimes work to the detriment of women, especially those in nonfactory employment (see article 7 of this document, and document 7). Still other middle-class feminists argued that women should not be hampered by regulations but should be free to "compete" with men in capitalist society.

This document is a resolution advocating protective legislation which was proposed at the International Socialist Congress held in Zurich in 1893. From that time on most local, national, and international socialist platforms contained "special" planks for women. This proposal was introduced by an Austrian delegate, Louise Kautsky. She and her husband Karl Kautsky, a Marxist theoretician, were prominent among Austrian and German socialists for many years. Louise Kautsky died in Auschwitz concentration camp in 1944.

A Socialist Platform for the Protection of Women Workers
Louise Kautsky (Austria), International Socialist Workers' Congress, Zurich, 1893

Considering that the bourgeois women's movement rejects all special legislation for the protection of women as interfering with the rights of woman and her equality with man, that on the one hand it ignores the character of our present-day society which rests on the exploitation of the working class by the capitalist class, women as well as men, and on the other hand fails to recognize the special role which has fallen to women through the differentiation of the sexes, namely their role as mother of children which is so important for the future, the International Congress of Zürich declares:

It is the duty of the labor representatives of all countries to advocate energetically the passage of the following measures which will offer legal protection to women workers:

1. Introduction of a maximum eight-hour day for women and a six-hour day for girls under eighteen.

2. Fixing an uninterrupted period of time off once a week of thirty-six hours.

3. Prohibition of night work.

4. Prohibition of women working in all jobs which are detrimental to their health.

5. Prohibition of work by pregnant women, two weeks before and four weeks after childbirth.

6. Appointment of women factory inspectors in sufficient numbers in all industries where women are employed.

7. Application of the above measures to all working women whether it be in factories, workshops, in home industry or as women agricultural workers. [The entire resolution was passed with the exception of article 7.]

The Congress also decided that: in order to protect women workers, and above all to forcibly inhibit the exploitation of

Protokoll des International Sozialistischen Arbeiterkongresses in der Tonhalle Zürich vom 6. bis 12. August 1893 (Zurich, 1894), pp. 36–37, 40.

women, it is necessary not only to reduce working hours but to accept the principle of "equal pay for equal work."

Document 24

These two selections are from autobiographies of Austrian socialist women. They were published in 1912 in *A Commemorative Book: Twenty Years of the Austrian Women Workers' Movement (Gedenkbuch Zwanzig Jahre österreichische Arbeiterinnenbewegung)*, edited by Adelheid Popp (see document 30). The series of autobiographies in this volume provide a rare and extremely useful glimpse into the world of socialist feminism and provide information on the early history of the movement and the contributions made by women to the growth of socialism. At the time these autobiographies were published it was hoped they would inspire other women to join in the socialist cause.

The first selection is by Anna Maier. Her experiences and the path by which she came to socialist activism were common to many working-class women. The second selection is from the autobiography of Therese Schlesinger-Eckstein (1863–1914), a middle-class woman who became a socialist leader. Like many others of her class, she first joined a middle-class women's organization but became disenchanted with middle-class feminists, whom she came to believe were unwilling to make a real commitment to working-class women. She joined the Austrian Social Democratic party in 1897 and remained active until the fascists came to power in the 1930s; she went into exile in France where she died in 1940 (see also document 5).

Becoming a Socialist
Austria, 1890s

Anna Maier: How I Matured

When I am asked what brought me in touch with socialism, I must refer back to my childhood [to begin my answer]. My father was a weaver, my mother a spooler, and other than that, they worked at whatever they could find. I am the youngest of 12

Gedenkbuch 20 Jahre österreichische Arbeiterinnenbewegung, ed. by Adelheid Popp (Vienna, 1912), pp. 107–109.

children and I learned very early what work is all about. When other children were out playing in the street, I would watch them with envy from the window until my mother would slap me to remind me that I had to work. It is easier [for a mother] to discipline a child than for a child to understand why she is being disciplined. When one thinks that at six, a child has to give up all the pleasures of youth. That is a lot to ask! When I went to school my only desire was to learn. But that desire was an illusion because I had to get up at 5 o'clock, do some spooling and then run off to school poorly dressed. After school I had to run home in order to do some more spooling before lunch. Then after school in the afternoons I had to spool again. I was able to accept that, but not being kept home from school to help with the work. But all the begging and crying in the world didn't help, I had to do what my mother said. When I was older and wiser, I often cursed all the splendours of nature because they had never meant anything to me.

When I turned thirteen my mother took me by the hand and we went to see the manager of a tobacco factory to get me a job. The manager refused to hire me but my mother begged him to change his mind, since she explained, my father had died. I was hired. When I was getting ready to go to work the next day, my mother told me that I was to keep quiet and do what I was told. That was easier said then done. The treatment you received in this factory was really brutal. Young girls were often abused or even beaten by the older women. I rebelled strongly against that. I tried anything that might help improve things for me. As a child I was very pious and used to listen enthusiastically to the priests telling stories from the Bible. So, when things were going badly for me [at work], I would go to church on Sundays where I prayed so intently that I saw or heard nothing going on around me. When I went back to work on Monday, things were not any better and sometimes they were worse. I asked myself: Can there be a higher power that rewards good and punishes evil? I said to myself, no, that cannot be.

Several years went by. The *Women Workers' Newspaper* [*Arbeiterinnen-Zeitung*] began to appear and a few issues were smuggled into the factory by one of the older women. The more I was warned to stay away from this woman, the more I went to her to ask her if she would lend me a copy of the newspaper since I didn't have enough money to buy my own. At that time work hours were very long and the pay was very low. When my friend lent me a copy of the newspaper, I had to keep it hidden and I couldn't even let my mother see it if I took it home. I came to understand many things, my circle of acquaintances grew and when a political organization was founded in Sternberg, the workers were urged to join—only the men, the women were left out. A party representative came to us since I was already married by then. When he came by for the third time I asked him if I wasn't mature enough to become a member of the organization. He was embarrassed but replied: "When do you want to?" So I joined and I am a member of the party to this day.

I attended all the meetings, took part in all the demonstrations and it was not long before I was punished by the manager of the factory. I was taken off a good job and put in a poorer one just because I had become a Social Democrat. Nothing stopped me though; I said to myself, if this official is against it, out of fear to be sure, then it can't be all bad. When the tobacco workers' union was founded in November 1899, I joined and we had some big battles before we were able to make progress. Through these two organizations I have matured into a class-conscious fighter and I am now trying to win over mothers to the cause so that future children of the proletariat will have a happier youth than I had.

Therese Schlesinger: My Road to Social Democracy

After the birth of my daughter, I was stricken with such a terrible case of child-bed fever that for almost two years I was either bedridden or in a wheelchair and I have never completely recovered from that terrible illness. About the same time my husband contracted tuberculosis and died; I became a widow after two and a half years of marriage and at a time when I was only barely able to get around on crutches. Then six months after my husband's death, my child was afflicted with such a severe, complicated case of pneumonia that the doctor said she wouldn't live. She eventually got better but she was so sickly for a few years that caring for her took most of my time. Yet despite that I often heard or read about the suffrage demonstrations of the Viennese working class and how the workers were brutally attacked by the police. When I read about a young woman worker who had spoken at a mass demonstration, thoughts of the French Revolution rushed into my head as I remembered how excited I was when I read about it as

Gedenkbuch 20 Jahre österreichische Arbeiterinnenbewegung, ed. by Adelheid Popp (Vienna, 1912), pp. 125–31.

a young girl. I longed to put away my own troubles as I was increasingly motivated to take part in one of the great struggles of my time.

Even [as a young girl] I thought it possible that I might one day play a role in the workers' struggle. I didn't have any idea how I might do that and was convinced anyway that I would be turned away since I was from a middle-class background. But as my own convalescence progressed and as my child grew stronger, I realized I could not escape the desire which I had cherished in my youth, namely, to help in the liberation of those deprived of their rights.

At that moment it was my friend Marie Lang who sought to interest me in the goals of the women's movement, which, as she pointed out, were to raise women of all classes out of oppression and legal discrimination. The General Austrian Women's Association had just been formed shortly before this time [1893] and essentially based its principles on socialist, if not decidedly social democratic, foundations. It advocated the admission of women into the universities, the opening of the professions as well as the improvement of protective legislation for women, the expansion of welfare institutions, the freeing of schools from clerical influence, women's suffrage and the abolition of state-regulated prostitution.

It was not difficult for my friend to get me excited about these and other goals and as soon as I was able to move about again I paid a visit to a meeting of the General Austrian Women's Association.

There I met Auguste Fickert, the distinguished champion of the bourgeois women's movement. From the beginning she expressed a lively interest in me just as I have held her in esteem for that gracious respect she has shown me. Once I took part in a couple of the discussions, they encouraged me to give a lecture and to work on the [women's] supplement in the *People's Voice [Volksstimme]*; the democrat Kronawetter had made that concession to the women's movement [in printing the supplement]. Shortly thereafter I was elected to the Board of the Association and for the next three years I spoke at most meetings and wrote for most issues of the supplement.

In the Association and especially from Auguste Fickert I heard a great deal about the goals of Social Democracy and was stimulated enough to read the *Workers' Newspaper [Arbeiter-Zeitung]* and the *Women Workers' Newspaper [Arbeiterinnen-Zeitung]* as well as the scientific publication of German Social Democracy, *The New*

Time [Die neue Zeit]. I also attended the lectures on social ethics given by Dr. Emil Reich, a lecturer at the University of Vienna. In the spring of 1896 the Ethical Society organized a comprehensive Inquiry into the condition of women workers in Vienna.* All political parties and many associations were invited to put representatives on the commission which conducted the hearings and Mrs. Rosa Mayreder and I were chosen as the delegates from the General Austrian Women's Association for this commission.

The picture of misery and inhuman exploitation which came out of the testimony given to the commission by so many women workers from all branches of industry disturbed me terribly. I was moved to lead a fight against the oppression and exploitation of women on behalf of those so sorely oppressed.

I immediately decided to teach myself more about the principles and theories of Social Democracy. I wanted to read Marx's *Kapital* since I saw that it was often referred to in articles of *The New Time.* I cannot describe how challenging it was for me. Many articles in *The New Time* had already prepared me for the difficulties but it still seemed like a sheer unscalable mountain. The contents of the first chapters were so difficult that for a long time I got terrible headaches if I even looked at the outside of the book. But I didn't give up, I read each paragraph over and over again and worked to write it down in my own words until it made sense. I was so happy when the other chapters went so much easier. Later I realized how inappropriate it was to begin with a book that was so difficult to understand. For the first time I was able to meet personally some Social Democrats at the sessions of the Inquiry. First some women comrades, Popp, Boschek and Glass, and then Dr. Adler, Pernerstorfer, Dr. Verkauf, Smitka and others who significantly increased my interest in the party.

The first International Women's Congress took place in Berlin in the late summer of 1896. It was organized by bourgeois women and I was sent as a delegate of the General Austrian Women's Association. I was to give two talks, first a report about the women's movement in Austria and then one on the Inquiry about working women which I have already mentioned. As I was making my first report—I had already talked about various facets of the bourgeois women's movement—I turned to the subject of the social

*John Fout is currently working on an extensive journal article that will analyze the testimony given at this inquiry.

democratic women's movement and the *Women Workers' Newspaper* when the chairwomen, Lina Morgenstern, suddenly informed me that my time had run out despite the fact that those who had spoken before me had been given unlimited time. I saw in this action—whether I was right or not doesn't matter—an anti-working-class bias and I let it be known that I wanted to leave the Congress and sought to take my second talk off the agenda. There was a storm. The co-chairwoman, Minna Cauer, and several other women, urged me to give up my protest saying it was all a misunderstanding and trying to convince me that I could use my material on the women workers in my second talk. So I gave my talk on the Inquiry two days later. My description of the misery and privation to which the women workers were exposed which had been shown by the Inquiry shocked the audience, which was for the most part composed of teachers, officials and writers of both sexes. They had heard precious little before this about the living conditions of the industrial working class. I also spoke out during a discussion on the morality question and, amid vigorous protests, expressed my conviction, which was only in partial agreement with the speaker's moral preaching, that prostitution is directly connected to the capitalist system itself. . . .

After I returned to Vienna from the Congress, Comrade Popp invited me to a meeting of women workers at which organizational matters and a report on the Berlin Congress were on the agenda. I was very pleased by this invitation and accepted it, never thinking that the talk at the meeting would be given by me. I was delighted and then surprised as Còmrade Popp so strongly praised my behaviour at the Berlin Congress. I was called upon to speak but declined because I was very embarrassed—but finally did it. . . .

I was now ever more frequently entrusted to give talks at social democratic meetings although I did not formally belong to the party. The decisive step was very difficult for me because the Board of the General Austrian Women's Association did not want to let me go at this time and Fickert, Lang and Mayreder sought, in the friendliest way, to convince me that I could serve the cause of women workers within the framework of their organization. They pointed out that the organization needed a newspaper and they were counting on me to found it. But because of that I felt compelled to bring this division of my allegiance to an end and so in 1897 when the Social Democrats took part in an election campaign for the first time, I became very involved in it. My friends in the bourgeois women's movement themselves realized that my place was rightfully in Social Democracy and they wished me all the best when I joined.

Document 25

This selection from *Women in the Soviet Union: The Role of Women in Socialist Construction* by Fanni Nurina presents an "official" view of the gains women had made in Soviet society by the early 1930s. Nurina takes pains to demonstrate that the Soviet government encouraged women to be active in politics and that it brought significant numbers of women into party and government offices. She does not point out, however, that few women were promoted to high-level positions where policy was made.

Women and Socialism in the Soviet Union: An "Official" View
Fanni Nurina, U.S.S.R., 1934

The Role of Women in the Government of the Proletarian State
The proletariat of the U.S.S.R., which won a victory in 1917 over the exploiters in a sixth of the globe, has abolished all the laws which made women unequal in production, social life, the family and all other spheres.

The youth of the Soviet Republic reads with perplexity about the brutal laws of the days of tsarism which were ended by the October Revolution. It is difficult to believe now, when women are taking an equal part in the government of the state and are holding positions from chairman of village soviets to People's Commissar and member of the Central Executive Committee, that only sixteen years ago Article 7 of Part I of Volume X of the Code of Laws held full sway in tsarist Russia. The article read:

> The wife is obliged to obey her husband as the head of the family, to love, honor and obey him, to do his pleasure and be attached to him.

...Under the constitution of the Soviet Union there are no

Fanni Nurina, *Women the Soviet Union: The Role of Women in Socialist Construction* (New York, 1934), pp. 68, 71-6.

limitations to the rights of citizens from the point of view of sex or creed. But this is not only formal equality such as the "equality" of women in the bourgeois-democratic and fascist countries, which is to this day limited even formally in such matters as the absence of the right of women to vote in a number of "democratic" countries. The Soviet constitution only sanctions limitations for the class enemy. The right to elect and be elected to the soviets, the organs of government, according to the constitution is not limited to any sex, creed, race, or nationality, the only limitation being that the voters must be workers of brawn and not less than eighteen years of age. . . .

Lenin never tired of repeating, however, that laws alone are insufficient, that even the best laws are useless if they remain on paper, if constant and systematic attention is not given to their enforcement, that therefore even the "best laws" introduced by the bourgeois constitution for women have in reality only one end: to keep the toiling women from participating in the revolutionary struggle against the bourgeois system.

The Communist Party of the Soviet Union created in the first years of the Soviet power a special department—the Women's Department—which was charged with the task of drawing the toiling women into socialist construction, seeing to their emancipation, seeing to the creation of all the necessary conditions for their truly equal participation in every field of socialist development in the Land of Soviets. Women's delegate meetings were organized, to help the backward working and peasant women gain a full understanding of their rights and utilize them to the utmost limits. From year to year the persistent work of the Party among the toiling women brought results. From year to year the participation of the toiling women in the soviet, Party and other organizations grew.

However, the participation of the working women in the election campaign did not at once yield the necessary effect in the sense of the election of a sufficiently large number of women to memberships in the soviets. It is one thing to elect and another thing to promote from the rank and file the most advanced women capable of taking charge of a responsible and difficult section of the Soviet government, of being members of the city soviet and still more of assuming the duties of its chairman.

Systematic work was conducted to train the most active working women for responsible positions in the government and enable them to discharge their duties with honor. Lenin said that every woman cook must learn to govern the country. In the Soviet Union all the necessary conditions exist to enable the working woman to master this task in the shortest possible time.

In 1929 there were elected to the city soviets 29,064 women or 26.4 per cent of the total against 9.8 per cent in 1922; 13.2 per cent in 1923; 18.6 per cent in 1924-25; 19.7 per cent in 1925-26 and 21.2 per cent in 1927.

Gradually the active women members of the city soviets gained recognition and respect for their able handling of the work and with each year the number of women chairmen of city soviets has grown.

The attraction of the peasant women to the government of the State proves to be a much more complicated and difficult problem. Here the old customs, the backwardness and darkness made themselves felt much longer and much more painfully. The class enemy in the villages, the kulaks, supported by the priests, developed a frantic struggle against the equality of the toiling peasant women, granted by the Communist Party and the Soviet power.

However, the peasant women eventually recognized this "true friend" and began to take an active part in the life of the village soviets. Beginning with 1927 the activity of the peasant women in social life has steadily grown.

The peasant women who were elected members and especially the chairmen of the village soviets found it extremely difficult at first.

At the Fourteenth Congress of Soviets the women delegates told of the difficulties which they encountered in their work, of the endless prejudices hampering them in the discharge of their duties. Comrade Frolenko, a delegate from Siberia, told how upon being elected chairman of the village soviet she was subjected to constant ridicule: "If you had a husband, he would give you a good hiding once or twice, and you would cease loafing," she used to be told. At first she was forced to come to the meetings of the soviet almost stealthily.

A woman delegate from Tver (Kalinin) told how she had been ridiculed, called "a she-commissar," and how only after energetic work for a full year which brought good results, the attitude towards her was definitely changed and she began to be addressed by name and patronymic and treated with due respect....

When for the first time thousands of peasant women, most of whom have had no experience in this work, were elected to leading offices in the village Soviets and district executive committees, they found it difficult to attend to their new duties. In many cases they lacked the technical knowledge to handle their work, had to overcome various difficulties, for instance in some villages, no man would consent to work as secretary to a woman chairman of the soviet.

In order to help this new body of rulers of the Soviet land who brought with them a vast store of creative energy, conscientiousness, devotion to the cause and a desire to carry out their duties with the highest efficiency, there were created both in Moscow and in the regional and provincial centers special training courses for women members of village soviets. Neglecting housework and even the children, many a middle-aged peasant woman took up this new and difficult work. It was with great difficulty that their fingers became accustomed to pen and pencil. The peasant women learned to understand the Soviet constitution, studied arithmetic and the language and spoke with great enthusiasm of the fact that they were no longer daunted by any work no matter how arduous, that now they could get along without reluctant secretaries who refused to work under a "female," that now they were well prepared and capable of coping with their new duties.

A large number of peasant women appointed to leading positions in the soviets gained experience not only by their direct practical work, which is the best possible school, but also by going through various educational and political courses.

There are many hundreds of village soviet women chairmen who have gained great authority in the village by their excellent work, by their struggle against the kulaks and by their organization and consolidation of collective farms.

The growth in numbers of working and peasant women participating in the elections to the various soviet bodies, such as the village and city soviets, the district executive committees and the congresses, naturally resulted in a growth in numbers of women members in the district, regional and central departments of the Soviet government. The more the women displayed their abilities in the practical Soviet work, the more authority and support did they gain and the easier did it become to appoint them to higher offices. From year to year the number of women delegates to the All-Russian and All-Union Congresses of the Soviets grows. Slowly but surely the Party has paved the way for the participation of the active women in the government of the state. These women are now holding responsible offices not only in the village, city and region, but also in the All-Russian and All-Union institutions.

At the Thirteenth Congress of Soviets women constituted 9 percent of the membership, and at the Fourteenth Congress 16 percent. Of special importance was the fact that the women appointed to leading offices in the government are mostly working women or toiling peasants. Among the women delegates to the Thirteenth Congress of Soviets 36.6 percent were working women, and 31.9 percent peasant women. Thirty-three women were elected members of the All-Russian Central Executive Committee by the Thirteenth Congress of Soviets (8.3 percent), and 54 women or 13.5 percent by the Fourteenth Congress. Another 35 women were elected candidates to membership in the All-Russian Central Executive Committee at the Fourteenth Congress (23.3 percent).

Every new election of a working woman and particularly of a peasant woman to the All-Russian Central Executive Committee at first aroused considerable distrust among the delegates to the Congress. The women nominated for membership to the All-Russian Central Executive Committee frequently displayed hesitation, asking to be removed from the list of candidates on the ground that "our own people will make life miserable for us at home."

This period is now becoming more and more a matter of the forgotten past.

VII

Women and Nazism

In the 1920s and early 1930s the Nazi party called for the removal of women from all areas of political and economic life and the reversal of the gains women had made since the beginning of the German feminist movement in the 1860s.* The Nazis insisted that women must not compete with men for jobs or take part in politics. Under National Socialism women could have only one role—all women were to be mothers in the service of the Nazi state. Yet many German women enthusiastically supported Hitler and the Nazi party. They did so because the Nazis successfully played on their fears, frustrations and insecurities, just as they did on those of men. Moreover, in the role of mothers of the race, Nazism offered women high status and a sense of purpose.

Most German women had not benefited from the meager gains made by the middle-class and socialist feminists movements. Reforms such as increased access to higher education and professional jobs had affected only a few upper- and middle-class women, and even they still encountered intense prejudice. Increasing numbers of lower-middle-class and working-class women worked in low-level, dead-end white-collar jobs, and those who worked in industry did the most routine, underpaid work. Despite the protective legislation enacted since the early twentieth century and the reforms of the Weimar period, these jobs were still far from pleasant by the 1930s (see document 15). Most married women also had the responsibility of caring for their children and doing housework and were under increased pressure to devote more time and attention to these tasks. Thus many women were anxious to leave the exploitation of the work place and take care of their responsibilities as wives and mothers. (See part three, chapters IX, X, XI.)

*This discussion is largely based on Claudia Koonz, "Mothers in the Fatherland: Women in Nazi Germany," in Renate Bridenthal and Claudia Koonz, eds., *Becoming Visible* (Boston, 1977), pp. 445-73.

While modernization brought few benefits to most German women, it increased the tension in their lives and often their sense of insecurity. Many women felt threatened by the rapid pace of social change which they believed undermined traditional values. Changing standards of morality, especially increased sexual freedom, appeared decadent to some women and posed a threat to the security of many dependent wives (see part four, chapter XIV). From the late nineteenth century, at the time women were reducing the size of their families, governments and political parties tried to halt the declining birth rate by encouraging women to have more children and assuring them that motherhood was their true vocation (see part four, chapter XIII). Furthermore, many middle-class women, who had been brought up to be dependent wives and mothers, resented feminist demands which they felt threatened the traditional family and attempted to push them out into the world of men. To make matters worse, the enormous male death toll in World War I threatened the ability of German women of all classes to find husbands. After 1929, unemployment and the hardships caused by the Depression increased women's difficulties and dissatisfaction. Adolf Hitler offered a simple solution to unemployment and women's dilemmas: He would find husbands for all German women, remove married women from the work force, and redistribute their jobs among unemployed men. Husbands would then support their wives while women happily raised large numbers of young "Aryans."

Long before the Nazi seizure of power in 1933, women organized in support of Hitler and the Nazi party. (They were never encouraged to become party members themselves, although some did.) Their leaders argued that German women did not have respect or equality in modern Germany and evoked a mythical Nordic past in which women had been equal fighters with men in the building of the German "race." They insisted that women's and men's spheres were different but equally important and that the so-called emancipation of women was a hoax. Women should return to their traditional roles and not seek to compete with men. Men in turn must give honor and recognition to women. They called on National Socialism to restore women to dignity and equality by allowing them, as mothers of the race and the preservers of German culture, to play an important role in the great national struggle. While the Nazis accepted the view that motherhood was a women's proper function, they had only contempt for women. They used women, as they used men and children, according to the needs of the party and the totalitarian state. In return for the glorification of motherhood, the Nazi's demanded total subordination.

After the Nazi seizure of power of 1933, Hitler ordered all women who had husbands or fathers to give up their jobs. Single women, too, were forced out of work. The primary goal of Nazi policy toward women was an increase in the birth rate. Thus monetary incentives were offered to "Aryans" to marry and have children. Loans were made to couples provided neither spouse was Jewish and the wife promised not to work. The amount to be paid back was reduced with the birth of each child. The Nazis banned contraceptives, closed birth control clinics, and increased the penalties for abortion. In the late 1930s "breeding camps" were established where selected unmarried Germans were sent for the purpose of impregnating the women. Those who did become pregnant could await childbirth in homes for unwed mothers which the Nazis provided.

Great pains were taken to organize women and make them efficient housekeepers and mothers. Classes were conducted in home economics, child care, and cooking. Young women were organized into youth groups, and married women were organized as consumers. Women's charitable organizations were used to raise money for Nazi causes. While women were exhorted to organize, sacrifice, and build National Socialism, no woman was ever allowed to make policy or question women's assigned tasks. Indeed, women had to adjust to shifts in policy which changed the demands made on them. In the late 1930s as the Nazis prepared for war, they realized that they needed women's labor in the work force. Thus, they rewrote their history and claimed that until the modern industrial period women had worked and made an important economic contribution. The Nazis would correct this injustice and restore women to their traditional roles and status. From now on German women were to be mothers *and* workers in the service of the Nazi state.

Document 26

Guida Diehl, the author of the first selection here, founded the Newland Movement, a right-wing organization dedicated to Christian principles, in 1917. After 1932 Diehl and the organization became supporters of the Nazis and Diehl was made the leader of the "Fighting Women's Union for National Socialism." In this selection, Diehl clearly articulates the major themes of pro-Nazi women leaders in the years before 1933.

When Hitler came to power, all women's organizations were ordered to accept Nazi leadership or disband. The parent organization of the middle-class feminist movement, the Federation of German Women's Associations *(Bund Deutscher Frauenvereine)* chose the latter course and disbanded in June 1933, a few days after accepting "with deepest regret" the resignation of the League of Jewish Women *(Jüdischer Frauenbund)*.* Many prominent German feminists who opposed the Nazis went into exile or were sent to concentration camps. However, most of the local women's organizations which were affiliated with the Federation of German Women's Associations decided to remain active and work for National Socialism under Nazi leadership. Their activities were organized under the National Socialist Women's Association *(NS Frauenschaft)*. Members of all women's organizations had to adhere to the "Principles of National Socialist Women's Organizations," which are reproduced here from a version published by Guida Diehl in 1933.

Nazi Women
Germany, 1933

A New Type of Woman by Guida Diehl

A new type of woman must be created through Germany's struggle for freedom. She must combine the features of the old [pagan] Germanic woman with those of the Christian German woman. She must help create a strong womanhood that will find the solution to the difficult problem of woman's role in the machine age. She will be a fighter; strong, of set purpose and powerful, yet at the same time motherly, warm, loving and serving. This new woman will be equal to the difficulties and challenges of our tumultuous age.

Let us remember that our two epic poems, the *Nibelungen* and the *Song of Gudrun*, depict types of women which no other nation

*Marion A. Kaplan, "German-Jewish Feminism in the Twentieth Century," *Jewish Social Studies* 38 (1976), p. 51.

Guida Diehl, *Die deutsche Frau und der National Sozialismus* (Eisenach, 1933), pp. 111–13.

can boast. In the powerful Brunhilde we have a heroic woman who fights a life-and-death struggle...[she] must avenge with death Siegfried's violation of her honor, deeply as she loves him.... Or take the splendid *Song of Gudrun*. What a noble, proud and austere figure of a woman who keeps faith with her betrothed in suffering and torment, not meekly enduring, but fighting proudly with stubborn strength. These women have nothing in common with a submissive Gretchen or Klärchen, who were created in an age when men shed gentle tears and women dissolved in sentimentality.

Or let us take a look at the powerful women in the Norse legends with their chastity, their unshakable fidelity, their respected and equal position in the fighting peasantry. That kind of womanly spirit must again come alive among us, for we need a Germanic rebirth. But we also have before us the models of Christian women who were not soft and ecstatic at all but strong and powerful (Maria!). Anyone who understands how to read the New Testament sees a noble and good spirit in those women. We are proud that no woman took part in the shameful murder of the most sacred fighter on earth, our Lord Jesus Christ. No woman misjudged him, mocked and disgracefully abandoned him. And we find as many woman martyrs as men among the early Christians, women who became heroines because they fought equally for the kingdom of the Lord. Since there were indeed women evangelists, it is totally wrong to interpret the phrase [of St. Paul] "women should be silent in the churches" to mean that women were suppressed in those times of struggle....

Heroism is by no means exclusively a male trait, and the fighting woman of today is in no way mannish. It is rather her very motherhood that impels her into the struggle for freedom. This German woman simply asks her man to fight the battle of liberation while she herself stands up for the spiritual battle of liberation behind the front, nursing and strengthening the resurgence of heroism. This tumultuous age with all its difficulties and challenges must create a new type of woman capable of partaking in the achievement of the Third Reich and of fulfulling the womanly task that awaits her.

Let us not forget that this new woman holds her honor high above all else. A man's honor rests on fulfilling the tasks of public life entrusted to him. He safeguards his honor by doing his work honorably and with firmness of character and pride. A woman's honor rests on the province specifically entrusted to her, for which she is responsible, the province where new life is to grow: love, marriage, family, motherhood. A woman who does not accept this responsibility, who misuses this province for mere enjoyment, who will not let herself be proudly wooed before she surrenders—which is nature's way—who does not in marriage provide a new generation with the basis of a family—such a woman desecrates her honor. For we live in a time when womanly worth and dignity, womanly honor and pride, are of the utmost importance for the future of the nation, for the next generation. Therefore, the proud safeguarding of her honor must be an essential characteristic of this new type of woman. The German man wants to look up again to the German maid, the German woman. He wants to admire in her this dignity, this pride, this safeguarding of her honor and her heroic fighting spirit along with her native, cheerful simplicity. He wants to know again that German women and German fidelity go hand in hand, and that it is worthwhile to live and die for such German womanhood.

Principles of the National Socialist Women's Organizations

The women of the National Socialist German Workers' Party are fighting for the German ideal.

We fight for the restoration of national power and the honor of Germany. Only a strong leader and a respected Reich can give and guarantee protection to us and our children.

We stand up for the promotion of the German economy and hence for the education and instruction of women about the importance of purchasing and using German goods. Nonessential products and luxury articles from abroad are banned in the household of the National Socialist woman.

We fight to keep the Aryan race pure and, therefore, for the elimination of all alien influences among the German people.

German shall be the spirit, German the language, German the law and German the culture.

We strive for the physical and mental toughening of our youth

Guida Diehl, *Die deutsche Frau und der National Sozialismus* (Eisenach, 1933), pp. 117–18.

through meaningful bodily training and for specialized intellectual and vocational schooling based on character formation of each sex.

By the example we women give them in self-discipline and constancy, they are to be formed into personalities that bring honor to the nation and enrich the life of the community.

We recognize as a necessity the great process of transformation in the life of women in the last fifty years brought about by the machine age, and affirm the education and integration of all the energies women possess for the benefit of the nation, insofar as they are not needed in the service nearest at hand, that is in marriage, family and motherhood. We strive for a new and genuine solution of the question of the role of woman.

We stand up for the preservation of the Christian faith. We feel responsible for our actions to our families, our nation, ourselves and to God.

*We fight for the honor and dignity of womanhood against the decline of morality and the destruction of a healthy love life, of marriage and the family; for a new structuring of the German-Christian family life, for the fitness of women as mothers in family and profession.

We fight with word and deed and with all the means at our command against the Jewish-Marxist spirit. We set up our affirmative national will as a bulwark against corruption from the camps of pacifism and Bolshevik communism.

We affirm our duty to the community and our readiness for all the tasks of social service.

Every woman who as wife and mother devotes unconditionally all her energies to our people and fatherland is a citizen of the coming Third Reich.

To hold up these principles publicly and in all places, faithfully and with never-flagging energy and to give our all in this battle— this we vow as women of the National Socialist movement to our Führer Adolf Hitler.

Document 27

These two selections were published in London in an effort to show the world what was happening to women during the early

---

*"This paragraph is missing in the official 'Principles,' but should be added for the sake of the important restructuring of family life" (Guida Diehl's comment).

years of Nazi rule. The author of the first selection, Hannah Schmidt, was a Swiss woman active in the International Women's League for Peace and Freedom (see document 21) who had worked closely with German feminists during the Weimar period. The second document is a letter written by a factory worker who directly experienced the Nazi solution to the woman question.

Women Against the Nazis
Germany, 1930s

"The Disfranchisement of Women," by Hanna Schmitt

In 1918 German women were given the active and passive franchise. From that time on, they were represented in the parliaments of the Reich, the states and the communities. The progressive and socialist parties in particular sent women representatives to these bodies. The only exception was the Nazi party and once the dictatorship was in power, it was this party that expelled women from parliaments and deprived them again of their public functions. Thousands of women who formerly had been active in state and communal positions experienced the hostile attitude of the new regime. In numerous cases they were turned out of hospitals and schools where they were employed as physicians, school principals and valuable teachers.

Mr. Goebbles tried to explain the measure in his own peculiar brand of dishonest pathos: "When we exclude women from public life, we give them back their honor." ...

I have observed for years the activities of this organization [International Women's League for Peace and Freedom] and learned to appreciate the labor of those women who, after the dissolution of the League [by the Nazis] had to leave their homeland to escape suffering in German prisons and concentration camps. Frieda Perlen, the chairwoman of the Stuttgart chapter, a tireless worker especially for German-French rapprochement, did not escape her persecutors. Her detention in a concentration camp broke her health and after her discharge she succumbed to her suffering. Three other friends, genuine and upright personalities, became stateless refugees. Why? Only

Hanna Schmitt, "Die Entrechtung der Frauen," in *Deutsche Frauenschicksale,* ed. by Union für Recht und Freiheit (2nd edition; London, 1937), pp. 17–25.

because they wanted the best for their country, because they stood up for peace and freedom....

Women when they are admitted to the universities are subject to work service duty in the so-called *Frauendienst* or "women's service." They are trained in anti-aircraft defense, for the signal corps and ambulance service, and get practice in the use of gas masks; in short, the first stage of their studies is given over to one theme only: readiness for war.

Women have disappeared from editorial offices and are deprived of professorships. There is no room for them in laboratories. If they are suspect for racial and ideological reasons, the regime persecutes them even more ruthlessly than men. For they are out of favor not only because of their convictions but also because of their sex, which, according to National Socialism, places them on a lower level than the male.

This is particularly evident in the economic and social life of women. An official decree issued on April 27, 1933, shortly after Hitler's seizure of power, said: "Management is to see to it that all married women employees ask for their discharge. If they do not comply voluntarily, the employer is free to dismiss them upon ascertaining that they are economically protected some other way."

Thousands of employees lost their positions by this decree, married as well as single women, who were simply told that parents or other members of their families could take care of them. It goes without saying that such a loss of income seriously threatens the existence of a family, considering the low wage level in Germany. Besides, the men who take the place of the women are not paid any better. Thus, poorly paid husbands are supposed to take care of their wives. If they cannot manage, the wives will look for work, but these days married women are treated worse than ever. Their wages are minimal for a maximum amount of work. Wage contracts are ignored. Only in munitions factories are they sought after as a reserve labor force in case of war. Due to the slavedriver system and the unsanitary conditions in the war industry, the health of the women is most seriously endangered....

And what about the private life of women? The Nazis claim to honor housewives and mothers above all. But this honor is denied to a great number of mothers. It does not cover, for example, the mothers of illegitimate children. They bear the burden of care but are morally disqualified and do not get the benefit of the necessary legal protection.

Marriage is subject to the severest restrictions. Women who have been in a concentration camp must provide proof before marriage that they are in perfect physical and mental health, racially pure and not dependent on public relief. The threat of sterilization hangs over many women like the sword of Damocles. Every woman with a physical defect, be it ever so slight, must make it known to the authorities. The doors are wide open for denunciations and vindictive vengeance.

According to official German statistics, more than 500,000 people were sterilized in the last few years; of these, 30,000 cases resulted in death. While in the U.S.A., which has sterilization laws also, 19,000 people were sterilized in 28 years, 55,000 people were subjected to this dangerous operation in a single year in Germany. With such massive surgical intervention, the necessary precautionary measures are naturally not observed. The magazine *German Justice [Die deutsche Justiz]* reports that by the end of 1934, 27,958 women were sterilized, with five per cent of the cases resulting in death.

The most tender and intimate relationship held sacred by all civilized peoples is that between mother and child. But with what brutality does National Socialism often tear asunder these bonds. If, for example, a mother is Jewish and the father Aryan, the child is taken away from the mother in case of divorce to avoid exposure to "Jewish influences." The fate of Jewish mothers is especially tragic in small towns. They must look on as their children grow up in isolation which has a devastating effect on the young minds. How heart-rending is the authentic report of a Jewish mother forced to live with husband and child in such a town. When she asked her little daughter what she wanted for Christmas, she tearfully replied, "Only a little playmate, mommy!" It is not surprising that Jewish families of means send their children abroad to be educated. There is a tragic saying among them, "Our children become letters.". . .

Women who are silent, women who serve, are not free women. For only free women can develop their characters to the fullest, be it in pursuit of studies or at work, as housewives and mothers. A nation that honors its women honors itself. However much it may boast of national virtues, a regime that oppresses the women shows contempt for the people and at the same time for those who are responsible for the future, the mothers of its children.

"Discharged—When You Are Too Old"

A woman worker in Leipzig writes:
I am 43 years old and single. Considering my age and economic situation, I have no chance of getting married. I must work if I am to earn my bread honorably. For the past 12 years I have been employed in a printing company. Day after day I've stood at the small platen press working as a feeder or at the Boston hand press or at the large, flatbed printing machine. Day after day I've checked the daily work list of no less than 16 items. Up to number 8, work is classified as "productive," from 9 to 16 as "unproductive." Work produced in filling orders for clients is "productive," such chores as cleaning the presses, changing ink, shipping, etc., are "unproductive." Our work day has 480 minutes and every single minute must be accounted for on the daily checklist; none must be missing. Even the time spent in the bathroom must be recorded under "unproductive" work.

Today I stood all day at the large Tiegel press feeding in 9,000 sheets. I've had it up to my neck! Whatever you do, it's never enough for the floor supervisor. You get nothing but scolding, never a friendly, polite word. Where could he learn manners and some regard for people? Not from the storm troopers, that's for sure! He is an active SA man, an old party member, so to speak, barely 28 years old. I've been at the plant for 12 years but it has never been such a madhouse in all those years put together. You are squeezed like a lemon. What you earn gets to be less and less and the deductions, voluntary and involuntary, get bigger and bigger.

And what I thought wouldn't be possible, happened today. I was given two weeks' notice along with nine other women workers. We are discharged and our places taken by men from the storm troopers' ranks. They'll do women's work for women's wages. How a family man can manage with 17 marks the gods only know. And what are we women suppose to do in the days to come? No Nazi can tell us!

"Entlassung, wenn zu alt," in *Deutsche Frauenschicksale* ed. by Union für Recht und Freiheit (2nd edition; London, 1937), pp. 217-18.

The National Union of Women Workers
of Great Britain and Ireland.

THE NATIONAL UNION OF WOMEN WORKERS was founded in 1895 by a group of women, who, in their social and philanthropic work, had felt the great need for co-operation among all the various organisations existing for the welfare of the community. From a much earlier date Conferences had been organised, and many local Unions, bound together by a Central Conference Council, had been started in large industrial centres, but it was felt that a more complete organisation would greatly extend their usefulness.

This National Union includes amongst its **" Women Workers "** not only those women who are engaged in industries or in business, but also those engaged in social, philanthropic, educational, and religious work, and last, but not least, women who work *for* or *in* the home.

Since its foundation the N.U.W.W. has grown, and is growing rapidly, in membership, in the number of its Branches or local Unions, and in the work of its Committees. Each year has seen a steady increase in the number of important **Societies affiliated to the Centre,** and also of local Societies affiliated to the Branches, so that, at the present time, the N.U.W.W. is recognised as the most influential and representative body of women in the United Kingdom.

Through its Central Office, and its Sectional Committees in London, it focusses and distributes information of use and interest to women. At its **Conferences and Council Meetings** important subjects are discussed ; and Resolutions passed by the Council, urging reforms or supporting Bills before Parliament, or suggesting Amendments, are sent to the heads of the different Government departments and to municipal and other Local Authorities.

The Executive Committee arranges **Deputations,** in co-operation with other Societies, when it considers it advisable to put the views of women on questions of public importance before His Majesty's Ministers.

The **Sectional Committees** deal with Legislation—i.e., Bills before Parliament affecting women and children—Industrial questions, Rescue work, Education, Public Health, Public Service—relating especially to the Administration of new Acts—the Study of Social Life and Conditions in India, and Work among Girls.

I desire to be enrolled as a Member of the National Union of Women Workers, and enclose
£   :   s.   *d. as an Annual Subscription to the Central Fund.*

Name...

Address..

....

Subscriptions should be made payable to the Hon. Treasurer, and forwarded to the N.U.W.W. Office, Parliament Mansions, Westminster, S.W. 1.

Membership application, National Union of Women Workers of Britain and Ireland, 1917–1918. This organization, founded in 1895, considered housewives and unpaid volunteers to be "women workers." (*Handbook and Report of the National Union of Women Workers of Great Britain and Ireland*, London, 1917–1918)

ASILE TEMPORAIRE POUR FEMMES

48, rue de La Villette. — PARIS

Asile de jour et de nuit pour les ouvrières sans travail et les domestiques sans place.

MODE D'ADMISSION

Les femmes sont reçues sur la présentation d'une carte qui donne droit à une semaine d'hospitalité ; cette carte d'une valeur de trois francs aura été délivrée par la personne qui s'engage à secourir la femme.

Les enfants qui accompagnent leur mère sont admis moyennant un bon d'un franc cinquante centimes.

Le travail dans la maison est obligatoire et le temps nécessaire pour se chercher de l'ouvrage est accordé à toute pensionnaire.

This admission card to a Parisian shelter for unemployed women gave the bearer the right to one week's stay (see document 2). The card states that children were allowed to accompany their mothers and that residents had to work in the shelter and actively seek employment. (*Actes du Congres International des Oeuvres et Institutions Feminine*, Paris, 1890, p. 166)

Dr. Aletta Jacobs, first woman doctor in the Netherlands and birth control pioneer (see document 49). (*Jus Suffragii: The International Woman Suffrage News*, February 1924, p. 71)

Opponents of women's suffrage frequently charged that granting women the vote would destroy family life and lead women to neglect their children. This poster, which attempts to refute those claims, was designed for use in London Underground stations, but was banned by subway authorities. (*Jus Suffragii: The International Woman Suffrage News,* August 1, 1914)

From the last decades of the nineteenth century women were barraged with advertisements for products which would help them become "modern" housewives and mothers and make them attractive to men. These are from the English magazine *Our Sisters* (1897).

" Madam, do you love your children ? " —SHAKSPERE.

Then it will be your first care to ensure to them health and happiness in the future, by providing them with the food which nature intended should be used for their proper growth and nourishment during childhood.

MELLIN'S FOOD

is an accurate article of diet, prepared on nature's plan.

Sample post free. Mention this paper.

Mellin's Food Works, Peckham, S.E.

Advertisements played on mothers' concern for their children and on women's guilt. Advertisements for baby food and medicines often implied that infant deaths and children's poor health were caused by maternal neglect. (*The Illustrated London News*, November 2, 1901, p. 670)

Russian women demonstrate, 1917. (*Jus Suffragii: The International Woman Suffrage News*, November 1, 1917, p. 17)

Women textile workers on strike in Crimmitschau, Germany, 1904. The banner states that the strike is in its twenty-second week, that the women are "Fighters for the ten-hour day," and proclaims "Long Live Solidarity." (*Crimmitschau 1903–1928*, Berlin, 1929, p. 130)

Part Three

◣◆◥

WOMEN AND THE FAMILY IN MODERN SOCIETY

The good wife is one who is strictly and conscientiously virtuous; she is humble and modest from reason and correction, submissive by choice, and obedient from inclination; what she acquires by love, she preserves by prudence; she makes it her delight to please her husband being confident that everything that promotes his happiness must in the end contribute to her own; she always rejoices in his prosperity, and by her tenderness and good humour lessens his cares and afflictions; as a good and pious Christian she habitually unites with her husband and children in all religious duties, and not only leads a holy life herself, but is continually giving good advice to her husband and family.

> *"Scraps from Portfolios," by Mrs. Tyrrell*
> *in the* Ladies Pocket Magazine,
> *Part 1, 1831, p. 21*

The wife, the mother, who is a worker, sweats blood to fill three tasks at the same time: to give the necessary working hours as her husband does, in some industry or commercial establishment, then to devote herself as well as she can to her household and then also to take care of her children. Capitalism has placed on the shoulders of the woman a burden which crushes her: It has made her a wage earner without having lessened her cares as a housekeeper and mother.

> *Alexandra Kolontai,*
> Communism and the Family
> *(London, 1918), p. 6*

Part three describes women's personal lives and family relationships and the changes these underwent in the nineteenth and twentieth centuries. It focuses on the various stages in most women's life cycle—childhood, young womanhood, marriage and motherhood, widowhood. It should be noted that women's relationships to other family members and their economic and social activities were different at each stage of their lives. Moreover, as children, single adults, and married persons, women had activities and experiences that differed from those of men. This was true for working- as well as middle- and upper-class women.

The first series of documents, in chapter VIII (numbers 28–30), describe childhood, including female children's education and working-class children's wage work. The next chapter (documents 31–33) describes the lives of working- and middle-class single women, unmarried women, and widows. The following chapter (documents 34–37) describes married women's lives, and the last (documents 38–41) presents examples of changing attitudes toward marriage and motherhood.

VIII

Childhood

The girlhood of a working-class woman was vastly different from that of a woman of the middle or upper class. The lives of working-class girls reflected the stark realities of poverty. Indeed, "childhood" was very short, especially in the early years of the nineteenth century, when both boys and girls began working at the age of five or six. As soon as they could, girls assisted their mothers in home industry or performed arduous work in mines, factories, and workshops and on farms. Older girls, actually as young as seven or eight, were often responsible for bringing up their younger siblings while their mothers worked long hours away from home. Young girls also minded children of other working mothers for wages.*

Employers eagerly exploited child labor since it was cheap and children were relatively easy to discipline. In textile factories during the early period of industrialization, whole families were sometimes employed together. Children were supervised by their parents and their wages were paid directly to their fathers. In the latter half of the nineteenth century technological advances, reform efforts, and government inspection and intervention led to a decreased use of child labor. Governments gradually passed legislation that restricted the ages and types of employment at which children could work and that called for them to be educated. In the last decades of the century compulsory education laws were enacted in most countries. In England, for example, children between five and fourteen had to go to school, although those between ten and fourteen could go half-time if they had to work. In

*For a discussion of the relationship of women's work and family status, see the important work of Louise A. Tilly and Joan W. Scott, *Women, Work, and Family* (New York, 1978). See also Patricia Branca, *Women in Europe Since 1750* (London, 1978), and *Silent Sisterhood* (Pittsburgh, 1975).

France education became compulsory for those between six and thirteen. By 1899 the minimum age for work in England was set at twelve (fourteen by 1918) and in France the legal minimum age of thirteen was established in 1882. But laws were easy to circumvent by parents who relied on their children's earnings and could not afford the luxury of sending them to school. Even when children did attend school, they still worked after school hours. Moreover, girls, probably more often than boys, left school entirely when family crises such as sickness or death required that they earn money for their families' survival. In Austria in 1898–1899, after the advent of compulsory education which allowed children to work half-time, girls had 2,559,990 half-day absences, while boys had only 1,992,756.*

The lives of working-class children changed as material conditions began to improve in western Europe in the late nineteenth century. The wages of small children became less necessary to families, and less possible with the enforcement of child labor and education laws, and children increasingly went to school for most of their childhood years. A falling rate of child mortality from the last half of the nineteenth century and a falling rate of infant mortality in the early twentieth meant that more children survived to adulthood. Moreover, families began to have fewer children, and when economic conditions permitted, mothers could spend more time educating and caring for the health and growth of the children they did have.

Although working-class girls received some primary education by the twentieth century, few completed much more than that before World War I. While parents might sacrifice immediate income in order to educate their adolescent sons for better jobs, most families were unwilling to forgo the wages of adolescent daughters to permit them to continue their education. Thus by the time they were thirteen or fourteen most working-class girls left school with only a rudimentary education and few skills. They then entered the work force prepared only for low-paying jobs in factories, shops, or offices or as domestics.

Childhood for middle-class girls was very different. While young girls helped their mothers with domestic chores and learned

*Katherine Anthony, *Feminism in Germany and Scandinavia* (New York, 1915), p. 49.

sewing and other needlework skills, they were not expected to become wage earners. Increasingly, girls of the middle class were educated to become "ladies," which meant learning ladylike accomplishments such as playing the piano, singing, dancing, and speaking a smattering of a foreign language. For much of the nineteenth century, girls learned these skills from their mothers, since a major part of a middle-class girl's formal education was provided by her mother at home (or by a governess for those from wealthy families). In France, for example, girls were usually educated at home until the age of ten, and then they might go to a convent school or *pension* (boarding school) to complete their education. In most other countries some girls, but by no means the majority, went to boarding schools while others attended local day schools. By the time a middle-class girl's formal education was over she was prepared to do little but help her mother with domestic chores and wait expectantly for marriage and motherhood.

Document 28

Books for girls which taught them how to spend their time and what they needed to know to become proper ladies, and which, at the same time, instructed mothers what to teach their daughters, were very popular among the French bourgeoisie in the middle decades of the nineteenth century. *A Little Girl's Week [La semaine d'un petit fille]*, whose "Introduction" is reproduced here, was first published in 1839; by 1867 it was in its fifth edition. Books such as this reflected the widely held attitude that a mother's first role in life, and the one she would find most gratifying, was teaching her daughters what they needed to know. The ideal was for mothers to instill correct values, habits, and attitudes in their daughters so that they would grow up to be good wives, housekeepers, and mothers.

Home Education for Girls
Louise D'Aulnay, France, 1867

I will not begin this as in a fairy tale: Once upon a time there was a beautiful and wise little girl who lived on cookies and sugar

---

Louise D'Aulnay (Julie Gourand), *La semaine d'une petite fille* (Paris, 1867), pp. 5–8.

plums. No. Marguerite, whose week I will describe to you, had no beauty except her youth, and in spite of her natural goodness she had a very hard time correcting all her faults, laziness above all.

Marguerite Harrel was ten years old. Until now she had lived just like other little girls, knowing nothing of life except the New Year's celebration, her dolls and candies, and family holidays when the kisses of her father and mother seemed even sweeter than usual. Like many of you she somehow learned to read. Her days were filled with walks and continual games, but there is an end to everything.

One morning, in the month of January, Marguerite entered her mother's room holding a book in which she seemed to have no interest whatever.

"My dear mother," she said with her ordinary playfulness, "how I enjoyed playing blind man's bluff yesterday! I wish it were already Sunday so I could see my cousins again. Oh! Monday is so boring. I never like it. Even when I am grown up, I will resent Monday. At least if it were nice outside, we could go out! But look how it is snowing! It is horribly cold. Are you going to the ball tonight, Mother?"

"No, Marguerite. I intend to devote the whole week to you to try to make you love studying. The delicacy of your health forced me to deny myself the joy that mothers experience in giving their children their first lessons. I only saw you suffering all the time— night and day I spent next to you. I gave in to all your whims; I was so afraid of losing you, my child! But today you are ten years old and you are in excellent health; yet, Marguerite, I have not noticed any change in you. Listen to me, I have a lot to say to you. Yesterday, I went to see Madame Amestin. Blanche, her daughter, and some of Blanche's friends were in the next room: it was a day off. Can you imagine how they were spending their time? You will never guess it! Blanche was reading while the others worked. The little friends began to chat and discussed all the young girls of their acquaintance. Your turn came, my dear Marguerite. "As for this one," said Blanche, "she has a good heart—but she is so lazy she will never accomplish anything. Really, she will play a sad role in society, ignorant and almost ugly!"

"Ugly!" cried Marguerite, beside herself. "Blanche dared to say that?" And the little girl began to cry.

"What is wrong with you?" asked Madame Harrel. "Is it possible that you by chance think yourself pretty?"

"Truly, yes, Mother—and if I am not pretty I will be very unhappy! But I am often told just the opposite. My dear mother, I beg you, tell me I am pretty—I want to resemble you so much!"

It would have been easy for Madame Harrel to humor the vanity of her daughter, for at that moment Marguerite's face was embellished by an expression of childish innocence that is always pleasing to a mother.

But besides the fact that Marguerite was not a beauty, Madame Harrel understood in an instant that it was necessary to smother the beginnings of vanity in a little girl as quickly as possible.

"My dear Marguerite, it is impossible for me to please you like that. I agree with Blanche. But tell me, what price do you attach to beauty? Is it that I don't caress you as much as Madame Amestin caresses Blanche? Are you not the object of all my thoughts? What difference does it make to me whether your eyes are smaller than those of your friend if I see tenderness in them? Why should your large mouth be of concern to me if it never lies? Instead of being unhappy about your lack of beauty, I am often joyful that you are not beautiful. At least I think my daughter will apply herself to acquiring qualities and talents which will make her loved. A sickness, an accident, ruins beauty and what remains? Later on, my child, I will make you understand me better."

"Never had I heard talk like this. You greatly surprise me, Mother. Really! you are not disappointed that I am not pretty? I have always thought you also loved me because of my face. It's funny," said the little girl, letting her arms fall and looking as though she were thinking for the first time in her life.

"Marguerite," said her mother, "do you want to become pretty?"

"Yes, Mother," the child replied excitedly.

"But will you accept the way I show you?"

"Everything, everything, Mother!"

"Let's see," said the good mother taking the chin of her daughter in her hand. "First of all, the little eyes are very insignificant. One would say these eyes were made for sleeping all day long. Ah! it's true that Marguerite sleeps a lot—she hasn't discovered the pleasure of studying. She yawns while learning her lessons and during her music lesson she looks at the clock twenty times, isn't that true?

"Well, the day you love to study your eyes will acquire a charming vivaciousness. Here is a mouth which is always pouting. That is because all the advice I give my daughter displeases her so she pushes her lip forward and deforms the one feature nature made passable. Your complexion, child, is that of a little girl who only scrubs in hot water with the corner of the washcloth. Your hair is dull because you won't give your maid enough time to wash and brush it. Really, should one be surprised that you are not pretty? Who could boast of being pretty under these circumstances? Well, Marguerite, do you still want to become pretty?"

"Ah! yes, yes, Mother."

"Well, my dear child, you must begin by working, by overcoming this laziness which you hide from yourself by constantly being on the move in the house or out taking a walk. I want to teach you how to use your time. Today is Monday, let us begin the week courageously. I will write down everything we will do in the next eight days, and I hope this week will serve as a model for all the others to come, for my child, life is made up of weeks."

"Eight days, my dear Mother, eight days of work! Ah! will that ever be long! Aren't you afraid I'll get sick? I will have to try so hard!"

"I am not in the least worried. On the contrary, I will be very reassured. The idleness in which you have lived until now is more harmful. As long as you are with me, you won't participate in the boisterous games of your brothers, games which do not become you in any way; you will be less piggy with your food, since lazy people always have a way of whiling away the time. Go on, it is agreed, you will work the whole week, isn't that true?"

Little Marguerite threw herself in her mother's arms and made a thousand promises. We will see if she kept them.

Document 29

The French Association for Child Rescue, like similar organizations in other European nations, was composed of middle-class women who believed it was their duty to extend their roles as moral guardians, educators, and protectors of their own children to the children of the working class. The main concerns of these women were to save children from physical and sexual abuse and moral endangerment, conditions which they believed would lead youngsters to crime, beggary and, in the case of girls, promiscuity or prostitution. They believed that their work in child rescue was the basis of all social reform and directed much of their activity toward the urban poor, whom they believed faced the greatest dangers. Mme. Pauline Kergomard, who gave the speech reproduced here at the International Congress of Women's Works and Institutions, was the organization's co-founder and vice-president. She was also an Inspector of Nursery Schools and a member of the *Conseil Supérior de l'Instruction Publique* (the highest advisory council on education in France), positions which had brought her into direct contact with the problem of abused children. At the end of her address she notes that although the Association had a male president and a male-dominated Board of Directors, it had been founded by women and was "indubitably" a feminine undertaking (p. 25). Particularly interesting is the Association's sophisticated and broad definition of child abuse. (See documents 12, 21, and 22 for other social reform organizations.)

Combating Child Abuse
Pauline Kergomard, French Association for Child Rescue, France, 1880s

The *French Association for Child Rescue,* which today numbers about 800 members, is a recent and essentially female creation. It thus has the right to be represented at this Congress....
Program of the French Union
The purpose of the *French Association* is to seek out, bring to those in authority, or gather in under its wing children who are physically abused or morally endangered, under the conditions set forth in the first article of its statutes.

Individuals under sixteen years of age are considered *children.*
Abused (children) are
1. Children who are the subjects of habitual and excessive physical mistreatment;
2. Children who, as a result of criminal negligence by their parents, are habitually deprived of proper care;
3. Children habitually involved in mendacity, delinquency, or dissipation;
4. Children employed in dangerous occupations;
5. Children who are physically abandoned.

"Union Française pour le Sauvetage de L'Enfance," rapport présenté par Mme. Pauline Kergomard, déléguée, *Actes du Congrès International des Oeuvres Institutions Féminines* (Paris, 1890), pp. 18, 21–25.

Children who are morally endangered are
1. Children whose parents live in a notoriously uproarious and scandalous state;
2. Children whose parents are habitually in a state of drunkenness;
3. Children whose parents live by mendacity;
4. Children whose parents have been convicted of crimes;
5. Childen whose parents have been convicted of theft, habitually encouraging the delinquency of minors, of committing an offense against public decency or an immoral act.

The *Association* establishes local Committees wherever possible.

Each local Committee is invited to establish a shelter for its own use. Local Committees shall keep the central Committee informed of all their undertakings.

Every active member of the *Association* promises to take an interest in every mistreated or morally endangered child he shall discover or encounter or who is brought to his attention.

First, he shall take down the first and last names of the child and the child's address.

If possible, he shall go that same day to the indicated address and conduct a brief preliminary investigation, the results of which he shall convey immediately to the local Committee, or if one is not available, to the central Committee.

If he is unable to do this, he shall send the name and address to the Committee the same day.

In either case, the Committee shall proceed without delay to conduct a meticulous investigation.

In the event that the investigation establishes that the child falls into one of the above categories, the Committee's representative shall suggest that the person exercising parental custody entrust the child to the Committee until the child's future shall be resolved.

If this person consents, the child shall be taken immediately to the temporary shelter.

Next, the Committee shall determine as rapidly as possible the conditions of the [child's] placement, in conformity with the first article of its statutes, and demand that the person having custody of the child agree to this placement. To this end it shall have that person sign a release identical to that now in use by the Public

Assistance Administration for the parents of children taken in under the program for the morally abandoned.

If consent is refused, or if the child does not fall into one of the categories detailed above, the Committee shall prepare a report summarizing the results of the investigation it has conducted. In every case a copy of this report shall be directed to the mayor of the city (or in Paris, the district) where the parents live.

If circumstances appear to warrant it, another copy shall be sent to the prefect or sub-prefect and, in Paris, to the director of Public Assistance.

Finally, a copy shall be sent to the public prosecutor of the Republic in every case in which acts revealed by the investigation appear to fall under the jurisdiction of the law. A summary of pending action shall be sent to each member of the *Association*....

The *Association* is functioning, as I have said. Certainly, it is far from realizing our ideal of perfection. But as each day brings its progress we hope, bit by bit, to make it a model society, completely liberal, that is, it is to be above all sectarian antagonisms.

While we wait for the law to **arm** us solidly against the undeserving parents from **whom we have** already wrenched some victims; while we wait for **it to permit** us to take all the children who roam the streets to our temporary shelter; while we wait for it to permit us to search the hovels where there is torture and depravity, we have set ourselves the task of:

1. Snatching children from the horrible hornets' nest of a police record by saving them from first convictions;
2. preventing them from being confined or released from confinement too early, which would fatally return them to the streets and bring them back before the courts;
3. improving their conditions at the police station or detention center while they await trial.

To this end we have established our headquarters at the Palais de Justice and, thanks to the humanitarian feelings of almost all the magistrates...we make ourselves known to the accused on their arrival, we negotiate with certain parents to have them sign over custody to us, we send children to farmers in the country (of whom we now have one hundred twenty for this purpose), we release to the Public Assistance Administration those who fall under their jurisdiction; as for the others, M. Rollet [the Association's representative] pleads that they be kept in custody until their twentieth year with conditional freedom, that is to say that the penal authorities should send them to us after a period of confinement so that they can then be placed in the country like the others.

Then, too, we have improved the conditions under which children are detained at the Police Station and Detention Center, girls being in greater need of this than boys. Not long ago the girls held in the Detention Center—some were four years old, some sixteen—were all placed together; now there is a separation [by ages], quite an elementary one, alas! But at least there are now two divisions.

Not long ago they slept three to a cell—without surveillance. Today there is a dormitory where observation is easy.

Not long ago they had nothing to keep them busy and spent their days telling each other their sad pasts. Today they sew—the Association has furnished them with material and sent a sewing teacher—today they read, because the Association has assembled a library.

Not long ago they stayed in the Detention Center in the same sordid clothing and unwashed state as the day they were arrested. Today there are baths and changes of clothes.

Oh! there is a great deal still to be done, but the Association is happy with the results it has achieved.

Document 30

Adelheid Popp (1869–1939) was born to a poverty-stricken family in a small town in Austria. She became an influential socialist leader. In the 1890s she was editor of the *Women Workers' Newspaper [Arbeiterinnen-Zeitung]*, a socialist publication, and she was a member of the Austrian Parliament in the 1920s. Her autobiography is a poignant account of the misery endured by working-class children in the nineteenth century. She vividly portrays the struggles of her mother, who, like countless other working-class women, had to assume the burdens of feeding and raising her family alone when her husband died. Popp's childhood experiences illuminate the devastating affects of illness, alcoholism, and, most of all, poverty on family life. Despite compulsory education laws Adelheid received only the most minimal education. From the time she was eight years old she was forced to work to help support her family. By her own account, her childhood was over by the time she was ten. (See also document 24.)

A Working-Class Childhood
Adelheid Popp, Austria, 1880s

Most persons, if they have grown up under normal conditions, look back in times of heavy distress, with gratitude and emotion to their happy, beautiful, careless youth, and sigh, perhaps wishing, "If it could only come again!"

I face the recollections of my childhood with other feelings. I knew no point of brightness, no ray of sunshine, nothing of a comfortable home in which motherly love and care guided my childhood. In spite of this I had a good, self-sacrificing mother, who allowed herself no time for rest and quiet, always driven by necessity and her own desire to bring up her children honestly and to guard them from hunger. What I recollect of my childhood is so gloomy and hard, and so firmly rooted in my consciousness, that it will never leave me. I knew nothing of what delights other children and causes them to shout for joy—dolls, playthings, fairy stories, sweetmeats, and Christmas-trees, I only knew the great room in which we worked, slept, ate, and quarrelled. I remember no tender words, no kisses, but only the anguish which I endured as I crept into a corner or under the bed when a domestic scene took place, and my father brought home too little money and my mother reproached him. My father had a hasty temper; when roused he would beat my mother, who often had to flee half-clad to take shelter with some neighbour. Then we were some days alone with the scolding father, whom we dared not approach. We did not get much to eat then; pitying neighbours would help us till our mother returned, impelled by anxiety for her children and household. Such scenes occurred nearly every month, and sometimes oftener. My whole heart clung to my mother; I had an unconquerable dread of my father, and I never remember to have spoken to him or to have been addressed by him. My mother told me later that he was vexed because I, the only girl of five to live, had dark eyes like hers.

I can still remember one Christmas Eve when I was not quite five

Adelheid Popp, *The Autobiography of a Working Woman* (Chicago, 1913), pp. 15-23, 28-29, 31-33.

years old. For this once I nearly obtained a Christmas-tree. My mother wanted just once to show me, her youngest child, what the Christ Child was. For many weeks she had constantly striven to save a few farthings in order to buy me some little cooking utensils. The Christmas-tree was adorned with chains of coloured paper, gilded nuts, and hung with modest playthings. We waited for our father to light the candles; he had gone to the factory to deliver some goods. He was to bring money home. Six o'clock struck, then seven, then eight—our father did not come. We were all hungry and wanted our supper. We were obliged to eat the nice poppy balls, apples, and nuts, to eat without our father, after which I went to bed without seeing the candles burn on the Christmas-tree. My mother was too much put out and anxious to light up the tree. I lay sleepless in my bed. I had looked forward so much to the Christ Child, and now he stayed away. At last I heard my father come; he was not received kindly, and another angry scene took place. He had brought less money than my mother expected for he had visited a public-house on his way. He had nearly six miles to go, and he wanted to warm himself. He had then sat longer than he intended, and came home tipsy. At the noise which ensued I looked up from my sleeping place—and then I saw how my father cut the Christmas-tree to pieces with a hatchet. I dared not scream; I only wept—wept till I fell asleep.

The next day my father felt some pity for me, for he gave me a few pence to buy tin kitchen things for myself. Compassionate persons gave me an old doll and playthings of their children's which had been discarded for other, more beautiful gifts....

My father was struck with a malignant illness—cancer—which brought us into great poverty. He would not remain in the hospital; but he was obliged to have medical help and medicines, and these swallowed up nearly all our earnings, and our circumstances became worse and worse. As often as I was sent to the chemist's with a prescription my mother complained as to how long it would last. One day he was so ill that the clergyman was fetched to confess him and to give him the last sacraments. That was a great event for me. All the inmates of the house knelt in our room and we with them. The smell of the incense filled the air, and the sobs of my mother were audible between the prayers. My father died a few hours later. My mother never forgot that he died without a word of reconciliation with her or of remembrance for his children.

I felt no sorrow when I wore the black clothes, the hat and veil lent me by a well-to-do family; I rather felt a sense of satisfaction at being so well dressed for once.

My mother was now the breadwinner for her five children. My eldest brother was indeed eighteen years old, but he could be no support to us, as he had learned a trade that was decaying. He resolved to try his fortune abroad, and went off. Two brothers who till now had worked with their father were apprenticed; the youngest, a child of ten, went to school.

My mother had great strength of will and much innate good sense. She was inspired with a wish to show that a mother can also provide for her children. Her task was most difficult, as she had learned nothing but domestic work. An orphan early, she had never been to school, and could, therefore, neither read nor write. She was also an enemy of the "new-fangled laws," as she called compulsory education. She considered it unjust for other men to dictate to parents what they were to do for their children. On this point my father had sympathized with her, and my brothers, when ten years old, had to help him in his work—weaving. Three years' schooling was sufficient, according to my parents' ideas; one of their frequent sayings was that he who had learned nothing when ten years old would learn nothing later. My youngest brother must now leave school. . . .

There was the sick brother [the youngest], and no wages coming into the house. My mother had no work, and the brother next to the youngest had run away from his master because he had been so cruelly treated. This was a winter, too, in which no snow fell for a long time, so that nothing could be earned by sweeping away this bread from heaven. My mother shirked no trouble in order to find work. Sometimes she would wash clothes somewhere, and then I had to go to her at noon and she would share her meal with me. We used to fetch from the restaurants the water in which the sausages were cooked; this with bread made an excellent tasty soup for us. My sick brother received from compassionate neighbours soup and many other good things. All tried to cure him. All good and bad household remedies were tried. My mother brought an ointment from the town, which had been prepared by an old woman and was to have wonderful results. Others came and laid dry, pounded plums, mixed with sugar, on his wounds. Herb baths were made for him, so-called sympathetic treatments were tried—all in vain; his wounds did not heal. Then I was obliged to begin to help earn.

I knitted stockings for other people, and ran messages. We worked at anything that was offered us to avoid succumbing to our need. When the brother next to the youngest at last found work with a mother-of-pearl worker, I was bidden there to mind the children. Finally I was taught how to sew on buttons, and I now sewed mother-of-pearl buttons on to silver and gold paper. That was always my occupation when I was out of school or during the holidays. When I had sewn on 144 buttons (a gross) I had earned one and a half Kreuzer (nearly a farthing and a half). I never managed to earn more than twenty-seven Kreuzer in a week....

My mother had received work in the spring in the garden of the Duchess, by which our situation was somewhat improved. But now my many faulty attendances at school were punished. As my mother could not write, I had not often had a written excuse for my absence. The school authorities had had a return of the attendances, and my mother was condemned to twelve hours' imprisonment. As she had now work, she neglected to comply with the injunction to take her place for the "punishment." She also deemed it incredible that they would imprison her, an honest woman, who had always conducted herself honourably. But at six o'clock in the morning on Easter Saturday two policemen appeared and took her away. She was almost out of her mind at having such shame put upon her as being forced to walk through the streets between two policemen. She could only find comfort in the knowledge that her whole life was spotless and pure. Afterwards she was bidden to the headmaster, and he represented to her that she ought to send me regularly to school, as I was very gifted. She was also assured that "something might be made of me." My guardian was also made to come. But he contented himself with admonishing me to be good and pious. But of what use was it to go to school when I had neither clothes nor food?

When this year's schooling was over, my mother decided to migrate to the town. I was now ten years and five months old, and I was no longer to go to school, but to work....

I received my removal certificate at school, which declared that I was ready to go into the fourth class of the elementary school. This was my sole equipment for the life of work which I was now to begin. No one protested against my being withdrawn from the legal eight years of school attendance. I was not registered on the police books. As my mother could not write, I was obliged to fill up the registration form. I ought, of course, to have entered myself under the heading "Children," but as I did not consider myself a child—I was a working woman—I left this heading not filled in, and remained unregistered by the police. Other people did not observe this omission.

We moved to the town, to an old married couple's, into a little room, in one corner of which was their bed, and in another my mother's and mine. I was taken into a workshop where I learned to crochet shawls. I earned from fivepence to sixpence a-day, working deligently for twelve hours. If I took home work to do at night, it was a few farthings more. I used to run to my work at six o'clock in the morning, when other children of my age were still sleeping. And they were going to bed, well fed and cared for, when I was hastening home at eight in the evening. Whilst I sat bent over my work, making one row of stitches after another, they played, or went for a walk or to school. I took my lot then as a matter of course; only one eager desire came to me again and again—just for once to have my sleep out. I wanted to sleep till I woke of my accord—that seemed to me to be a most splendid and beautiful thing. If I had sometimes the good fortune to be able to sleep on, it was indeed no happiness, for want of work or illness was the reason for it. How often on cold winter days, when my fingers were so stiff in the evening that I could no longer move my needle, I went to bed with the consciousness that I must wake up all the earlier. Then after my mother had wakened me she gave me a chair in the bed, so that I might keep my feet warm, and I crocheted on from where I had left off the previous evening. In later years a feeling of unmeasured bitterness has overwhelmed me, because I knew nothing, really nothing, of childish joys and youthful happiness.

IX

Single Women

During the period from the late eighteenth to the early twentieth century major changes occurred in the working, personal, and family lives of single women. Most single women were young women who expected to marry eventually. But a small number of women by choice or force of circumstance remained unmarried throughout their lives. Although the experiences of working- and middle-class women were different, there was a transition toward wider occupational choice for most women, and, for some, more personal independence.

In the early part of the period young working-class women, like their forebears in pre-industrial days, were likely to work in domestic industry or as servants on farms. As industrialization opened new opportunities, many women found work in factories and as servants in middle- and upper-class urban households.

Domestic service remained a major area of employment for unmarried women until the last part of the nineteenth century. It provided needed employment for young rural women without skills and it eased the transition to city life. Once they were established in the city, young women often left domestic service entirely or alternated between work as a servant and other kinds of jobs.

Single women who migrated and did not have live-in domestic positions faced the problem of finding a place to live. Some employers operated boarding houses or dormitories, but most young women had to find housing wherever they could. They rented space with families or in a boarding house, but this was often no more than part of a room in which to sleep. Low wages forced working women into overcrowded, unsanitary, and dismal living conditions.

Generally, daughters who left home did not lose contact with their families but their relationships with their parents changed.

While their sisters who remained at home used their wages to support their families, women who migrated did not always send money home. This was especially true after they had lived on their own for a number of years. Their meager wages went for their own support, to provide themselves with a dowry so that they could marry (although this was less necessary as time went on) and, if they could afford it, to buy clothing or pay for entertainment. Parental authority was weakened when daughters left home, and so was parental protection. Young single women on their own were particularly vulnerable to sexual and economic exploitation. Out-of-wedlock pregnancy and the inability to support themselves and their children led many to turn to prostitution.

In the late nineteenth and early twentieth centuries a major change occurred in working-class women's work and personal lives. Technological advances and the expansion of white-collar employment led large numbers of young women to abandon domestic service, in some cases for improved factory jobs but primarily for white-collar work in retail shops, government offices, and private businesses. Although working conditions were far from ideal in these occupations (see documents 2–7, 30), young women preferred them to domestic service because they offered more personal freedom, daily contact with other young women, and greater opportunities to meet men. Single women were now more likely to live with their parents, who themselves might be second- or third-generation urban dwellers.

The peer group became the focal point of social activity for women whether they lived alone or with their families. Single women went to dance halls and on Sunday outings with women and men their own age. They often met their future husbands at these activities, and parents lost the control they once had over the choice of their daughter's husband. When they could, young working women spent substantial portions of their earnings on entertainment, clothing, books, and magazines. In fact, unmarried daughters had more personal and economic independence than their mothers, who could rarely afford the time, energy, or money for this kind of recreation and personal expenditures. But these changes also brought new pressures. Sexual attractiveness, which had not been an issue when parents selected their daughters' husbands, became an important factor in courtship and marriage and in women's self-image. Popular culture and new social conventions encouraged women to be sex objects; continued spinsterhood was a sign that a woman was not sexually appealing to men.

By the 1930s young working-class women were receiving at least some secondary education, they had a wider range of employment opportunities than ever before, and they had more freedom in their personal lives than their mothers and grandmothers had had when they were young. But most still had jobs with long working hours, low pay, and no hope of advancement, and women who remained unmarried usually suffered from inadequate incomes. Since single women also suffered social stigma, it is not surprising that most did not wish to remain single for very long.

Young middle- and upper-class women faced far different circumstances, but their lives, too, changed over the course of the nineteenth and twentieth centuries. For most of the period they were expected to live at home until marriage, and be subject to parental control. They were also expected to live up to a rigid moral code, be innocent (ignorant, actually) of sexual matters, and be passive and obedient. They were generally discouraged from showing any interest in advanced education or affairs of the world since these were deemed unsuitable for the "delicate" female sex. But many young women chafed at the boredom of the waiting period between school and marriage, a life that one German woman described as largely consisting of "tea with friends where one ate red pudding with white sauce or white pudding with red sauce."* Although this life style persisted into the twentieth century, by the middle of the nineteenth some women began to rebel against the limited range of educational, occupational, and personal opportunities open to them (see documents 8–14 and 47–53). They understood the adverse affects of single women's restricted lives on their intellectual and emotional development and on their future relationships with their husbands and children. One feminist remedy was the opening of higher education to women. After considerable struggle, women in France succeeded in gaining admission to university study in 1861, and English women could obtain degrees by 1878. In Germany, women could not be fully matriculated in universities until the twentieth

*Helen Lange as quoted in Marion A. Kaplan, "German-Jewish Feminism in the Twentieth Century," *Jewish Social Studies* 38 (1976), p. 39.

century. Efforts to expand educational opportunities were accompanied by campaigns to open the professions to women. By the early twentieth century large numbers of young middle-class women expected to obtain some higher education and/or work during their single years.

Most middle-class women, whether or not they pursued a career while single, expected to marry, and after marriage be supported by their husbands and devote themselves to raising their families for the rest of their lives. But these expectations were not fulfilled for all women. Some never married at all and a few divorced. (Even though divorce became easier to obtain in some countries, it was still a rarity in the late nineteenth and early twentieth centuries.) For most women, however, marriage ended with the death of their husband, a common occurrence since women typically married older men. They then entered a second period of single life, but one that was very different from the first.

In many respects widows were freer and more independent than either married or young single women. In the first part of the nineteenth century widows had more legal rights and more personal freedom under the law than did married women since in most countries married women's property, earnings, and persons were legally under their husband's control. But throughout the period for both working- and middle-class women, widowhood could be a difficult time, financially and emotionally. They had to care for and support their children alone or, if they were elderly, cope with illness and infirmity. These problems were particularly acute for working-class widows, but middle-class widows who were not adequately provided for and could not find work experienced poverty and deprivation and some even ended up in the workhouse (see documents 2 and 19). A woman could be freer in widowhood or she could be poorer and lonelier than ever before in her life.

Document 31

Harriet Martineau, the author of the first excerpt here, was born in Norwich, England, in 1802 and died in 1876. During her lifetime she witnessed and helped foster changes in the opportunities for and attitudes toward unmarried women's work and education. She was educated mostly at home by her brothers since her mother held the view, unusual for the early nineteenth century, that both girls and boys should receive an education. She never married and when her father, a wool manufacturer, lost his fortune and died, she supported her mother and sisters by one of the few occupations for which women of her class were trained— needlework. An intelligent and energetic woman, she turned to writing and produced works on social, economic, and historical topics as well as children's books. Keenly aware of the hardships and limitations placed on women by an upbringing which sought to make them ornamental wives, she advocated better education so that women could be independent and self-supporting.

By the end of the nineteenth century there were some improvements in the lives of middle- and upper-class young women in western and northern Europe. As the second selection here, from the English *Woman's Penny Paper*, indicates, urbanization and modernization brought a loosening of social restraints. However, that was not the case everywhere; young women continued to be carefully chaperoned and physically restricted, especially in southern Europe.

"Our Social Life Has Changed": Young Women in the Victorian Period
England, 1820 and 1889

Age 18 (1820)

When I was young, it was not thought proper for young ladies to study conspicuously; especially with pen in hand. Young ladies (at least in provincial towns), were expected to sit down in the parlour to sew—during which reading aloud was permitted—or to practice their music; but so as to be fit to receive callers, without any sign of blue-stockingism which could be reported abroad. Jane Austin, the Queen of novelists, the immortal creator of Anne Elliott, Mr. Knightly, and a score or two more of unrivalled intricate friends of the whole public, was compelled by the feelings of her family to cover up her manuscripts with a large piece of muslin work, kept on the table for the purpose, whenever any genteel people came in.

Harriet Martineau's Autobiography, 2 vols., ed. by Maria W. Chapman, (Boston, 1877), vol. 1, pp. 77–78.

So it was with other young ladies, for some time after Jane Austin was in her grace, and thus my first studies in philosophy were carried on with great care and reserve.

Chaperones (1889)

In an age like ours it is natural that we should outgrow some of our old institutions, and we find ourselves repeating, by way of excuse, that circumstances alter cases. With the rigid decorum of fifty years ago, have fled many customs and appurtenances then thought indispensable. Will the chaperones of Society be angry at being called "old institutions"? It is very greatly to be feared that some will....

Our social life has changed; perhaps it would be more truthful to say, is continually changing. We do not need to quote instances of this. One could hardly walk a quarter of a mile in any street of London without seeing instances of it, particularly in dress and manners of women, in the things they do, in the words they say. When hansoms were first introduced, what lady went in one alone? Now what lady goes in anything else? Only three classes of unfortunate people—the timid ones, who would rather not see more of a horse than they can help; those with more luggage than the roof of a hansom will carry; and lastly, and this of the three is by far the most numerous class, those who can't afford it. Then, since customs are changing, it is quite certain that they will change in the ball room as well as elsewhere. Who has not been told that three dances was the limit of what might be granted to the most favoured partner? Now what chaperone is able to enforce this golden rule of our forefathers? It is well to think a little what a chaperone goes to a ball for. She goes on purpose to see that her charge behaves herself as such an ethereally clothed being should. That was the originating idea of a chaperone. But the chaperone, even if she were placed where nothing could escape her eye in the ball room, knows nothing of what goes on outside it, where most of the flirting takes place. No, if ball rooms were the only part of the house used on these occasions, chaperones might be very efficient in warding off "detrimentals," but since such is not the case, chaperones can hardly be said to achieve what they aspire to perform in the way of guardianship....

"Chaperones," *Women's Penny Paper*, vol. 1, no. 6 (March 2, 1889), p. 2.

Letting a girl go to a dance without a chaperone is a sort of putting girls on their honour. Let it be remembered we are not arguing for a girl to have the freedom of a young man, as some do, or that mothers young enough to enjoy dancing should not go out with their daughters. Society's fiat that a mother with a grown-up daughter should not dance, we think hard, and rejoice to see how often it is set at nought. At a public subscription dance, it must be admitted that a chaperone is a necessity. What we would urge is that it should not be considered wrong that a girl in good society should go to a dance at a friend's house unchaperoned. That it should no longer be felt when a girl is known to have come alone, that her parents were guilty of neglecting her by allowing her to go there unattended. When brothers take their sisters it is considered quite correct, but surely brothers can hardly be looked upon as taking the place of chaperones. It will be said, perhaps, that since it is a fact that all girls do not make themselves respected, they had better have their chaperones with them, to warn them after too long an absence, or to counsel no further dances with a too openly favoured partner. A steady head may save a giddy one from folly by warning glances and whispered cautions, yet experience, the best of all teachers, tells us, there is little use in warnings or even prohibitions. What is suppressed in public grows in private. As we have before said, the ball room never sees the greater part of the flirtation. The girl in most need of her chaperone's care is the one the soonest taken out of its reach. Let us try and teach girls from their early days the dignity of their womanhood, and that amusement, for which all young natures rightly crave, need not be looked for beyond the limits of propriety, but there is plenty of it (and of excitement also) in perfectly harmless pleasures, amongst which dancing holds a prominent place. Should this state of affairs ever become perfectly general, a state we mean when hostesses as a matter of course "mother" all the girls who have come alone into their drawing rooms, then there would be less scandal, because more simplicity in our manners.

Document 32

By the late nineteenth century urbanization, smaller living quarters, a desire for greater privacy, and the increased mobility of the middle class meant that widows and unmarried women were not always able to live with their adult children or other relatives. But this selection by Louise Otto, an editor of the German feminist journal *New Paths [Neue Bahnen]*, indicates that even if they were able to live with their relatives, single women might not always enjoy that arrangement. In this article, which appeared in 1881, Otto presents surprisingly modern arguments in favor of independent living for unmarried women and stresses the joys of living alone.

"Small—Clean—Alone": The Joys of Living Alone
Louise Otto, Germany, 1881

"Small—Clean—Alone" is an apt slogan for women who live alone, who have no family, either their own or one for whom they work, in which they can make themselves useful. Widows with no children or only married ones, young women who either didn't want to get married or lacked the opportunity, those who have an independent income, a pension or earn a salary so that they do not have to live in the home of strangers—they all will gladly confirm the above words and will find consolation for many other privations because they can do as they please within their own four walls. Be her home ever so *small*—as long as it is *clean*, not only clean of dirt and unpleasant odors but also free of distracting problems which bring with them burdensome and unsympathetic people—it is better to be *alone* than with such things and people even though it is nice to be in the vicinity of those we enjoy, appreciate and love.

If it could be statistically established how many elderly and unmarried women live alone in their own small lodgings consisting of one room, or at best two, a few closets and a kitchen, the number would amaze you.

It was not so in bygone days. Widowed mothers-in-law and grandmothers, aunts and every kind of distant female relative moved in with family members. Households were set up in such a way that anyone of means owned a spacious house where a room could be found for a single lady to live and sleep, and where she could make herself useful to the family and the home. Many

"Klein—rein—und allein," *Neue Bahnen: Organ des Allegemeinen Deutschen Frauenvereins* 14, no. 3 (1881), pp. 18-20.

household tasks needed feminine hands: bread-baking, soap-boiling, the preserving of meat, vegetables and fruit for winter (all tasks taken over by industry today), the supervision of children (who spend most of the day in school or Kindergarten now), the greater hospitality of a former life style, when pleasures were enjoyed at home and acquaintances were gladly welcomed. Thus, a relative living alone was cheerfully taken in by the family. She was not entirely dependent but rather found companionship and in return had the satisfaction of offering a helping hand which was fully appreciated.

All this has changed. Expensive apartments usually offer no spare room for a relative, nor is her help needed since there isn't enough work even for a servant girl. So nothing is gained by two parties moving in together, neither for the married couple, whether they have children or not, nor for the grandmother or mother-in-law or aunt. In the best of cases, mutual respect is maintained but differences in habits and outlook can cause annoyances; at worst, all mutual consideration is set aside making such a living arrangement utterly unbearable. Mother-in-law or aunt becomes a burden; she herself feels it and ruefully realizes too late that she has given up her independence, freedom and peace of mind for what she expected would be a more pleasant and comfortable existence. She has given up those blessings of life one has the right to expect in old age and which make it bearable.

Let us visit one of those small apartments where old ladies of culture live alone and take care of themselves with the help of a cleaning woman for the heavy housework and the basic shopping. In the entrance hall everything is neat and bright, there is no reminder "wipe your feet" as one finds outside the front door in so many places. Inside everything looks clean, orderly and harmoniously arranged. We may find in the hallway some superfluous household effects close to the heart of the occupant. We look at them with respect rather than with mockery. In the kitchen everything is orderly at all hours of the day. Though she cooks only for herself, she sees to it all the more that every little pot and pan is in its place. And the rooms—how they reflect the spirit of the occupant! Here is a table for flowers or individual flower-stands with houseplants, there is at the window, a bird-cage open so that the little occupant can fly in and out, for no danger threatens it in the room. The furniture has grown old with its owner but it is well preserved, reminding her of the magic of her youth and its experiences as do the pictures on the wall. Those pieces of furniture that show the most use—the sewing machine, the writing desk and the piano—reflect the individuality of the occupant. A spirit of orderliness and contentment permeates all. To be sure the occupant can feel quite lonely on days when no visitor drops in and she cannot go out, when there is nobody to talk to except her little bird. But books, newspapers and above all her memories keep her from boredom. All too often, when she comes home dissatisfied from a visit with relatives where she found worries, mutual misunderstandings and bad tempers because of some mishap, she is glad to leave behind the confusion of opinions, moods, apprehensions and intentions, and return to her quiet home where she is her own mistress and can make herself feel comfortable and cozy: "Small—Clean—Alone." So she is doubly contented whether she be widow or an old maid.

The more well-to-do or those who earn money by giving private lessons or writing, etc., can live even more comfortably in many respects. They can set up a household on a larger scale and have a servant girl. Every grandmother, mother-in-law, aunt, etc., living and working under these conditions, is able to open her home warmly to children, grandchildren and relatives, and she in return will be welcome when she goes for a visit, be it for hours, days or weeks. She can look forward to a happy old age if she stays by herself and remains independent.

Visiting is quite different from living together. The latter is the rock upon which the best of friendships between the nicest people are wrecked. Moving in together may appear pleasant and may offer many advantages, and specifically great savings. But how do these compare to the advantages of continued freedom and independence in old age?

This is why the faces of so many elderly ladies living by themselves are suffused with the glow of inner peace, while those who are disappointed in their expectations for their declining years have rigid features marked by discontent, bitterness and resentment since they can no longer enjoy life.

Document 33

The memoirs of Julliette Sauget (1886–1969), parts of which appear here, is an engrossing account of the life of a French woman in the early twentieth century. After a childhood of rural poverty, she migrated to Paris, where she worked as a domestic. Later she took advantage of expanding educational and employment opportunities and eventually improved her situation. Many of her experiences as a young single woman were shared by millions of others across Europe. Julliette's story is fascinating because she experienced so many of the changes that occurred in women's lives in the first half of the twentieth century. She clearly articulates commonly held attitudes toward, among other things, work, unmarried motherhood, independence, and perseverence.

A Rural Woman: Childhood, Working as a Domestic in Paris, Keeping Her Illegitimate Child, *Memoirs*
Julliette Sauget, France, 1886–1920

1. Birth and Childhood in a Large, Poor Family in a Rural Township of the Somme

I was born on Christmas Day, 1886, in a hamlet of the district of Rue (Somme), situated on the edge of a marsh. My family was very poor. My father, a woodcutter, worked for a big property owner in the area. I belonged to a family burdened with children: eleven (five boys and six girls), of whom ten were raised in modest circumstances (one daughter died accidentally at an early age). I was the next to last. Births in my family were regularly spaced every two years. Therefore, my poor mother was always worried about providing us with food. We owned only a small cottage and a little adjoining garden. We had a cow, a horse, a sow, and some fowl. But our main income was my father's small wages. His work consisted of cutting down trees in the marsh and helping out with the beet harvest. Very little money came into the house, and my mother, when I was grown up, often told me that in her nightly prayers, she would ask: "My God, grant that there will be bread in the cupboard tomorrow for my children.". . .

A curious custom took hold in my family: the boys went to the local public school while the girls were sent to the nuns' school, who instructed us for free because of our poverty. While my brothers obtained their grade school diplomas, the same was not true for my sisters and me. Just when I was about to take the

Julliette Sauget et Julliette-Marthe Mouillon,˙ "Un example de migration rurale: de la Somme dans la capitale. Domestique de la Belle Epoque à Paris (1904–1912)," *Etudes de la région parisienne* 44, no. 27 (1970), pp. 3-7.

examination for my diploma, the nuns did not want a graduation ceremony at Rue and proposed that I take the examination at Abbeville. Since my mother did not allow such a trip, I was never able to obtain the diploma. For us, this was only a small detail, since as soon as school was over we were to be placed in neighboring farms or in private homes, to relieve our impoverished parents. Thus my brothers and sisters were all farm workers and domestics for a more or less long period of time....

When I was seventeen and a half years old, I left Rue and my family to go to Paris. My departure took place in rather distressing circumstances. My father had severely scolded and slapped one of the sisters, and I decided out of loyalty to her to leave home. I left for Paris with my oldest sister, who was married there and who was spending a few days of vacation at Rue....

2. The Life of a Domestic in Paris: Frequent Changes

...I had neither skills nor training for office work. In Paris, I stayed at my sister's. My first wish was to be a lacemaker. But I soon realized the difficulties: low wages and the lack of lodgings of my own, for I could no longer stay with my married sister, who lived in cramped quarters. This eldest sister, who had started out in Paris as a maid, advised me to look for a job as a domestic in a family. I therefore went to an employment agency and I began as a servant in the house of a man who rented carriages, on the rue Doudeauville, in the 18th arrondissement. That was in 1904. I was lucky to find two good employers, very kind to me and without pretense since I took all my meals with them at the same table. No doubt, I sometimes found them coarse and boorish, but the months passed without too many problems. However, after eight months of service, I found that I had to leave the place. I slept in my employers' apartment and not in a separate maid's room.

Now there was a seventeen-year-old boy in the family. One night, I found him in my room and he wanted to sleep with me. I pushed him away and the next day, I naively told my employers at mealtime what had happened. This was greeted by a great burst of laughter and I understood that I could no longer stay in this family without running grave risks. My sister took me in and I looked for a new position....

The years 1905–1906 were marked by a large number of successive positions. I wanted to work for the real bourgeoisie so I could learn a lot and be in contact with other house servants. I was still very much a rustic, naive, and without experience in how to manage a house or cook well. I believed that everyone took me for a silly goose. Through the placement bureau, I obtained a new position in the same 18th arrondissement, in the home of a merchant, rue Léon, where I remained for six unmemorable months. In my first two positions I earned 25 then 30 francs a months in addition to lodging, food and laundry. I like changes and it took very little cause for me to decide to leave an employer. After my first two positions, I was to experience frequent changes.

3. *Trials and Help: The Quest for Independence*

My last job as a domestic was at a doctor's, a Rumanian Jew, on rue Châteaudun, an ailing doctor who treated only those patients who were able to come to his office. My work was varied (receiving the patients, housework, laundry, ironing, serving meals) and I was well treated. It was at this doctor's house that I discovered I was pregnant.

As a matter of fact, while frequenting the Elysée-Montmartre dance hall, I had met a Uruguayan electrical engineer who was in training in Paris. He wanted to marry me and take me to South America. In spite of the state in which I found myself and the difficulties which awaited me, I refused to leave for the New World. I did not want to become an expatriate and the advantageous situation of my child's father did not change my decision. Rather than a promising future in America, I preferred to stay in France, with all the cares which were sure to follow....

In my misfortune, I was greatly helped by my employers. The doctor's wife helped me with the less difficult work and hired a woman for the harder tasks. The doctor made me go to the Charity Hospital, where the birth of my daughter took place at the beginning of 1909. I intended to resume my job, but a head nurse advised me to seek a position as a wet nurse at the Lying-in Hospital of Port-Royal. I was accepted and I remained there for four months with my daughter. I was paid little, but I had the advantage of being able to keep my child. Unfortunately, my health deteriorated and I had to leave for a rest home. After several weeks, the head of personnel at this home advised me to take a job as a wet nurse in a bourgeois household. I would be able to keep my daughter, who would have to be weaned, which grieved me greatly. With a heavy heart, I gave my milk to a little girl who was a stranger to me and I quickly discovered that my child would not accept milk from the bottle. Anxious, I left my job as a wet nurse and went to ask for advice and assistance from the family of the Jewish doctor on the rue Châteaudun who had been so kind to me during my pregnancy and at the birth of my daughter. The doctor's wife again took me into her service and I entrusted my daughter to one of my sisters in Amiens, waiting until I could bring her up myself. I stayed two more years at the doctor's on rue Châteaudun. But how surprised I was to learn from my employer that I had to recognize my daughter officially since she was an illegitimate child, which I did, six months after her birth, at the city hall of the 9th arrondissement, before two witnesses....

I then had time to reflect on my precarious situation. I received little money from my daughter's father, who had returned to America. I wanted to raise my child myself and I did not want to be dependent on anyone. I was first a porter in a glass warehouse for the Saint-Gobain Company where my brother was a driver-delivery man. I was then finally able to bring up my child and have more peaceful moments. But in 1912, as a result of a competitive examination, I began work for the Welfare Services of the Seine department as a hospital attendant. From that time on I was more secure about the future. My modest income was assured. I rented a small apartment and I took advantage of the hospital's day-nursery and lunch room. By dint of will power, discipline, work, and deprivation, I passed the nurses' examination after going to night school. Right after the First World War, I married a representative of the Saint-Gobain Company, who was to become a director of commerce, while I ended my career in 1935 as supervisor of the hospitals of Paris.

X

Married Women

In the nineteenth and twentieth centuries, the vast majority of European women married. Indeed, rates of marriage rose and the average age at which women married fell in most countries. While marriage remained an economic necessity for most women, both working- and middle-class women increasingly chose their own husbands and expected to find emotional fulfillment in marriage.

All aspects of married women's productive and reproductive lives underwent significant transformations.* In pre-industrial times the home was a center of economic production where husband, wife, and even very small children worked. In this domestic economy women combined childbearing, child rearing, and household responsibilities with economically productive work. With industrialization the primary work place shifted from the home to factories and workshops, and workers became wage earners. Under this system married working-class women experienced greater difficulty balancing childbearing and child rearing with paid employment outside the home, especially when this meant long hours away from home, no facilities for child care, and low wages (see part one, chapter I). Furthermore, since married women were barred from many occupations, they often had difficulty finding steady employment. Thus, in the early stages of industrialization and urbanization women tended to work regularly when they were single and when their children were very young, and to abandon full-time employment outside the home when the oldest children were able to earn wages. Mothers could then devote more time to caring for younger children and their household responsibilities.

This does not mean that working wives did not earn part of their families' incomes in the nineteenth and early twentieth centuries. In fact, census data which show that the majority of married women did not work are misleading. In all countries married

*See note, p. 117.

women worked when their husband's or children's wages were insufficient for subsistence or when they were unemployed. In countries where agriculture was still very important (in France and Italy, for example), married women continued to constitute, as they traditionally had done, a large proportion of the work force. In these as well as more industrialized nations married women also worked in factories and workshops, although with the exception of the textile industry they were usually confined to the least industrialized sectors. In general married women sought work that allowed them to combine wage earning with the care of their children. This work was often sporadic and temporary and the kind that escaped the tally of the census takers. Married women labored in various types of home industry, sewing clothing, ribbons, artificial flowers, and other goods. They were also street peddlers, they took in laundry, cared for the children of other working mothers, and were charwomen. A widespread means of earning money was taking in boarders. Their wage earning was not always continuous, but many married women, just how many it is impossible to know, certainly did work for wages.

When men's wages increased and health and diet improved, there was less need for wives to work. They still earned wages when it was necessary for their families' subsistence and, when possible, in order to raise their families' standard of living. But since women's wages were very low and their family responsibilities burdensome, it was in their own interests and the interests of their families for mothers to concentrate on necessary domestic tasks wherever possible. Therefore the functions of husband and wife within the family became increasingly separated; the wife's primary concerns were taking care of the home, feeding the family, and raising children, while the husband was considered the primary breadwinner. These tendencies were reinforced in the late nineteenth century in western Europe when the demand for much of the wage-earning work married women did, such as home sewing and peddling, decreased. Although new jobs were open to women, particularly in white-collar occupations (see part one, chapters I and II), these as well as many industrial employments were often restricted to young single women, who were considered more reliable, more manageable, and more sexually appealing than married women. Thus many women came to expect and, in view of working conditions, to look forward to giving up full-time employment when they married.

Whether they worked for wages or not, women still worked in their homes without pay. Working-class wives were housekeepers and household managers; they were responsible for their families' budgets (working-class husbands often turned over their wages entirely to their wives), they bought and prepared food, made and mended clothing, did the washing and ironing, cleaned and saw to the furnishing of their homes. These were all crucial activities since a wife's skill in handling family finances could often mean the difference between subsistence and starvation. As wages rose and a wider variety of food and consumer goods became available, the wife was expected to improve the cleanliness and comfort of the family's home and the quality of their food. These were not easy tasks since even until the middle of the twentieth century most working-class families lived in cramped quarters, which usually lacked modern conveniences, and could not afford labor-saving devices.

Most married women had a third occupation—bearing and raising children. In this area too, their responsibilities increased. In western Europe child mortality fell in the late nineteenth century and infant mortality declined in the twentieth. More children lived to maturity and, with the enforcement of compulsory education laws, they remained financially dependent on their parents until adolescence. After leaving school they usually worked and lived at home until marriage. This meant that there was more work for the mother. Working-class mothers were assured by middle-class reformers that if they took proper care of their infants and young children and saw to their education, their offspring would not only survive but would grow up to be healthy, happy adults. To achieve these goals mothers had to devote more time to child rearing, especially when their children were young. For many working-class women the only feasible way to do that and meet all their physical and financial responsibilities was to have fewer children. In western Europe birth rates began to decline after the 1870s (although they did so earlier in France) and families became smaller. Fewer children meant that a woman might be healthier and might have more time for each child, for her housework, for paid employment to raise the family's standard of living, and, possibly, for herself.

It is not surprising that while the family remained patriarchal and the wife's dependency increased, the mother became the center of the home and family life. Moreover, family life appears to have become more important as working men realized shorter work hours and increased leisure time. The family Sunday outing, for example, became an important form of recreation in many countries. But home was essentially a woman's sphere, and women's daily concerns were different from men's. While some women were isolated in their homes, most, especially urban dwellers, could count on the support, advice, and companionship of women relatives and friends who shared their way of life and understood their needs. Working-class women lived out most of their days in a woman's world, a married women's culture focused on family responsibilities and shaped by women's unique experiences.

Among the middle class, wives were not expected to be wage earners, and so men's and women's spheres were even more sharply separated. Within their realm, wives were expected to live up to a demanding set of standards and roles. Life was obviously far easier for them than for working-class women, but the image of the middle-class housewife promoted in literature—the lady of leisure, submissive in all things to her husband, securely resting on her pedestal while served by a retinue of servants and governesses—was simply not true for the vast majority of middle-class married women. While many may have desired the trappings of gentility, only among the upper class and the wealthier middle class could wives afford to lead lives of leisure. In fact, unlike men of their class (and like women of the working class), most middle-class women performed physical labor in their homes on a daily basis.

For most of the nineteenth century a middle-class family could generally afford only one servant, a maid of all work. She was usually a young rural woman or a poor city girl unaccustomed to the middle-class life style and standards of cleanliness. Houses and families were often large so there was too much work for one servant to do. In London in the middle of the nineteenth century, for example, houses were three or four stories high, containing eight to ten rooms, and families averaged five to seven persons. The woman of the house did a good deal of the housework, scrubbing, polishing, carrying water, and tending fires. Moreover, as the availability of single live-in domestics decreased, middle-class women turned to daily workers, charwomen, who might only come one or two days a week. This occurred at the same time that standards for a middle-class life style were rising.

Urbanization and modernization multiplied middle-class women's responsibilities and placed great pressures on them. The large increase in the size of the middle class meant that many of these women were new to their status and roles. They were expected to manage the household budget and to maintain and upgrade their families' standard of living within what were still limited resources for most. As incomes rose, so did the requirements for housecleaning, clothing, and food preparation. Furthermore, urbanization and the mobility of the middle class meant that many women did not have the support and aid of other female family members that they had had in the past. Often alone, overworked, and insecure, they turned for advice to books, magazines, and the formal and informal women's networks. Unfortunately, this advice, which often insisted that women be perfect wives, perfect mothers, and perfect housekeepers, only increased their work loads and anxiety. Moreover, from the end of the nineteenth century women were bombarded with advertising which touted new labor-saving devices for the home. Women were eager to have these products because they believed they would ease household tasks and make them better housewives and because they were symbols of middle-class status. But many of these labor-saving products could actually increase women's work. While a coal-burning stove, piped-in water, and a sewing machine undoubtedly eased a woman's lot, the acquisition of a washing machine might mean that laundry was no longer turned over to a laundress and her husband and children expected cleaner clothes and linen more often.

Housework, though, was not considered a middle-class woman's primary occupation. Her main responsibility and the source of her most meaningful work was motherhood. As the nineteenth century progressed, motherhood was exalted more and more in books, magazines, and sermons. It was held up as the ideal for all women and the source of their greatest prestige. These authors and preachers promoted relatively new attitudes toward child rearing which held the mother responsible not only for her offsprings' physical care but for their happiness too. Mothers were blamed for high rates of infant and child mortality and were instructed in how to upgrade infant feeding, sanitary measures, and child care. Mothers were also told to see to their children's emotional development, since their children's future happiness and success depended on it. They were expected to devote as much time and physical and emotional energy as possible to child rearing and developing strong bonds with their children.

Even earlier than working-class women, middle-class women began to reduce the size of their families. Smaller families meant that middle-class women could lead less circumscribed lives, a goal middle-class feminists had been working toward from the middle of the nineteenth century. Indeed, by the twentieth century women who did not have many children might be able to take advantage of the hard-won gains women had made in intellectual, educational, and employment opportunities.

There were other changes, too, in the early twentieth century. Feminists demanded greater equality in marriage and in divorce, and openly advocated women's right to control their own sexuality and reproductive lives. The idea that a woman's identity was subordinated within marriage to her husband and children was quietly resented by many women and openly attacked by others. But although many women could not or did not want to live up to the roles of perfect wife, perfect mother, and perfect housekeeper, there was powerful pressure on middle-class women to conform to these standards.

Document 34

Middle-class women depended on their servants, but the relationship between mistress and domestic was complex, and often tension-filled and mutually unsatisfactory. As the following article from the *English Woman's Journal* indicates, even women accustomed to live-in servants could be forced to reduce their household help when their husbands died or suffered a financial reversal. This did not mean that these women then lowered their expectations or demands concerning housekeeping. The worker who replaced the full-time servant was usually a married woman who worked on a daily basis. Already burdened by her own family responsibilities, she was paid a pittance and expected to conform to her employer's often unrealistic standards. Although this document indicates that there was some change in attitudes toward servants by the second half of the nineteenth century, the charwoman was still the object of an unending series of complaints. Relationships did not improve as the supply of young live-in domestics decreased in the late nineteenth and early twentieth centuries and middle-class women regularly turned to charwomen.

The Middle-Class Housewife and the Problem of Troublesome Domestics
England, 1860

My mother cannot understand modern domestics and their ways of going on. She has been a housekeeper these fifty years, and she never thought that things would come to such a pass as they have arrived at.

Poor dear old mother! accustomed in earlier and brighter days to a respectable number of well-trained old-school servants who stayed a dozen years in a place, who wore linsey-woolsey petticoats and blue checked aprons, only on Sundays substituting white linen for the latter; girls whose best gowns—they did not call them "dresses" in those days—lasted a fabulous number of years and were then converted into quilts to last as long again; girls whose notions of respect and duty to their earthly masters and mistresses were only held second, so says my mother, to their duty to God. It certainly does seem hard for her, now she is old, to look back on such servants as she talks about and reconcile herself to silks, flounces, veils, parasols, and crinoline.

And, thus it fell out, that so long as we were able to afford one solitary domestic of the modern school, there was war between her and my mother, despite my intervention, on every subject wherein the ways of the damsel differed from those of her predecessor of fifty years ago. . . .

It was almost a relief to me when circumstances at length compelled us to give up our single servant, and be contented only with a charwoman to wash on Mondays and clean on Saturdays. I reflected with immense satisfaction, that under the new arrangement there *must* be peace sometimes. If my mother should even alternately instruct and find fault with the occasional "help" for two days in the week, and then occupy two more in commenting on her delinquencies, I should still gain materially; for four days of grumbling would be better than six, not to mention the absence of

"Two Chapters About Charwomen," *English Woman's Journal*, May 1860, pp. 185-91.

that gay Sabbath attire which used to be so offensive to the dear old lady's eyes.

The first individual who filled the post of charwoman, pulled the same way as my mother, or, at any rate, never contradicted her; and, poor thing! her clothing was not likely to offend, for it was all too scanty and we were fain to eke it out by the gift of sundry cast-off but yet more substantial garments than she possessed. Poor Mary! she was bravely fighting to keep her little children from the stain, as she deemed it, of pauperhood, during a season when work was scarce and the willing hands of the good man at home were lying idly across his lap for want of something to do.

So he was in the house minding the youngsters, and feeling his compulsory idleness far greater evil, both for soul and body, than the heaviest labor; while his cheerful little partner took her turn at bread-winning, and washed and scrubbed, early and late, to earn her shilling a day....

I said we congratulated ourselves on the absence of servants and the presence of a charwoman, but one woeful Monday morning, when the clothes were all ready to begin washing, I came downstairs, as I thought to let in Mary, and found her little Jack instead. He had a sorrowful tale to tell. It was written in his scared face, all channelled over with tears and dirt, and he sobbed out, boring his grimy knuckles into his eyes the while, that "father was very bad in bed and mother couldn't come." This was the last hair. Mary's stubborn back was bowed now, poor soul! there was nothing for it but the parish, for she must stay at home and nurse the sick man. It was some comfort that she found a reward for her willing, ungrumbling servitude, practiced from house to house. Her employers each gave a little aid to bring her through her time of trouble, and this sickness proved the "dark hour before the dawning." But we never had Mary's household services again. The good man got work and by and by a still smaller edition of little Bill appeared, so the house-mother's hands were filled in her own home.

We naturally, however, applied to Mary to recommend someone to take possession of the vacated wash-tub and scrubbing-brush. But she would not recommend, she would only mention her neighbour Peggy Flannagan, who said "she'd be glad of a day's washing."

So we lost Mary, and Peggy reigned in her stead for some six weeks....

But Peggy differed greatly from her predecessor, Mary. She was not clean in her person, and my mother declared that her presence was not desirable within a few feet. Moreover she had no notion of putting things in their places, but always left all her working materials in the apartment where they were last used. It was not therefore pleasant, when one wanted a sweeping brush, to have to sit down and think which room Peggy had swept the last, and so on with all the paraphernalia for dusting and scrubbing. But this was not the worst. My mother, accustomed to receive almost reverential respect from her old servants, could not endure poor Peggy's familiar ways....

For some weeks after Peggy's departure, I worked unassisted; but a severe cold compelled me again to seek aid. After spending almost as much time as would have sufficed for the work itself, I at last met with an individual who expressed herself willing to *oblige me* by coming. But from her first entering the house she appeared so anxious to impress upon us the fact that she was conferring a favor, that the sense of debt became positively oppressive. She hesitated about engaging herself for a future day, and very often stayed away, even when she had promised to come, for such very trifling reasons, that we thought it was simply to show how dependent we were upon her.

Now, though I am quite willing to acknowledge the mutual obligation which exists between the employer and employed, I do *not* agree with my charwoman that she is the only person who ought to be considered as conferring a favor. I desire to treat her with all kindness, showing every possible regard to her comfort, and I expect from her no more work than I would cheerfully and easily perform in the same time. But when I scrupulously perform my part of the bargain, both as regards food and wages, not too mention much thought and care in order to make things easy for her and which were not in the agreement at all, I think she ought not only to keep faith with me if possible, but to abstain from hinting at the obligation she confers in coming.

It is not pleasant, as my mother says, to beg and pray for the help for which we also pay liberally. But it is worse for my kitchen helper to be continually reminding me that she need not go out unless she likes, and that it was only to oblige me she ever came at all. I do not relish this utter ignoring of her wages, etc., or her being quite deaf because I choose to offer a suggestion as to the propriety of dusting out the corners, or when I mildly hint that I should prefer her doing something in my way....

But if I were to detail all my experiences, I should never have done. I have had many good and willing workers; but few on whose punctuality and regularity I could rely. With married women there is often the will to be punctual and regular, but the many claims of home render it impossible to put it in practice. Most young women of good character and conduct are engaged as resident servants, not liking to risk the uncertainty of work incidental to a charwoman's life; and old ones are frequently addicted to snuff and claim a prescriptive right to cold meat, feeling themselves injured if you put a fragment into the pantry for future picking.

Document 35

The article below, which appeared in a popular Swiss women's magazine in 1895, was part of a vast body of literature aimed at modernizing the "perfect" middle-class wife. She now had to be a perfect housewife too: a caretaker in command of the minutest details of household management, a careful consumer of the latest products, and a "doer" who was never without new housekeeping projects to occupy her time. Cleanliness, order, and modernity were her watchwords. Achieving these and raising her children were considered the middle-class woman's proper full-time occupations.

The Good Housewife
Switzerland, 1895

The linen closet is the pride of every good housewife and deserves a little attention in these columns. The demands of luxury and elegance are such nowadays that even here where simple white and meticulously stacked linen used to be the rule, a pleasing change and harmonious colors are sought in place of tiresome white surfaces. It goes without saying that prettifying the linen closet must not be done at the expense of solidity, impeccable

"Der Wäscheschrank," *Schweizer Frauenheim*, no. 21 (May 25, 1895), pp. 291–92.

quality and cleanliness; these are merely to be enhanced by pleasing arrangements and colorful decoration.

There are two time-tested precautionary measures to be observed for the upkeep of our linen treasures: after laundering they must be left to dry thoroughly; whenever possible, spread them out separately overnight to eliminate any lingering dampness. Then always place the freshly laundered linen at the bottom of the shelves to make sure of proper rotation.

How a housewife arranges her linen closet depends on her skill and individual taste. She may want to use a narrow ribbon to keep articles of a kind together, or use the new practical movable ribbon. She can line the shelves with paper or a fabric. All this is up to her and cannot be prescribed. Still, a few suggestions on how to adorn your closet may be welcome, for it is surely not presumptuous to assume that brides and young housewives are among our readers.

Ribbons that are tied with a bow-knot have many opponents and rightfully so; they are a nuisance when one is in a hurry to take out some article. Instead a silken colored rubber-band tied with a snap-fastener, leaving out, however, the silken bow because the ribbons are fastened underneath.

The shelves can be lined in a variety of ways, most attractively with shirting, and a flannel strip along the borders that harmonizes with the ribbons. An embroidered border or strip of lace attached to the front face of the shelves gives a charming effect to the whole arrangement. Some pretty sample patterns will appear before long in these pages.

Instead of shelf borders, the following decorations can be used which have practical advantages and facilitate finding different articles. This is especially important in times of sickness when strange hands have to get at the closet. Cut out 16 to 20 quadrangles alternately from pastel blue and red flannel, 8 to 12 cm. in length and 12 to 15 cm. in width. Write on each piece with India ink and in Roman type the names of the articles in question: handtowels, napkins, covers, etc.; embroider the names in satin stitches with white silk and frame them with red lines on the blue flannel and with black lines on the red flannel. On the reverse side the patches should be rounded off and taken in. Then cut some larger pieces of white flannel, stitch and sew them on the quadrangles. Depending on the size and content of the shelves, pin three or four of these decorated patches at equal distances on the front face of the shelves with the rounded part downward.

A light fragrance in the linen is very pleasing. Since sprinkling nonstaining flower petals among the articles is impractical, one can hang small scented bags on a nail on the back wall, one for each shelf. These sachets can be made from remnants of silk, filled and tied with a gold string or a narrow silken ribbon. If you want to adorn them even more, you can paint or embroider them.

Sweet woodruff and lavender lend themselves nicely for scenting your closet. The former are tied into small bouquets, sewed into muslin and placed among the linen. Lavender should be picked long-stemmed, the bouquet tied right below the flowers, and the stems folded up around the flowers so as to fully encircle them. They are then tied together above and inserted from below into a colored silk pouch and topped with a bow. In this manner, a kind of small flask is produced preventing the flowers from falling off.

It is hardly necessary to add that a list of contents attached to the inside of the closet door is a must. And so, content and with peace of mind we can close the door of our linen closet.

Document 36

Middle-class women confronted a double set of often conflicting standards in the late nineteenth century. On the one hand they were expected to uphold traditional values and preserve their feminine instincts and "womanliness." At the same time they were encouraged to follow the modern, "scientific" techniques of motherhood as prescribed by experts. Failure to live up to both sets of requirements led many women to feel inadequate and anxiety-ridden. Articles such as these two from a regular column in the English *Our Sisters* (see document 11 for another selection from this source) were intended to aid women in their dilemma; in fact, they often increased women's worries. At the same time that experts advised middle-class women on how to cope with modern life, they criticized the way women were meeting their responsibilities and cast doubts on their ability to do so without outside aid and advice.

In books and articles published all across Europe high infant mortality rates were blamed squarely on mothers. Maternal ignorance, lack of careful attention to infant feeding, and the desire to be "modern" and not breast-feed babies were said to be the major causes of infant death. It is interesting to note that although traditional authorities and male doctors generally decried "artificial feeding," this woman's magazine did not insist that breast feeding was the only appropriate method in the modern era. Aware that women were increasingly turning to bottle feeding, this magazine devoted a good deal of space to a discussion of proper feeding and sterilizing techniques.

Advice to Mothers on the Feeding of Children
England, 1897

Up-to-date smart 19th Century women are apt to smile their superiority at the ways of the old fashioned women. But some of them were very good. Trained nurses did not abound so the average woman took more interest in the case of the sick. Now-a-days we can hire a nurse to do the duties we ought, in a measure, to be qualified to do ourselves.

The woman of centuries gone—although, perhaps, she could neither read nor write—had a very real instinct of womanliness; the instinct to comfort the sick and "mother" the well. I always like to think of some of those we read about, wise in herbs and simples and decoctions, ministering not only to their own households, but to whole villages. No doubt their "possets" and "teas" were nauseous compounds, and of very little medicinal value, but these good women knew that nursing and comforting and "cossetting" were the main essentials in the art of healing.

The Home Doctor and Nurse
Every woman who has charge of a household should have a practical knowledge of nursing, simple doctoring and physicing. The professional doctor must be called in for real illness. But the Home Doctor may do so much to render professional visits very few and far between. And her knowledge will be of infinite value when it is necessary to carry out the doctor's orders....

A Hungry Baby
One of the "first causes" of much illness is improper feeding in childhood. Pages might be written on the appalling ignorance which prevails on the subject of baby-feeding. Farmers who raise stock muzzle their young calves lest they might eat unsuitable food

Annesley Kennealy, "Home Doctor and Nurse," *Our Sisters*, December 1896, p. 10; January 1897, p. 9.

and lose health and value. Yet these same men would be startled at a suggestion to restrict their babies' food, and they would explain that babies are not prepared for market, while calves are!

Recently I came across the grandchild of one of our richest and cleverest peers. The baby had two nurses clothed in spotless white; his mail-cart was trimmed with silver fittings, and he was a delicious bundle of lace, fluffy furs, and white satin. But he was as surely being starved to death as any baby in the slums: His young mother said, rather vaguely, she was afraid, if he had too much food, he would "get liver." The poor bairn was afterwards put on a nourishing regimen and is flourishing finely.

The Mother Builder

It is a curious fact that architects who design and builders who carry out their plans must have a training for this work. But the Mother Builder is supposed to have to know by instinct how to put in each tiny brick which builds up the "human." The results of leaving it to "instinct" is that the child starts out with bad foundations and a jerry-built constitution. In my next paper I shall set forth to explain how the baby may be built up into a stalwart, comely citizen of whom his mother may well be proud....

There can be no domestic subject so important as the case of children, and no subject on which the mother can less afford to be ignorant.

When one considers that one child in every three born dies before the age of five years, it is evident how wide-spread must be the ignorance as to the feeding and care of these little ones. It is a matter of surprise to those who understand the constitution and needs of infants that, considering the conditions under which the large number of them are reared, the mortality is not greater.

It only shows what a firm hold some children have, and what splendid healthy men and women they would make if only they were properly fed, properly clothed and properly cared for.

The Risks Babies Run

To begin with, the popular superstition that a young baby must be "hungry" because it lives on milk, and is on this plea the recipient of scraps and bits of vegetables, potato and gravy, crusts, and other heterogeneous articles of diet, has much to answer for. Then, the artistic sense of the mother which leads her to display mottled necks, dimpled arms, and chubby legs, instead of warmly

covering these charming portions of baby's anatomy, goes hugely
to swell the death-rate. Baby-comforters, starchy foods, and bread
and milk, have much to answer for in the high mortality of infants.

The Hand-Fed Infant
Dickens, in one of his novels, calls attention to the dangers and
difficulties attendant on the path of the "hand-fed" baby. And yet a
large proportion of modern babies must be brought up by hand,
for so many of the women of today are quite unable to nurse their
infants.

And it is, under these circumstances, that the babies suffer. Not
because hand-feeding is bad, but because so few people understand
it, and because there are so many superstitions to be broken down.

A breast-fed baby—if its mother is in good condition—should
have nothing but mother's milk. Towards the beginning of the
seventh month this diet should be supplemented by two meals each
day of a malted food, such as Mellins', and Frame Food proprietors
will send ¼-lb. packet sample free for 3d. postage.

A Bottle Baby
I would have a placard on the walls of every Girls' School to this
effect: "The food of a bottle baby should consist of milk and barley-
water." It will be a red-letter day in the annals of Babydom when
the elementary fact is imbued into the minds of budding
femininity. For after all, it is really more important for the girl to
learn the rocks and promontories on which a small human life
may be wrecked than to be acquainted with the Capes and Bays of
Northern Finland!

Mother's Milk
Under healthy conditions the milk which nature has provided
for infants is that on which they thrive best. But with the hurry and
excitement of modern life, much of nature's plan has been
prevented. To nurse her child to the best advantage of both, the
mother needs to be in a more placid, restful state of mind than the
majority can attain to in this century of high pressure. So that,
however unwilling a mother may be to realize that the food she is
able to give is not the best for her child, she must face the fact, if
needs be, and strive to so study the question of artificial feeding as
to make up for the deficiencies of her own milk supply. If the
mother's milk be good, the path is so easy! For nature supplies just

the right quantity at the right time: so that, if the mother will take trouble to nurse her child regularly, and at suitable times, the whole process will go by clockwork. But if the mother be of an excitable temperament, or eat unsuitable food, or if she be unhealthy, the child may be slowly starved, although, apparently, taking a sufficient quantity. A mother's breasts give about one pint of milk during the 24 hours for the first few weeks, and this quantity increases until in the later months it reaches three pints. Calculations have been made from this fact as to the nourishment necessary to infants at varying ages, and artificial feeding has been based on these calculations.

Document 37

This autobiographical sketch by a married working woman was solicited by the German Textile Worker's Union. It was printed in 1930 along with 150 other short autobiographies by women textile factory workers as part of a series of reports on the working conditions and personal lives of the union's members. Each woman was asked to comment on "my work day and my weekend." (For another autobiography from the same source, see document 15.)

Triple Toil: The Life of the Working Wife and Mother
Germany, 1930

Since my husband became unemployed, I have been forced to go to work. In order that things don't become too disordered I must bear a share of the housekeeping for my family, which consists of my husband, three children, aged three to thirteen, and me. My residence is in the district of Zeitz, and my work place is a wool combing factory where I am a cleaner. Since I have almost an hour train ride, I get up early, about a quarter after the hour (4:15 A.M.). The train leaves at 5:10 A.M. and arrives at 5:55 A.M. Since our work day begins at 6:00 A.M., I have to run a long-distance race from the train station to the factory in order to be on time. At the factory I clean carding comb machines until 2:15 P.M. My train for home does not depart until 5:13 P.M. I have to wait so long at the train

Mein Arbeitstag—Mein Wochenende: 150 Berichte von Textilarbeiterinnen ed. by Deutscher Textilarbeiter-Verband (Berlin, 1930), p. 251.

station. I am home about 6:00 P.M. Then there is more work to do at home. I have to prepare the food, get ready for the next day and look after the children's clothes to see that they are intact and clean. When you aren't there all day things are abused a bit more because the little misbehaviors aren't seen. In the evening, you are worn out and exhausted from the long hours so the clothes, the underwear and stockings have to be mended on Sundays. Sometimes I have to sacrifice my sleep too since I attend the party and worker welfare meetings and even preside over the latter as chair. On Saturday I arrive home about the same time. Then I usually go shopping at the cooperative society for food for the whole week. Every four weeks I have to do a huge washing for the family by myself. What is more, on the night before (Saturday), I have to get everything ready so I can begin early Sunday morning. As a rule [my] Sunday starts about 7:00 A.M., since there is house cleaning and clothes mending to do. Then lunch is prepared. About 2:00 P.M., Sunday actually begins for me. It is ended with a visit to a worker organization or with a walk. So it goes, day in, day out, week after week, the daily life of a working woman. The worker's fate.

XI

—•—

Changing Attitudes toward Marriage and Motherhood

As the nineteenth century progressed, a growing amount of literature and public discussion was devoted to the joys and responsibilities of motherhood and the means by which motherhood and motherliness could be promoted. Aimed primarily at middle-class women, a "cult of motherhood" was promoted and tied to a "cult of true womanhood" and a "cult of domesticity." In its fullest form this ideology argued that motherhood was not only a natural condition for women, but the highest and most noble state a woman could attain. It was in the role of mother that a woman would find meaning in her life and her greatest rewards; failure to aspire to or succeed at motherhood doomed her to failure as a woman. Versions of the cult of motherhood were expounded by governments, churches, doctors, self-appointed authorities, both male and female, and most feminists. Feminists generally viewed motherhood as women's unique, but not necessarily only, role and wanted the importance of motherhood fully appreciated and not denigrated. In its most pervasive form, however, the idealization of mothering saw it as a woman's raison d'être and required women to center their lives on children, home, and husband. The promotion of this highly restrictive definition of womanhood increased at the very time women's roles and aspirations were rapidly changing. In fact, the proponents of motherhood, who claimed to uphold tradition, actually defined what women's behavior and attitudes *should* be rather than describe what these actually were. While the ideals of "perfect motherhood" undoubtedly helped to shape women's expectations and self-perceptions, many women found conflicts between their personal experiences and an ideology that stressed the joys of motherhood.

Working-class women could hardly afford the time, money, or energy that perfect motherhood required. Middle-class reformers, through lectures, home visits, and publications, attempted to bring improved standards of infant and child care, nutrition, and cleanliness to the working class. But most working-class mothers, especially those who were employed away from home, could not conform to middle-class standards, even if they wanted to.

To help overburdened mothers care for their children, socialist parties, some but by no means all trade unions, and many middle-class feminist groups called for maternity benefits and paid maternity leaves for working women, day-care facilities, and child-health and lunch programs. (See document 23.) Some of these reforms were slowly adopted but only on a limited basis through the nineteenth and first part of the twentieth century. In France, for example, *crèches* (baby nurseries) were established after the 1840s in some cities, and well-baby clinics and centers for the distribution of sterilized milk were opened in the 1890s. (The last two were established in Britain after 1900.) Ironically, while these and similar programs did not even begin to meet the needs of working mothers, they were repeatedly denounced as attacks on true motherhood and family life. When governments did pass reform legislation, such as limiting the hours women could work or establishing child-care programs, their primary justification for doing so was not women's personal or economic needs. Rather male legislators stressed the obligation of the state to protect the life and health of its future citizens and soldiers.

Although heavy demands were placed on working-class women, the cult of motherhood was directed primarily at middle-class women. But for many of these women, too, the joys of motherhood proved illusory. Many, especially those women who had benefited from increased educational opportunities from the last half of the nineteenth century, felt stifled by lives devoted to husbands and children which excluded other options. From the middle decades of the nineteenth century, but more apparently toward the end of the century, some women chose not to marry and have children. While their numbers were small, such single women were disproportionately represented in the professions, the arts, and the leadership of the women's movement. Most of these women did not reject marriage as such; rather they felt compelled to forgo the traditional roles because of the difficulties of combining the responsibilities of wife and mother with professional work and intellectual achievement. Rather than disparage motherhood many feminists sought greater dignity for mothers and career women and worked for reforms that would allow middle-class women to be both professionals and mothers if they wished. Most feminists, whether of the right, center, or left, held up motherhood as woman's highest achievement. A good many middle-class feminists believed that women's maternal responsibilities excluded them, at least those with young children, from seeking careers. Others argued that it was because of woman's role as mother of the race that she was entitled to and had the qualifications for wider social and economic roles. Although some feminists insisted on promoting women's needs as individual, independent human beings, most pro- and antifeminists, whether communist, socialist, liberal, or reactionary, included women's role as mother in their arguments for widening or restricting women's activities and opportunities.

Document 38

The letter below was written by an anonymous reader of the Austrian middle-class feminist magazine *Women's Documents [Dokumente der Frauen].* The publication was devoted to presenting firsthand accounts of women's experiences. The letter that follows was written by a young mother to her doctor. The views expressed reflect those of the editors, particularly Rosa Mayreder, who, in her book *Critique of Feminity, [Zur Kritik der Weiblichkeit],* attacked the forces that pushed all women into the same mold and denied them their individuality and intellects (see document 24).

A Dissatisfied Mother
Austria, 1899

Dear Doctor! I realize that in all probability I will invite your vigorous condemnation by writing this letter today but the sincere interest which you take in us [mothers] merits to be candidly repaid and should not be answered with just a few banal and hypocritical phrases.

You consider me very fortunate. Married, if not in the best of

"Brief einer Mutter von F.B...R," *Dokumente der Frauen,* vol. 1, nos. 1-13 (March–September 1899), pp. 719-722.

circumstances, with a rosy one-year-old baby to whom I can dedicate all my motherly care. What greater fortune could one ask for?—So you think, as a man.

I think and feel otherwise. I am dissatisfied, nervous, and exhausted.

"Oh yes, for your nervousness," I hear you say, "you must refrain from all excitement, get plenty of good, refreshing sleep, and avoid coffee, tea and alcohol."—I know all that already, before you even order it. I follow all the rules which are supposed to be compatible with the occupation of mother. And yet nothing helps. The causes of my discontent, my anxiety, my neurasthenia, lie much deeper; they lie in the unavoidable circumstances which nature has conferred upon me as a consequence of motherhood. Oh yes, be amazed, horrified, whatever you want, but believe me, we women, we who have thoughts and aspirations, we who through serious intellectual activities have come to a higher state of civilization—we are so far removed from contact with nature that the so-called sweet joys of motherhood cause us more tortures than a quiet, normal thinking man can imagine.

I know for certain that for many women the moment a child is born their whole world dissolves, their own ego no longer exists, their selflessness goes so far that they no longer know any of their own pleasures, and since they continuously descend to the level of the child's intelligence, they are ultimately lost to any other kind of intellectual activity. As the child begins to develop his mental powers and widen his circle of interest, he sets an intellectual standard for the mother educating him. Then he is left to his own devices, because other children follow whose care and protection now completely consume the already mentioned mothers. These are the mothers who through tradition, education and talent have become "true women," who personify all the attributes so highly treasured by the male consumer: resignation, sacrifice and an absence of "ego." . . .

The fortunate women are those whose financial circumstances permit them to hire a reliable nurse for their children. But of course the mother will always have to supervise and not leave the child with her any longer than necessary, especially in cases where the governesses or nurses are not adequately trained. However, she will at least have some time for herself and her husband and not have to sacrifice her individuality for motherhood—not so with me and others who do not have abundant wealth to dispose of. Not only do I myself suffer grievously from it since my intellect is not allowed its full reign, but my husband loses his friend for I lack the time and desire to participate in his interests, his reading or what is going on in the world. Physically I also feel increasingly lifeless and miserable. I was accustomed to getting a great deal of exercise but now I must be satisfied with sitting every day in the garden with the child or pushing the baby carriage back and forth. I have only a servant girl and she has very little free time after her work in the kitchen and the house to use watching the child. Much as I dislike entrusting the little one to the care of a strange person whose loyalty and reliability I can by no means guarantee, I have to do so since that gives me the time I need to do my most urgent household business.

When the child finally goes to sleep, I am so drained from all the unending, taxing idleness and watching that I am unable to read or think about anything. You don't know how much pain it causes to be dragged down by unavoidable conditions into a morass of dullness and indifference toward the outside world; but I lack the strength to hang on. For a long, long time I have attempted in the evenings while the child sleeps to pursue my intellectual interests, to keep alive my sympathy for life's surge. But it takes an iron will and indestructible strong nerves to do justice to both the child and myself. I can't do it.

"Yes," you will say, "those must be especially unfavorable circumstances, for I have never heard such things from a mother before." No! No more unfavorable than those of many women of modest means. And I assure you that hundreds of women feel the fetters of motherhood as hard as I. They just don't dare to admit this either to themselves or to others, for centuries-long custom depicts the relationship of the young mother to the child as the embodiment of all happiness and satisfaction and so woe to those who don't experience this happiness to the utmost. "Debasement, denial of the holiest instincts," you will think to yourself. It may be that you are right. But one cannot simply command the progress of culture to stop because of the requirements presented by motherhood just when that progress finally begins, even if somewhat delayed, to awaken women from a vegetable-animalistic semiconsciousness....

In Germany they are beginning to develop wonderful institutions for working-class children through private charity; day-care centers in which the poor, small creatures whose fathers and mothers have to earn a living for the family by hard physical labor can be competently fed and cared for during the day for a very small fee.

I have often taken this idea a step further in my thoughts. I wondered if it were not possible to establish similar institutions, with all the resources of modern hygiene and equipped under first-rate medical supervision, to which the mothers of the middle class who cannot hire a nurse (governess) could take their children for a few hours or half a day for a suitably small amount of money. In how many families with today's social conditions does the woman have to try to earn something, and for these women especially institutions of that kind would be a real blessing. And wouldn't prejudice soon be overcome—she would realize, I believe, that her child would be better provided for in this way during the time she could not devote to him, than by a domestic otherwise occupied in the kitchen where accidents so often occur....

Something else to consider. If the mother gets sick, then nobody watches after the children; the older ones look for friends among the children in the street and while the mother is sick the one- and two-year-olds are left more than ever to the domestic servants who have other responsibilities. In such cases the children, with a doctor's certification of the mother's illness, could go to the institution for free....

And so, dear doctor, you now know about my secret ideas for alleviating the hardest burden of mothers. I have informed you of all this, first, because I wanted to be honest and secondly, because I believe you can now better understand many women you have hitherto judged harshly because you have received deeper insight into our feelings and thoughts.

Document 39

In Germany the call for the protection of women during pregnancy and for paid maternity benefits was taken up by all segments of the women's movement, from the socialists to the conservatives (see document 23). One of the most ardent campaigns was conducted by the Society for the Protection of Motherhood and Sexual Reform [Bund für Mutterschutz und Sexualreform]. Legislation prohibiting the employment of mothers in industry for three weeks after childbirth had been enacted in Germany in 1878, but like similar early legislation in other countries the law had not provided for compensation for the mother during her absence. Paid leaves were introduced in 1882. By 1907 when the *Bund* presented the petition below to the Reichstag, women in industry could have up to six weeks paid leave following childbirth. The *Bund* wanted these benefits extended to women in other kinds of employment, paid leaves for all workers in the last weeks of pregnancy, and a premium paid to mothers who chose to nurse their babies. Most of these provisions were enacted in 1911.

The *Bund* believed motherhood should be freely chosen and stressed women's rights to a sex life whether married or not. But like most other proponents of maternal protection in Germany, England, France, Scandinavia, and other countries, the *Bund*'s members did not base their arguments solely on women's own needs. Rather they stressed that motherhood should be protected and encouraged because it was in the state's interest to do so. Everywhere in Europe it was argued that insuring mothers' health and allowing them time to care for their children would lower infant mortality rates, halt the decline in the birth rate, improve the health of children, and thus provide healthier youths to serve in the military to ensure the future of the race and the nation.

The Manipulation of Motherhood
Germany, 1907

Concerning Maternity Insurance

To the Esteemed Reichstag:

The respectful undersigned League for the Protection of Motherhood makes a request for the following change in our insurance legislation:

"that comprehensive maternity insurance, which passed according to the attached resolution at our General Assembly on January 12-14, 1907, be incorporated in the (present) sickness insurance [program]."

Motivation

1. Women's work in industry grows in every increasing percentages. In certain industries the number of women has

Helene Stoecker, ed., *Petitionen des Deutschen Bundes für Mutterschutz, 1905–1916* (Berlin, 1916), pp. 9-12.

reached the level of men and in others the former has overtaken the latter. Thus the number of mothers in factories grows from year to year. Likewise, other branches of national industry such as home industry, trade and agriculture show a strong increase in [the number of] women in general and of married women in particular. Thus, this is not a temporary situation, nor is it a symptom of illness in the social fabric: rather it is the inevitable result of favorable economic conditions. It is the duty of the state, therefore, to create new ways which will allow the mother to work without damage being done to the whole nation.

2. The protection which women factory workers have today during pregnancy and after delivery under the national health insurance [program] is a very important beginning to the approach which we have charted.

However, rural workers, domestics, those in home industry, and *the vast majority of working women* are completely unprotected. Great social ills which threaten the future of our people are arising from this inadequate protection of mothers by the state. We call to your attention:

a. *Infant Mortality*

Germany's infant mortality rate is worse than that of almost all other civilized countries. In the year 1904, 19.4 percent of the legitimate children and 31.4 percent of the illegitimate children died in their first year. In the years from 1900 to 1904 almost a million German children died in infancy. The deaths of these young children, which some have rightly called a "modern infanticide," occur on the one hand because of overwork and malnutrition during pregnancy, because of poor care during the lying-in period and a shortened period of recuperation for the mother, and on the other hand because of artificial feeding and unsatisfactory care of the infant.

b. *The Decline in the Number of Men Fit for Military Service*

Those children who remain alive despite the lack of protection from their mothers develop weak bodies because of the absence of the mother's milk and are subjected to repeated debilitating illnesses. Yet in most cases, working mothers must give up nursing the children since there are no facilities for nursing mothers at work and because, in order to earn money, they often go back to work after three or four days. This weakening of children's bodies results in the diminution of the number of men fit for military service.

c. *The Increase of Abdominal Injuries in Working Mothers*

Numerous mothers develop severe abdominal injuries as a result of lack of protection during pregnancy and insufficient nourishment during the postnatal period, which forces them to get out of bed prematurely, and because of a lack of proper, well-ordered postnatal care. The fortunes of the family are destroyed, the mother is driven to an early grave and the health insurance [program] is overburdened.

3. Thus we can say that a large part of the German people suffers racial deterioration which is likely to undermine our hopes for the future. There is one means of improving this situation. It is the protection of the mother during the time she gives to the state the citizens upon whose existence the state rests.

Document 40

Ellen Key (1849–1926) was a Swedish activist and prolific writer whose books were translated into many languages. She influenced women throughout Europe and in America and was especially influential in Germany, where the *Bund für Mutterschutz* adopted many of her ideas. Like many feminists, Key turned to history and anthropology to find the origins of women's roles and came to the conclusion that they were biologically determined. Women were destined for motherhood; if their maternal instincts were not realized, they would remain unfulfilled human beings. Key argued that society must elevate motherhood and recognize that each woman, whether married or unmarried, had the absolute right to become a mother.

Key, who never married, was vilified because of her insistence that every woman had the right to be a "sex-being" and bear children outside the bounds of legal marriage. But she gained the support of many conservative feminist groups and was eventually honored by the Swedish government. More liberal and radical feminists, while often agreeing with her basic premises, rejected her insistence that women's and men's spheres were inevitably different, and they were disturbed by the possible implications of her ideas. Although Key later embraced the suffrage issue, in 1896 she argued against seeking the vote on the grounds that women should concentrate their efforts on elevating women's natural activities instead of seeking new areas of work and power in competition with men.

The Renaissance of Motherhood
Ellen Key, Sweden, 1914

Fifty years ago no one would have thought of writing about the nature of motherliness. To sing of motherhood was then just as natural for ecstatic souls as to sing of the sun, the great source of energy from which we all draw life; or to sing of the sea, the mysterious sea, whose depth none has fathomed. Great and strong as the sun and the sea, motherhood was called; just as tremendous an elemental power, a natural force, as they—alike manifest, alike inexhaustible. Every one knew that there existed women without motherly instincts, just as they knew of the existence of polar regions on the globe; every one knew that the female sex, as a whole, was the bearer of a power which was as necessary for life's duration as the sun and the sea, the power not only to bear, but to nurture, to love and rear and train. We knew that woman, as a gift from Nature, possessed the warmth which, from birth to death, made human life human; the gift which made the mother the child's providence, the wife the husband's happiness, the grandmother the comfort of all. A warmth which, though radiating most strongly to those gathered around the family hearth, also reached those outside the circle of her dearest, who have no homes of their own, and embraced even the strange bird as it paused on its journey. For motherliness was boundless; its very nature was to give, to sacrifice, to cherish, to be tender, even as it is the nature of the sun to warm, and of the sea to surge. Fruitfulness and motherhood received religious worship in the antique world, and no religious custom has withstood the changes of the times so long as this. . . .

Motherliness, which in the beginning was but the animal instinct for protecting the young, became helpfulness, compassion, glad sympathy, far-thinking tenderness, personal love—a relation in which the feeling of duty had come to possess the strength of instinct, one in which it was never asked *if*, but only *how*, the duty should be fulfilled. And though the manner of showing the feeling has undergone transition, the feeling itself, during all the ages that it has acted in human life, has developed until, in our day, it has grown far beyond the boundaries of home. The man's work is to

Ellen Key, *The Renaissance of Motherhood* (New York, 1914), pp. 97, 98, 103-104, 108-109, 113-15, 119-20.

kindle the fire on the hearth, the woman's is to *maintain* it; it is man's to *defend* the lives of those belonging to him; woman's to *care* for them. This is the division of labour by which the race has reached its present stage.

Manliness and womanliness became synonymous with the different kinds of exercise of power belonging to each sex, in their separate functions of father and mother. That the mother, through her imagination dwelling on the unborn child, through her bond with the living child, through her incessant labors, joys, and hopes, has more swiftly and strongly developed her motherliness than the father his fatherliness, is psychologically self-evident. The modern psychologist knows that it is not the association of theory, but the association of feeling, which is the most important factor in the soul-life. But besides feeling, which like the roots of the plant, must remain in the dark soil that the tree may live, we have *will* to guide our thoughts. What is present in the soul, what directs our action, what spurs our effort, *that* is what we, with all our will, as well as feeling, hold dear. Thus there accumulated in the female sex an energy of motherliness, which has shown itself so mighty and boundless a power that we have come to claim it as a constant element and one not subject to change. And this energy grew so great because the hitherto universally conflicting elements in human life reached their oneness in mother-love; the soul and the senses, altruism and egoism blended.

In every strong maternal feeling there is also a strong sensuous feeling of pleasure—which an unwise mother gives vent to in the violent caresses with which she fondles the soft body of her baby—a pleasure which thrills the mother with blissful emotion when she puts the child to her breast; and at the same moment motherliness attains its most sublime spiritual state, sinks into the depths of eternity, which no ecstatic words—only tears—can express. Self-sacrifice and self-realization come to harmony in mother-love. In a word, then, the nature of motherliness is altruism and egoism harmonized. This harmony makes motherhood the most perfect human state; that in which the individual happiness is a constant giving, and constant giving is the highest happiness....

Scientific investigation into the form through which, consciously or unconsciously, the power of motherliness was expressed in the laws and customs of the past, and further research into that compound of feelings and ideas which shaped and gave rise to the traditions of savage tribes, came simultaneously with the era of Woman-Emancipation. At the same time there took place a deep transformation in the view of life, during which all values were estimated anew, even the value of motherliness. And now the women themselves borrow their argument from science, when they try to prove that motherliness is only an attribute woman shares with the female animal, an attribute belonging to lower phases of development, whereas her full humanity embraces all the attributes, independent of sex, which she shares with man. Women now demand that woman, as man, first of all be judged by purely human qualities, and declare that every new effort to make woman's motherliness a determining factor of her nature or her calling, is a return to antiquated superstition.

When the Woman Movement began, in the middle of the last century, and many expressed fears that "womanliness" would suffer, such contentions were answered by saying that that would be as preposterous as that the warmth of the sun would give out. It was just in order that the motherliness should be able to penetrate all the spheres of life that woman's liberation was required.

And now? Now we see a condition of things alluded to in the first chapter, a constantly decreasing birth-rate on account of an increasing disinclination for motherhood, and this not alone among the child-worn drudges in home and industry, not alone among the lazy creatures of luxury. No, even women strong of body and worthy of motherhood choose either celibacy, or at most one child, often none. And not a few women are to be found eager advocates of children's upbringing from infancy outside of the home. Motherhood has, in other words, for many women ceased to be the sweet secret dream of the maiden, the glad hope of the wife, the deep regret of the aging woman who has not had this yearning satisfied. Motherliness has diminished to such a degree that women use their intelligence in trying to prove not only that day-nurseries, kindergartens, and schools are necessary helps in case of need, but that they are *better* than the too devoted and confining motherliness of the home, where the child is "developed into a family-egoist, not into a social modern human being.". . .

All women, even as now all men, must learn a trade whereby they can earn their livelihood—in case they do not become mothers, as well as before they so become, and after the years of their children's minority; but during those years they must give themselves wholly to the vocation of motherhood. But for most women it ought still to be the dream of happiness, some time in their lives, to have fulfilled the mission of motherhood, and during that time to have been freed from outside work in which they only in exceptional cases would be likely to find the same full outlet for their creative desire, for feeling, thought, imagination, as is to be found in the educative activity in the home. But so unmotherly are many women of this age that this view is considered old-fashioned and (with the usual confusion of definition) *consequently* impossible for the future.

When already they say the women of today want to be "freed" from the inferior duties of mother and housewife, in order to devote themselves to higher callings, as self-supporting and independent members of society, how much more will that be the case with the women of the future! As these "higher" callings, however, for the majority consist, and will continue to consist, in monotonous labor in factory, store, office and such occupations, it is difficult to conceive how these tasks can possible bring greater freedom and happiness than the broad usefulness in a home, where woman is sovereign—yea, under the inspiration of motherhood, creator—in her sphere, and where she is directly working for her own dear ones....

If this "freedom" is the ideal of the future, then, indeed, my view of motherliness, as indispendable for humanity, is reactionary; but it is reactionary in the same way that medicine reacts against disease. And has our race ever been afflicted by a more dangerous disease than the one which at present rages among women: the sick yearning to be "freed" from the most essential attribute of their sex? In motherliness, the most indispensable human qualities have their root....

Motherliness must be cultivated by the acquisition of the principles of heredity, of race-hygiene, child-hygiene, child-psychology. Motherliness must revolt against giving the race too few, too many, or degenerate children. Motherliness must exact all the legal rights without which woman cannot, in the fullest sense of the word, be either child-mother or social-mother. Motherliness thus developed will rescue mothers not only from olden-time superstition, but also from present-day excitement. It will teach them to create the peace and beauty in the home which are requisite for the happy unfolding of childhood, and this without closing the doors of the home on the thoughts and demands of modern times. Motherliness will teach the mother how to remain at the same time Madonna, the mother with her own child close in her arms, and Caritas, as pictured in art: the mother who at her full breast has room also for the lips of the orphaned child.

Document 41

Alexandra Kollontai (1872-1952) joined the Russian Social Democratic Labor Party in 1898. She became a Bolshevik in 1915. Kollontai headed the Women's Bureau (Zhenotdel) of the Communist party, which was founded in 1917 and was the first commissar of public welfare (see document 25).

Kollontai believed that the establishment of a socialist society was the only way to achieve women's liberation. But she realized that the overthrow of capitalism was not sufficient to end the oppression of women. She believed that could only be achieved by the elimination of women's subordination to and dependence on men within the family. Kollontai wanted women to be able to participate fully in economic, social and, political life on an equal basis with men. To accomplish this, women had to be freed from domestic drudgery and the responsibility of bringing up children; she called for the separation of the kitchen from marriage.

Communism and the Family
Alexandra Kollontai, U.S.S.R., 1918

In Soviet Russia, owing to the care of the Commissariats of Public Education and of Social Welfare, great advances are being made, and already many things have been done in order to facilitate for the family the task of bringing up and supporting the children. There are homes for very small babies, day nurseries, kindergarten, children's colonies and homes, infirmaries, and health resorts for sick children, restaurants, free lunches at school, free distribution of text books, of warm clothing, of shoes to the pupils of the educational establishments—does all this not sufficiently show that the child is passing out of the confines of the family and being placed from the shoulders of the parents on those of collectivity?

The care of children by the parents consisted of three distinct

Alexandra Kollontai, *Communism and the Family* (London, 1918), pp. 15-20.

parts: (1) the care necessarily devoted to the very young babies; (2) the bringing up of the child; (3) the instruction of the child. As for the instruction of children in primary schools and later in gymnasiums and universities, it has become a duty of the State, even in capitalist society. The other occupations of the working class, its conditions of life, imperatively dictated, even to capitalist society, the creation for the purposes of the young, of playgrounds, infants' schools, homes, etc., etc. The more the workers became conscious of their rights, the better they were organized in any specific State, the more society would show itself to be concerned with relieving the family of the care of the children. But bourgeois society was afraid of going too far in this matter of meeting the interests of the working class, lest it contribute in this way to the disintegrati)n of the family. The capitalists themselves are not unaware of the fact that the family of old, with the wife a slave and the man responsible for the support and well-being of the family, that the family of this type is the best weapon to stifle the proletarian effort toward liberty, to weaken the revolutionary spirit of the working man and working woman. Worry for his family takes the backbone out of the worker, obliges him to compromise with capital. The father and the mother, what will they not do when their children are hungry? Contrary to the practice of capitalist society, which has not been able to transform an education of youth into a truly social function, a State work, Communist society will consider the social education of the rising generation as the very basis of its laws and customs, as the corner stone of the new edifice. Not the family of the past, petty and narrow, with its quarrels between the parents, with its exclusive interests in its own offspring, will mould for us the man of the society of tomorrow. Our new man, in our new society, is to be moulded by Socialist organizations such as playgrounds, gardens, homes, and many other such institutions, in which the child will pass the greater part of the day and where intelligent educators will make of him a Communist who is conscious of the greatness of this sacred motto: solidarity, comradeship, mutual aid, devotion to the collective life.

The Mother's Livelihood Assured

But now, with the bringing up gone and with the instruction gone, what will remain of the obligations of the family toward its children, particularly after it has been relieved also of the greater

portion of the material cares involved in having a child, except for
the care of a very small baby while it still needs its mother's
attention, while it is still learning to walk, clinging to its mother's
skirt? Here again the Communist State hastens to the aid of the
working mother. No longer shall the child-mother be bowed down
with a baby in her arms! The Workers' State charges itself with the
duty of assuring a livelihood to every mother, whether she be
legitimately married or not, as long as she is suckling her child, of
creating all over maternity houses, of establishing in all the cities
and all the villages, day nurseries and other similar institutions in
order thus to permit the woman to serve the State in a useful
manner and simultaneously to be a mother.

Marriage No Longer a Chain

Let the working mothers be re-assured. The Communist Society
is not intending to take the children away from the parents nor to
tear the baby from the breast of its mother; nor has it any intention
of resorting to violence in order to destroy the family as such. No
such thing! Such are not the aims of the Communist Society. What
do we observe today? The outworn family is breaking. It is
gradually freeing itself from all the domestic labors which formerly
were as so many pillars supporting the family as a social unit.
Housekeeping? It also appears to have outlived its usefulness. The
children? The parent-proletarians are already unable to take care of
them; they can assure them neither subsistence nor education. This
is the situation from which both parents and children suffer in
equal measure. Communist Society therefore approaches the
working woman and the working man and says to them: "You are
young, you love each other. Everyone has the right to happiness.
Therefore live your life. Do not flee happiness. Do not fear
marriage, even though marriage was truly a chain for the working
man and woman of capitalist society. Above all, do not fear, young
and healthy as you are, to give to your country new workers, new
citizen-children. The society of the workers is in need of new
working forces; it hails the arrival of every newborn child in the
world. Nor should you be concerned because of the future of your
child; your child will know neither hunger nor cold. It will not be
unhappy nor abandoned to its fate as would have been the case in
capitalist society. A subsistence ration and solicitous care are
assured to the child and to the mother by the Communist Society,

by the Workers' State, as soon as the child arrives in the world. The child will be fed, it will be brought up, it will be educated by the care of the Communist Fatherland; but this Fatherland will by no means undertake to tear the child away from such parents as may desire to participate in the education of their little ones. The Communist Society will take upon itself all the duties involved in the education of the child, but the paternal joys, the maternal satisfaction—such will not be taken away from those who show themselves capable of appreciating and understanding these joys." Can this be called a destruction of the family by means of violence? or a forcible separation of child and mother?

The Family a Union of Affection and Comradeship

There is no escaping the fact: the old type of family has seen its day. It is not the fault of the Communist State, it is the result of the changed conditions of life. *The family is ceasing to be a necessity of the State, as it was in the past;* on the contrary, it is worse than useless, since it needlessly holds back the female workers from a more productive and far more serious work. Nor is it any longer necessary to the members of the family themselves, since the task of bringing up the children, which was formerly that of the family, is passing more and more into the hands of the collectivity. But, on the ruins of the former family we shall soon behold rising a new form which will involve altogether different relations between men and women, and which will be *a union of affection and comradeship, a union of two equal persons of the Communist Society, both of them free, both of them independent, both of them workers.* No more domestic "servitude" for women! No more inequality within the family. No more fear on the part of the woman to remain without support or aid with little ones in her arms if her husband should desert her. The woman in the Communist city no longer depends on her husband but on her work. It is not her husband but her robust arms which will support her. There will be no more anxiety as to the fate of her children. The State of the Workers' will assume responsibility for these. Marriage will be purified of all its material elements, of all money calculations, which constitute a hideous blemish on family life in our days. Marriage is henceforth to be transformed into a sublime union of two souls in love with each other, each having faith in the other; this union promises to each working man and to each working woman simultaneously, the most complete happiness, the maximum of satisfaction which can be the lot of creatures who are conscious of themselves and of the life which surrounds them. *This free union,* which is strong in the comradeship with which it is inspired, *instead of the conjugal slavery of the past—that is what the Communist Society of tomorrow offers to both men and women.*

Part Four

WOMAN AND HER BODY

The right to abortion does not depend on crimes which the conventions of romantic tradition deem worse than death, and which laws justifiably treat as second only to murder....

Neither does the right to abortion depend on the uncertain and unpredictable result of possible genetic patterns in the child....

Abortion should not be either a perquisite of the legal wife only, nor merely a last remedy against illegitimacy. It should be available for any woman, without insolent inquisitions, nor ruinous financial charges, nor tangles of red tape. For our bodies are our own.

> F. W. Stella Browne, "The Right to Abortion,"
> in F. W. Stella Browne et al.,
> Abortion *(London, 1935), pp. 30–31.*

Being a woman on this earth is like being in a prison. For a woman's life is filled with legal clauses, regulations, attitudes and prejudices which hold her so tight and oppressed that it is almost unbearable.

But that oppression is giving way and soon will end. The complete equality of women before the law, in everyday life, in everything, will soon be achieved just as it has in the political sphere.

Until then all those beautiful words about the emancipation of women are empty phrases; what good is the right to vote if women are just unwilling baby-making machines?

Woman's struggle will not be complete until she achieves the right to control her own body. If a man does not have to be forced into the act of procreation, a woman should not be forced to bear children.

> Dr. Else Kienle, Frauen aus dem Tagebuch einer Ärtzin
> *(Berlin, 1932), pp. 308–309.*

Being born female did more than define and limit a woman's education, employment opportunities, and roles in her family. It was also a crucial factor in determining her chances of being a healthy and well-nourished person. There were often significant differences in the diets, health, and standards of living of males and females within the same country, class, and even within the same family. These differences went beyond sex-specific health problems and variations in life expectancy. It appears that from the pre-industrial period right through the depression of the 1930s women were more likely than men to be malnourished and to suffer the consequences of an inadequate diet. Women also faced health problems related to pregnancy and childbirth which, like other ailments, were complicated or caused by the physical strains of women's triple burden of wage work, housework, and child care.

Being born female also meant that reproduction and child rearing were a woman's major concerns for a good portion of her life. During the nineteenth century women began to have fewer children and national birth rates fell. Historians and demographers have offered a host of economic, social, and political reasons for this decline in fertility, but until recently most of these explanations have focused on men and male concerns and have ignored women's role in decisions to limit births, the means women employed to control the size of their families, and the effects of reduced fertility and smaller families on women's own lives. The documents below address these issues directly. The first chapter of this part (documents 42–45) describes women's general health and nutritional problems and pregnancy and childbirth. The next chapter (documents 46–50) describes women's use of birth control and their efforts to obtain effective means of contraception and safe abortions. The last chapter (documents 51–53) focuses on women's sexuality and changing attitudes toward sexual behavior.

XII

―•―

Health, Nutrition, Pregnancy

The period since the late eighteenth century has witnessed dramatic improvements in general levels of health, nutrition, and life expectancy of people in western industrialized nations. But many of the benefits of modern life came more slowly to women, especially working-class women. Moreover, industrialization and urbanization created new and serious health problems. Working-class people who suffered under abysmal and unhealthy working conditions were forced to endure overcrowding and unsanitary living conditions as well. Ironically, as married women spent less time in factories and mines, thus avoiding the health hazards found there, they spent more time in cramped, sunless urban slums which were also injurious to health.

The diets of most working-class people were inadequate throughout the nineteenth century and for many remained so in the first half of the twentieth. Bread was the staple food and often consumed the largest share of a family's budget. Even by the late nineteenth century the working-class diet consisted largely of bread, tea or coffee, fat (butter, margarine, or animal fat), sugar, potatoes, some cheese, a little meat, and perhaps some fish. But meat and other protein foods were not distributed evenly within a family; most of these were reserved for men. In times of financial stress, wives, who were responsible for the family budgets, would cut back on their own food while trying to keep up their husbands' rations. Women believed that they had to keep their husbands well fed so that they would continue working and supporting their families. To ensure this, wives skimped on their own food even when they, too, worked for wages (see documents 1 and 44). In the twentieth century, diets improved for some people, but fresh fruits and vegetables and milk were often missing, and women and girls continued to be more likely than men to have inadequate nourishment. In France and Germany wives who were not employed away from home ate at home and economized on their food while their husbands generally ate their midday meals in restaurants or workers' cafeterias. In some German towns governments or private groups operated restaurants that provided low-priced, reasonably well-balanced meals for working men. But it was not considered respectable for working women to go to these places.* One recent study suggests that girls below the age of menarche suffered the greatest degree of nutritional deprivation and as a result were more prone than any other group within the population to contract tuberculosis, a major cause of death in females in the nineteenth and early twentieth centuries.†

But even though they might eat less well than men, women's nutritional needs were often greater. Many women did physical work that was as hard as or harder than men's and they did arduous housework in addition, which men did not. In order to meet all their responsibilities wives frequently got less sleep than their husbands. Pregnancy and nursing required increased caloric intake but it was often impossible for women to obtain additional food. If a woman had to give up regular paid employment in the latter stages of pregnancy or after childbirth in order to nurse a child, she might be forced to cut back on her food consumption at the very time her nutritional needs were greatest. In the nineteenth century mothers frequently prolonged nursing as a means of birth control. But since pregnancies and births were still frequent, this practice could prolong the interval of increased nutritional need and potential malnutrition.

Middle- and upper-class women did not suffer the same kinds of nutritional and physical deprivations, but urbanization, neglect, and the ideals of ladylike behavior all took their toll on wealthier women's health. Stuffy, heavily curtained rooms, lack of exercise, a diet laced with sweets and an emphasis on feminine "delicacy" all contributed to ill health. These women's tight, restrictive clothing was the cause of many physical ailments, particularly weakness of the abdominal and back muscles, which could have serious consequences during pregnancy and childbirth. Just before the turn of the century a movement for dress reform arose which called for an end to the wearing of corsets, petticoats, and other

---

*See Minna Wettstein-Adelt, *3½ Monate Fabrik-Arbeiterin* (Berlin, 1893), chap. 2.
†Sheila Ryan Johansson, "Sex and Death in Victorian England: An Examination of Age- and Sex-Specific Death Rates, 1840–1900," in Martha Vicinus, ed., *A Widening Sphere* (Bloomington, Ind., 1977), pp. 163–81.

uncomfortable and cumbersome garments. Proponents of dress reform believed that simplifying women's dress was an important step toward better health and women's emancipation.

Middle-class women also suffered from a host of "nervous" disorders (see document 38) and complaints of fatigue, sleeplessness, and anxiety and general ill health were common. These conditions and women's use of drugs and alcohol may well have been reactions to the physical strains, restrictions, and the boring regimen of women's lives. Frequent bouts of ill or delicate health may also have been ways of avoiding sexual intercourse, which many women found distasteful and which brought the danger of pregnancy. Unfortunately for middle- and upper-class women, a delicate constitution was considered an attribute of a lady, and so women and their doctors tolerated and considered normal very low standards of health and physical well-being.

Women of all classes experienced medical problems relating to their reproductive systems and childbirth. Middle-class women increasingly turned to male physicians to treat these and other ailments, and to attend births. Poor women, who could not afford doctors' fees, relied on traditional folk remedies, the advice of friends and druggists, and the services of midwives. For most of the nineteenth century, few working- or middle-class women could afford to see a doctor very often. But given the ignorance, sexism, and potentially harmful practices common among doctors, this was not entirely to women's disadvantage.

Little was known about menstruation and the menstrual cycle in the nineteenth century. Many doctors counseled women who wished to avoid pregnancy that the "safe period" was midway between menstrual periods—the time, in fact, when they were most fertile. Doctors also asserted that menstruating women were prone to, among other things, shocks, temporary insanity, and idiocy. It was not uncommon for doctors to advise young women that the best cure for their menstrual disorders was marriage and pregnancy.

For most of the nineteenth century the practice of obstetrics and gynecology remained primitive, ineffectual, and often harmful. In the first part of the century doctors commonly believed that the womb was a woman's central, controlling organ and that many of women's physical and psychological as well as reproductive problems were best treated by attacking the womb. Thus to cure ailments such as backache, nervousness, and sleeplessness, doctors placed leeches on the vulva or the neck of the womb, cauterized the cervix with a white-hot iron or silver nitrate, and injected various solutions into the uterus. Fortunately, these measures fell into disuse in the latter part of the century, but many treatments given women remained inadequate and often dangerous.

Yet middle-class women increasingly chose doctors as their birth attendants because they believed that would result in safer births.* Working-class women continued traditional childbirth practices for a much longer time; births were attended by midwives and women friends and relatives who stayed afterward to help with household chores and child care. Some midwives were trained graduates of schools of midwifery, while others, the majority, had no formal education but acquired their skills through experience. They had high status within the community and often aided women with their other health complaints and helped them abort unwanted pregnancies.

Midwives saw birth as a natural process and interfered as little as possible in the progress of nature. Doctors, who sought to take over obstetrics in the nineteenth century and eliminate the competition of midwives, viewed childbirth very differently. They considered it an illness which needed to be cured and frequently intervened in the birth process. In the early part of the nineteenth century doctors cauterized and bled women in labor and administered strong purgatives and emetics. Although these practices were later dropped, they continued to use drugs, manual manipulations, and forceps (which often caused lacerations in the mother) to speed up birth and the delivery of the placenta. They also performed Caesarian sections, but in the absence of sterile procedures, the rate of fatalities was frightful. Chloroform was in use in the second part of the century and it eased the pains of childbirth for some women.

The doctors' insistence on intervention and their lack of sanitary measures were major causes of the continuance of high maternal mortality rates long after child and infant mortality had declined in western Europe. The employment of a doctor as a birth attendant actually increased a woman's chances of contracting puerperal (childbed) fever, the primary killer of parturient women. By the 1880s Louis Pasteur had defined the cause of the fever, which came within a few hours or days of birth and frequently

---

*See Richard W. Wertz and Dorothy C. Wertz, *Lying-in: A History of Childbirth in America* (New York, 1977).

killed shortly thereafter, as bacteria that entered the wounds of childbirth and then the bloodstream. He also noted that the infection was carried from patient to patient on the hands of doctors who brought it right into the women's homes. (Death rates were even higher in hospitals, but very few, and only the poorest, women gave birth there.) Yet doctors continued to approach women in childbed with unwashed hands and unsterile instruments, and tens of thousands of women died each year from puerperal fever, right through the 1920s and 1930s.

In the twentieth century, among poor women, low levels of nutrition and health from childhood on and the absence of prenatal care were also contributors to maternal deaths, difficult births, and pregnancy-related problems. National health insurance programs often lacked maternity benefits entirely or excluded dependent wives in the early years of their existence. In England, the funds for maternity-care centers, which had been authorized during World War I (1918), were cut back in the 1920s and 1930s, as were maternal-health programs in other nations. Thus, right through World War II most poor women could not take advantage of medical advances that might have resulted in better overall health and less complicated pregnancies and births.

Some women believed that women's physical problems and their difficulties in obtaining safe, effective medical care would be eased if there were more women doctors and well-trained female medical personnel. At first, especially in England, women doctors were considered desirable primarily to safeguard the modesty of female patients. However, many women, including women doctors, came to believe that female physicians had a better understanding than men of women's medical needs and would provide them with more sympathetic and better health care.

Document 42

From the middle of the nineteenth century, middle-class reformers stressed the link between lack of exercise and women's poor health. This tract was written in 1859 by a member of the Ladies' Sanitary Association, a British organization devoted to "elevating the physical condition of society." It first appeared in the *English Woman's Journal* and was later reprinted and distributed through the journal's office.

Reformers such as this author urged educators to include

physical education in school curricula and encouraged middle-
class women and girls to swim, play tennis, and do exercises. In the
late nineteenth and early twentieth centuries Swedish and American gymnastics were popular with more enlightened women in
England, Germany, and Scandinavia, and dancing, particularly in
the style of Isadora Duncan, enjoyed a great vogue across Europe.
But the dominant ideal of feminine behavior did not include
athletic prowess, and many women and girls continued to be
unable or unwilling to get proper exercise.

The Importance of Physical Education for Girls
England, 1859

Women have it also in their power to put an end to the undue
exercise of the mental faculties, and the neglect of physical training
which are so general in girls' schools, and which so seriously
undermine the health of the pupils. Probably, in most schools far
more attention is now paid to the fulfillment of the conditions of
physical health than was usual ten or fifteen years ago; but a still
greater reform is urgently needed. The latest writer on bodily
exercise "expresses his firm conviction—a conviction arrived at
after making numerous inquiries into the matter, and with
considerable pains-taking to reach the truth—that there exist in
England, at the present day, thousands of schools for girls where
(through muscular inaction and other violations of the laws of
health) at least one-third of the pupils are more or less deformed;
and that there are a still greater number of schools where, among
thirty or forty girls, it would be difficult, in many cases impossible
to find a single one, who, after having lived under the regime only
a few months, would be pronounced by the well practiced medical
man as not evidencing symptoms of functional derangement." A
whole legion of medical writers have for many years been
complaining thus; but the evils complained of must continue till
educators feel their deep responsibility in the matter, and resolve to
allow no conventional prejudices, no parental whims, to prevent
them from adopting every means necessary to the healthy,
harmonious physical development of their pupils. To secure this
end, some more systematic and thorough method of exercise is

"The Details of Woman's Work in Sanitary Reform," *English Woman's Journal,*
July 1859, pp. 317-19.

needed than walks or dancing lessons, which, though beneficial so far as their influence extends, only brings into action some of the muscles. The system of bodily training distinguished as Ling's Rational Gymnastics, is the most perfect of any yet introduced. These gymnastics are practised with most beneficial results in some of the best conducted schools in London, and also very generally in those in Sweden, Russia, Prussia, Saxony, and Austria. An explanation of the peculiar excellencies of this admirable system would be misplaced in these merely suggestive pages, especially as it has been already given elsewhere. Swimming is another most beneficial exercise, the importance of which cannot be too strongly urged upon the attention of every educator; its claims as a means of self-preservation, independently of its value as a means of health and enjoyment, are sufficient to prove that it ought to form part of the education of all. Dancing should not be confined, as it now generally is in girls' schools, to the formal lessons given once or twice during the week, but the pupils should be encouraged to dance as a recreation in the playground when the weather permits. In winter evenings, too, when the day's work is done, a merry school-room dance—about as orderly as Mr. Fezziwig's—is a very healthful and exhilarating affair, at once destructive to chilblains and "the blues." Every encouragement should also be given to the practice of those out-door and in-door games which bring the muscles into vigorous exercise.

In many schools it is found very difficult to induce the elder pupils to take any interest in the means of physical development. Usually when a school-girl attains to the magnificent age of thirteen or fourteen she leaves active games to "the children." If she is a pretty, vain girl, she straightaway turns her attention to the mysteries of bonnets, mantles, and crinoline; if she is an ambitious, clever one, she begins "cramming" for examinations, and waxes great in crayon heads; if she is thoughtful and conscientious, she devotes herself to an unmerciful course of study, under the idea of "improving her advantages;" whatever she is, she votes exercise a bore and a hinderance, and takes as little as she can. The state of things is a necessary result of the plan of education usually adopted; girls are rarely taught the value of physical development and strength; they are stimulated by prizes and every possible inducement to cultivate the mind, while the claims of the body are tacitly understood to be of far less importance. But let every girl be constantly and thoroughly impressed with the fact, that the highest perfection and happiness of which her nature is susceptible can be obtained only through the simultaneous, harmonious development of all her faculties; let the belle of the school know that health heightens beauty; let the ambitious, studious girl be told of the dependence of mental upon bodily vigor; let the conscientious one be convinced, that to develop her whole being, is a duty she owes to her Creator, to society and herself.

Document 43

Neither school curricula nor parental education included the study of the human body and its reproductive system. Parents and teachers carefully avoided discussions even remotely related to sexuality and reproduction. As a result children grew up ignorant of their most basic biological functions. This ignorance caused grown women to feel helpless, embarrassed, and guilty when they or their children were ill or in pain, and it led to unnecessary physical and emotional suffering. By the beginning of the twentieth century feminists, sexual reformers, and many individual women dedicated to promoting better health for women (especially poor women—see document 44) urged an end to the enforced ignorance of biology and sexuality.

This document is a guide for mothers to teach their daughters about sex. It is in the form of a simple dialogue between mother and daughter and is an adaption of the work of a Dutch woman, "Nellie" (Mrs. Van Kol), which appeared in a Belgian socialist feminist publication in 1905. Although the article deals candidly and in detail with the female reproductive system, pregnancy, and childbirth and advocates a loving relationship between husband and wife, it never mentions sexual intercourse and leaves unanswered (and unasked) the question of just how egg meets sperm.

A Sex Education Guide for Mother and Daughter
Belgium, 1905

"Sex Education," part IV, by Mme. Van Kol ("Nellie")

"Mama, what happens to the baby while it is in the mother's body? What does it do? Does it sleep and wake up? Does it eat? Does it drink?"

Mme. Van Kol ("Nellie"), "L'education sexuelle," *Cahier Féministes*, December 15, 1904, pp. 7–8.

This was what Marie, a nice little girl, asked some time after having learned all that she had to know about the union of man and woman.

Like many children, she had been satisfied to learn that a baby grows in its mother's body and for some time she had not questioned beyond that. But since her mother had given her a frank and satisfactory answer to her question "How do babies come into the mother?" she had a lot to think about. For children, who are blessed with a healthy and active understanding, do not rest until they have grasped the problem in its entirety. They take its measure, think about it, and come back to it in conversations, questioning until their curiosity is fully satisfied. At first they keep their new discovery to themselves, as if in a treasure vault, and only later, when the need manifests itself, do they come out with it. Thus Marie's mind had been occupied by the question of reproduction for several days. Her mother was intelligent enough to guess what was going on in her daughter's mind; thus, she was eager to answer her queries in an affectionate manner.

"All right," she said, "I'll explain it all to you. But first we must sit down comfortably because this will not be a matter of just a few words.

"Here we go. In the lower part of a woman's belly there is a special organ, a kind of sack, having the shape and size of an average pear but which can expand a great deal. This organ is called the womb.

"Its narrow end, where the stem of the pear would be, faces downward; this is where the sack's opening is. Coming out of the left and right sides of the large end are two small tubes connected to the ovaries. These are very small organs situated at the left and right of the womb in which the eggs are formed. An egg, if it is fertilized, will develop into a baby. For this purpose an egg detaches itself from the ovary, passes through one of the tubes to the womb. If it is fertilized, it stays in the womb; if not, it disappears.

"This release of the egg is accompanied by a flow of blood from the sexual organs. This occurs painlessly in healthy women.

"It will probably be your turn for this to happen in a few months, but it will not frighten you because it is a natural occurrence. Just be sure to let me know so that I can show you a few useful precautions to take for two or three days each month.

"Let us return to our lesson. You have learned that fluid which comes from the man fertilizes the egg in the woman. From this egg a human being, male or female, will be born. This fluid contains organisms infinitely smaller than the egg and which have a very short life. When one of these little organisms attaches itself to an egg brought to the womb, it penetrates it and the egg thus fertilized undergoes some interesting changes.

"This new being is joined deeply to the soft lining of the womb to develop safely. It is a wonderful place. Without going into scientific detail I can tell you that one soon feels the disproportionately large head and the disproportionately small arms and legs. During this growth, the egg's outer membrane grows soft and fills with water in such a way as to cushion the shocks and jars around the little one. There it rests, still and hardy, without a bit of light or any sound reaching it. It experiences neither hunger nor suffering. Its mother's blood nourishes its body and tenderly protects it.

"As the egg grows larger, the womb naturally enlarges. In the spot where the fertilized egg is attached, a mass called the placenta takes shape—it is nothing but a complete system of veins and blood vessels linking the blood of the mother to that of the baby.

"The infant's blood flows into a tube called the umbilical cord, which comes out of the baby's stomach and ends in the placenta. There it is enriched by contact with the mother's blood and returns to the baby by the same umbilical cord. The growing baby does not have an independent life. It neither eats nor drinks. It is completely dependent on its mother. If she has all she needs, the infant lacks for nothing; if she is without what she needs, it suffers.

"After birth, the umbilical cord is severed. The little bit of it left on the new-born is tied up firmly, dries up, and falls off, leaving a scar we call the navel. The rest of it is expelled from the mother's body with the placenta, being ejected when it no longer serves any function.

"The act of birth consists of violent spasms by the womb which push the baby outward. You could say that everything in the mother's body gives way and tears to open up a passage for the baby through the sexual organs.

"The water held in the womb's sack flows out, easing the baby's passage. But for hours, mothers suffer beyond words to bring their babies into the world.

"Fortunately, all of them, almost without exception, love their babies even before their birth and eagerly and joyfully await them.

"A great consolation for the mother is to be aware of the father standing near the bed, to hear him speak tenderly and to be the object of his anxious care. A sensitive husband who loves his wife himself suffers at this time. He is aware that he experienced only pleasure in the act that brought the baby to life, while his mate has borne a burden that has grown heavier and heavier during pregnancy, and undergoes a great deal of pain in order to bring it into the world.

"There is nothing that can resist nature, that is for sure. But a good man like your father, Marie, is aware of more exacting obligations to his mate. In his wife, he respects his child's mother, the mother of all human kind. Thus he strives to assure his wife a place of respect in the family and in society.

"He takes care to provide his daughter with a healthy, natural upbringing so that she in her turn will experience successful childbirth. He grants the wife and mother rights and freedoms which allow her to be a responsible person, bound by ties of love to her husband, her children and her home.

"Such relationships do not exist in every country even among the most civilized people. But men of high standing, like your father, who bow respectfully before the mothers of mankind, use all their energy to work with women to win them their due place.

"A last word, my child, and very important! Before long you will be old enough to hear talk of love. Know how to look after yourself. Don't give yourself to someone who will flatter you and make pretty promises. The union of the sexes is not for pleasure; it can cause the arrival of a child. The child has a right to its father's care, not only for his material well-being, but for his moral upbringing as well. Therefore, do not let passion cloud your judgment. Give your body only to the man you judge worthy to be the father of your child. And always have confidence in your mother!"

The conversation ended with a tender embrace. Mother and daughter then went about their business, each lost in her own thoughts.

Document 44

Immediately before and during World War I, the British Women's Co-operative Guild (see document 6) waged a campaign for the enactment of a "National Scheme" of maternity care. During the war, when there was a good deal of concern in governments all over Europe with promoting higher birth rates, the Guild succeeded in having a Maternity Sick Benefit added to the National Health Insurance program. Maternity centers were also established to provide medical care and advice to women before and after childbirth.

As part of their campaign the Guild solicited letters from present or former Guild branch officers. The women were asked to comment on their experiences and difficulties with pregnancy and childbearing and how these affected their health. These women were asked to include in their responses how many children they had, how soon after each other they were born, if any died under age five, if any were stillborn, and if they had had any miscarriages. They were also asked to comment on their husbands' occupations and wages. The Guild received 386 replies and in 1915 printed 160 of them, four of which constitute this document.

Of the 386 women who responded, 348 had had a total of 1,396 live births, 218 miscarriages (15.6 per 100 live births), and 83 stillbirths (5.9 per 100 live births). Of the 348 mothers, 148 (42.4 percent) had had stillbirths or miscarriages. (They were not asked to comment on abortion, which was illegal.) These women reported that 122 infants had died under one year of age (8.7 per 100 live births), 86 of the 348 women having lost children in their first year of life.*

The women who wrote these letters were generally from better-off working-class families and were politically active. Yet their poverty and suffering were staggering. Husbands were frequently unemployed or underemployed, which forced their already over-burdened wives to seek wage work. These women often went without sufficient food while pregnant in order to pay for a doctor or midwife. Strenuous work, especially hauling and lifting heavy objects, and physical exhaustion caused them to miscarry and give birth prematurely. While they frequently blamed themselves for their children's deaths and defects, they were nonetheless aware of the means to end their suffering; over and over again these writers call for medical care and adequate nourishment for women, an end to women's ignorance about their own bodies, and, most of all, a respite from their ceaseless labors.

Maternity: Letters from Working Women, ed. by Women's Co-operative Guild (London, 1915), pp. 194–95.

Maternity
England, 1915

9. Bad Confinements

I shall only be too glad to assist you in giving my experience. In the first place, I have had eight children; seven is now living. I was twenty-three when I was married. My first pregnancy I suffered with my leg swollen and veins ready to burst. At my confinement the baby was hung with navel cord twice round the neck and once round the shoulder, owing to lifting and reaching, which caused me hours of suffering, and it caused my womb to come down, and I have had to wear something to hold it up until these late years. I am now fifty-eight; my husband has been dead seven years. I was left to fight life's battles alone. As my family increased I had to have my legs bandaged. I never felt a woman during pregnancy; as I got nearer I felt worse. At my confinements the greatest trouble was the flooding after the baby was born, and the afterbirth grown to my side. When that was taken away the body had to be syringed to stop mortification. I have had the doctor's arm in my body, and felt his fingers tearing the afterbirth from my side. While I am writing, I almost fancy I am talking with you. I hope I have not tired you with my letter.

Wages £1 to £2; eight children, two miscarriages

11. "I Was Awfully Poor"

My first girl was born before I attained my twentieth year, and I had a stepmother who had had no children of her own, so I was not able to get any knowledge from her; and even if she had known anything I don't suppose she would have dreamt of telling me about these things which were supposed to exist, but must not be talked about. About a month before the baby was born I remember asking my aunt where the baby would come from. She was astounded, and did not make me much wiser. I don't know whether my ignorance had anything to do with the struggle I had to bring the baby into the world, but the doctor said that my youth had, for I was not properly developed. Instruments had to be used, and I heard the doctor say he could not tell whether my life could be saved or not, for he said there is not room here for a bird to pass.

Maternity: Letters from Working Women, ed. by Women's Co-operative Guild (London, 1915), pp. 28-29, 30-32, 50-51, 153-54.

All the time I thought that this was the way all babies were born.

At the commencement of all my pregnancies I suffered terribly from toothache, and for this reason I think all married child-bearing women should have their teeth attended to, for days and nights of suffering of this kind must have a bad effect on both the mother and child. I also at times suffered torments from cramp in the legs and vomiting, particularly during the first three months. I hardly think the cramp can be avoided, but if prospective mothers would consult their doctors about the inability to retain food, I fancy that might be remedied. At the commencement of my second pregnancy I was very ill indeed. I could retain no food, not even water, and I was constipated for thirteen days, and I suffered from jaundice. This had its effect on the baby, for he was quite yellow at birth, and the midwife having lodgers to attend to, left him unwashed for an hour after birth. She never troubled to get his lungs inflated, and he was two days without crying. I had no doctor. I was awfully poor, so that I had to wash the baby's clothes in my bedroom at the fortnight's end; but had I had any knowledge like I possess now, I should have insisted at the very least on the woman seeing my child's lungs were properly filled. When we are poor, though, we cannot say what *must* be done; we have to suffer and keep quiet. The boy was always weakly, and could not walk when my third baby born. He had fits from twelve to fourteen, but except for a rather "loose" frame, seems otherwise quite healthy now.

My third child, a girl, was born in a two-roomed "nearly underground" dwelling. We had two beds in the living-room, and the little scullery was very damp. Had it not been for my neighbours, I should have had no attendance after the confine-ment, and no fire often, for it was during one of the coal strikes. My fourth child, a boy, was born under better housing conditions, but not much better as regards money; and during the carrying of all my children, except the first, I have had insufficient food and too much work. This is just an outline. Did I give it all, it would fill a book, as the saying goes.

In spite of all, I don't really believe that the children (with the exception of the oldest boy) have suffered much, only they might have been so much stronger, bigger, and better if I had been able to have better food and more rest.

Cleanliness has made rapid strides since my confinements; for never once can I remember having anything but face, neck, and hands washed until I could do things myself, and it was thought certain death to change the underclothes under a week.

For a whole week we were obliged to lie on clothes stiff and stained, and the stench under the clothes was abominable, and added to this we were commanded to keep the babies under the clothes.

I often wonder how the poor little mites managed to live, and perhaps they never would have done but for our adoration, because this constant admiration of our treasures did give them whiffs of fresh air very often.

My husband's lowest wages was 10s., the highest about £1 only, which was reached by overtime. His mother and my own parents generally provided me with clothing, most of which was cast-offs.

Wages 10s. to £1; four children.

24. Utterly Overdone

Sometimes we think that our own life does not seem to be of any importance, and our troubles are what should be, specially before the Maternity Benefit. When I was married, I had to leave my own town to go out into the world, as it were, and when I had to have my first baby, I knew absolutely nothing, not even how they were born. I had many a time thought how cruel (not wilfully, perhaps) my mother was not to tell me all about the subject when I left home. Although I was twenty-five years of age when married, I had never been where a baby was born. When my baby was born I had been in my labour for thirty-six hours, and did not know what was the matter with me, and when it was born it was as black as a coal and took the doctor a long while to get life into it. It was only a seven-months baby, and I feel quite sure if I had been told anything about pregnancy it would not have happened. I carried a heavy piece of oilcloth, which brought my labour. Anyway, the boy lived, but it cannot be expected that he can be as robust as if he had been a nine-months baby, but he is healthy, but not extra strong.

When he was six years old, I had my fifth baby, and had also a miscarriage, and then I went on strike. My life was not worth living at this rate, as my husband was only a working man, out of work when wet or bad weather, and also in times of depression. I had all my own household work to do, washing, mending, making clothes, baking, cooking, and everything else.

In those six years I never knew what it was to have a proper night's sleep, for if I had not a baby on the breast I was pregnant, and how could you expect children to be healthy, as I always seemed to be tired. If I sat down, I very often fell asleep through the day.

I knew very little about feeding children; when they cried I gave them the breast. If I had known then what I know now, perhaps my children would have been living. I was ignorant, and had to suffer severely for it, for it nearly cost me my life, and also those of my children. I very often ponder over this part of my life. I must not say anything about my mother now, because she is dead, but I cannot help thinking what might have been if she had told me.

Five children, one miscarriage.

122 Ironing and Kneading in Bed

I was married one year and five months before my first boy was born. I nearly lost my life. I was in labour from 1 o'clock in the morning until 7.5 at night. Then the doctor used instruments. He stated I had worked too hard, and not rested sufficiently, but I could not afford a girl. My husband then was only getting £1 1s. per week, and 5s. rent had to be paid out of it. The second baby came fifteen months after.... I had no milk for either. I was in labour with the second from Monday dinner-time until Tuesday night. Then the doctor gave me an injection of warm water; as I was torn so badly before he did not want to use the instruments. Two years after I had a miscarriage.... I then had to lie in bed for a whole month. I kept a small girl, and I used to do my own ironing and knead my bread in bed unknown to the doctor. I had a bed put down in the small parlour to save the girl and children running upstairs. I feel sure that if I had had a maternity benefit then to help me, I should not be suffering now inwardly. No mother can stay in bed very comfortably knowing things are going on anyhow while she is in bed. Then, again, during the time she is carrying the child, her mind is troubled, and she becomes fretful, hence a fretful, delicate child. The mother, when funds are low, goes without much food, pleading headache etc., so as to try and blind her husband. I think an expectant mother should rest at least half an hour every day, and especially towards the last should have no heavy work to do, such as washing and ironing. The extra weight she is carrying naturally throws the humours into her legs, the veins standing out like thick cords, and at night she cannot sleep for cramps and aches. The child is the asset of the nation, and the mother the backbone. Therefore, I think the nation should help to feed and keep that mother, and so help to strengthen the nation by her giving birth to strong boys and girls. She does not require weaklings, and insufficient food and overwork and worry is the root of this weakness, both in the case of mother and child. I only hope that sick visitors should see that it is the mothers that are getting the benefit of the maternity benefit, and not the husband, and often the landlord.

Wages 20s. to 23s.; two children.

Document 45

The plight of pregnant factory workers received more attention than did that of unemployed and economically "invisible" housewives. But since factory workers had all the burdens of their nonworking sisters and endured the factory system as well, their health problems were particularly acute and were not eliminated by the few weeks of pregnancy leave which they won in most countries in the early twentieth century.

In 1922 the German Textile Workers' Union undertook a campaign to improve the health and working conditions of its pregnant members. The Union sent a questionnaire to workers who were or had been pregnant and asked them to include comments about their experiences in their reply. They were asked to discuss their working conditions, especially the impact of their daily factory routine on their pregnancies, and also the psychological impact of working while pregnant. Some of these responses (three of which appear here) were published by the Union in a book entitled *Wage Work, Pregnancy and Women's Suffering [Erwerbsarbeit Schwangerschaft Frauenleid]*. This work also contained the results of the Union's study of the affects of working conditions on pregnant women's health. It reported that textile workers experienced increased tendency to miscarriage and premature birth, frequent damage to the womb and abdominal muscles and pelvis, varicose veins, thrombosis, and psychological damage caused by the stress and strain of the noise and work.

Letters from Pregnant Working Women
Germany, 1923

Dear Executive Committee:

I am in possession of your questionnaire dated August 24, 1923, and want to try and answer it for you as best I can. It is hard for me to report [about my pregnancy] and give you an accurate picture of it. I am a seamstress and have to sit all day long but when a piece is finished it has to be cleaned and then you have to stand the whole time. For the last eight or nine weeks I've had pains in the heart all the time and I go crazy sometimes with the pain. I work a short shift, only two days a week, but when they are over, it is as if I had worked the whole week. I have to climb three flights of stairs in the factory and that takes considerable exertion; heavy breathing, groaning and pains in the heart and then swelling in the legs which makes the veins stick out, and that causes pains when you do your work. You wish that the work could go to the devil or wherever but unfortunately where will you get sick benefits so you will have full [financial] support when the child is born? That's badly needed since children's things are so expensive.

With friendly greetings

I would like to respond to your letter of the 25th of the month as follows:

If one's monthly period is no fun for the working woman, being pregnant, especially with the vomiting during working hours, is much worse. In order to be able to work at all [when I was pregnant] I ate at six o'clock in the morning and then slept for another half-hour. The worse aspects of my job are the monotony of the work, having to spend so much time over the cylinders and hardly being able to complete the work of processing the products. The whole day is spent in dusty air, damp, dark—the lights have to be turned on by 3 o'clock in the afternoon—you count the quarter hours until it's time to get off work, and then the worst [job] is pulling the cords. Sometimes the machines go so hard that even a large man can hardly maintain them. Many of the men look at us [pregnant women] like we are crazy, and they use the most vulgar language to talk about us. At my husband's urging I stayed home

Erwerbsarbeit Schwangerschaft Frauenleid, ed. by Deutscher Textilarbeiter-Verband (Berlin, 1925), pp. 15–17.

the last six weeks before the birth and after three difficult days gave birth to a healthy girl. I've said farewell to the factory since I want to nurse and educate my child myself.

I only have one request. My husband and I naturally don't want another child right away, first partly because of the wife's health and second, we take the position that we don't want to bring more children into the world than we can provide for. Now I would be thankful to you if you would be able to give me information about prevention of pregnancy or about the means to do it. We have a doctor's book but we don't want to lay out so much money for dangerous measures. We would be happy if we could get a medical opinion about it. Since we are married and own our home, which we built ourselves, we could help ourselves.

In the hope of a speedy reply, I remain with best wishes.

I feel myself obligated to respond to your worthwhile letter so I can report some things about my pregnancy. Aside from some physical difficulties I experienced and the fact that the birth came six weeks early, which caused me some painful hours, I feel completely well again.

Having received your letter, I will write a few lines to you. I suffered a great deal during pregnancy, first from varicose veins in the feet as a result of so much standing and running around in the factory so that in the evenings I had swollen feet. Then I had the whites [vaginal discharge] and there was occasional burning so that I could hardly walk when it was warm and I had to wash myself many times during the day. Even after the birth the irritation continued for three weeks after the child came. The delivery went very well since this child was not delivered with forceps as my first one was. I have been a widow for two years and have fallen into the hands of a man who said he was not married. When I learned he was, it was too late—that's the way the world is. I have a four-year-old boy. My husband was murdered two years ago near Magdeburg and I received nothing for the child. I don't know what else to write.

Greetings

XIII

—•—

Contraception and Abortion

Birth rates fell dramatically in the late nineteenth century especially in western Europe, but the desire to limit births was not just a nineteenth- and twentieth-century phenomenon. Throughout history women have employed myriad and often exotic contraceptive techniques as well as abstinence, abortion, and infanticide to prevent and space births and to control the size of their families. In the late nineteenth and early twentieth centuries changes in social, economic, and physical conditions led large numbers of women to have fewer children. Women's desire to control the number of children they bore was not new. What was new, and ultimately revolutionary, was the insistence by women of all classes that access to safe and effective means of contraception and abortion was their right.

A variety of contraceptive devices, all more or less unreliable, were available to women during most of the nineteenth century. The sponge, a piece of cotton, lint, or fine wool inserted into the womb, and various pessaries and vaginal caps were used. Women also douched after coitus with vinegar, bicarbonate or baking soda or alum. A popular manual suggested they douche with solutions made from astringent materials such as white oak bark, hemlock, green tea, and raspberry leaves.* Women also employed traditional customs such as sneezing, coughing, or squatting after coitus or "squeezing the parts together" after their husbands ejaculated. Male condoms were available, and although their costs were lowered after the vulcanization of rubber in the 1840s, they were still too expensive for most working-class people. They were mainly used by middle-class men to avoid venereal disease. Coitus interruptus, which did not cost anything, was probably the most widely used method. The most effective birth control technique

*Norman Himes, *A Medical History of Contraception* (New York, 1970), p. 227.

known in the period, the vaginal diaphragm, was invented in the 1880s, but its diffusion was uneven and slow, especially among the poor.

When contraception failed, as it regularly did, women turned to abortion. Like contraceptive information, advice on abortion was passed along among women, often from mother to daughter, or between friends, neighbors and co-workers. Herbs, potients, vigorous exercises, and hot baths were the preferred methods since women considered them "natural" ways to abort. If these failed, objects such as quills, needles, or bark were inserted into the womb or various solutions were injected with a syringe. Women also obtained strong abortive drugs from pharmacists, and middle- and upper-class women, who could afford to, paid doctors to perform illegal abortions. Midwives frequently performed abortions for working-class women.

Women were all too aware of the dangers of these procedures. Several women who wrote to the Women's Co-operative Guild in 1915 (see document 44) decried the affects of abortion and miscarriages on women's health. Indeed, the continuing high rates of maternal mortality may have been linked to the debilitating affects of repeated miscarriage and abortion. But in the absence of effective means of preventing conception women almost routinely turned to abortion when they believed that bearing a child was the less desirable alternative.

It is impossible to determine how widespread the use of contraception, and particularly abortion, were, but surveys done in the early twentieth century indicate that birth control was practiced among all classes. Marie Stopes, who opened the first birth control clinic in England in 1921, reported in 1925 that some of the first 5,000 women who came to the clinic had previously used a variety of contraceptive techniques but with little success. Coitus interruptus had been used in 814 cases (with a failure rate of 81.82 percent), condoms in 198 cases (with a failure rate of 75.25 percent), 110 had used the quinine pessary (with a failure rate of 98.18 percent), 62 had used douching or syringing (95.16 percent failure), 62 had used various cervical caps (85.48 percent failure), 18 used the sponge (73.20 percent failure), 12 had used the safe period (100 percent failure), and 8 had used nursing (100 percent failure). Stopes pointed out, however, that the women who came to her clinic did so because they wanted more effective means of birth control, so their rates of failure were probably higher than the national average. The Stopes Clinic provided most of its first 5,000 patients with a small cervical cap, to be used together with greasy suppositories, generally quinine or chinosol.*

In Berlin, between 1911 and 1913 Dr. Max Marcuse questioned 100 working-class married women and found that 64 percent had used some form of contraception and 40 percent had had at least one abortion (see document 46). In most countries middle- and upper-class women appeared to have had greater success with contraception than poor women. They often relied on relatively expensive quinine pessaries, syringes, and condoms which, like abortofacients, were advertised in women's magazines, in doctors' health manuals, and even on soap wrappers. Contemporary observers in the nineteenth and twentieth centuries often claimed that as many as one-third or even one-half of all conceptions were aborted, but these claims are impossible to validate.

Although male doctors wrote books and pamphlets on birth control from the early nineteenth century and a few male and female advocates of birth control attempted to spread knowledge of techniques, the first practical and sustained efforts to provide the masses of women with contraception did not come until women themselves led the way. The first birth control clinic in Europe was opened in Holland in 1881 by Dr. Aletta Jacobs, the first woman doctor in the Netherlands. (Marie Stopes's "Mother's Clinic" in London was staffed by women doctors and nurse-midwives.) Other clinics founded and operated by men as well as women opened in the 1920s and 1930s. Unfortunately none of the methods offered by these clinics was totally reliable. Moreover, abortion and in some countries even advocacy of birth control or the dissemination of contraceptive information or devices were illegal.

In the 1920s and 1930s there were organized efforts in many countries to have these laws revoked and make birth control more available to poor women. A long struggle in Germany by a broad-based coalition led by the communists failed to have the anti-abortion statute struck down. French women could not even succeed in having laws which prohibited the sale of contraceptives overturned. There were some small successes, however. In England women obtained the right to abortion if it threatened the mother's

---

*Marie Stopes, *The First Five Thousand* (London, 1921), pp. 36, 42.

life in 1929 and if it was necessary for the mother's health in 1938, but these exceptions primarily aided middle-class women. In 1930, as the result of the campaign spearheaded by the Women's Co-operative Guild, the Ministry of Health allowed the new Maternity Care Centers to provide married women with advice on birth control if another pregnancy would endanger the mother's health. This decision was not made public, however, until Marie Stopes printed it in her publication, *Birth Control News.**

Perhaps the most significant development in this period occurred when women took the issues of abortion and contraception outside the informal women's network. They demanded that medical practitioners provide them with effective contraception and safe abortions and that governments recognize women's right to decide for themselves whether or not to bear children. They encountered serious opposition from both the right and the left, from those who believed their demands would lead to freer sexuality, a further fall in the birth rate, the destruction of the family, and/or wholesale changes in the relationship between the sexes. Of course, many of the advocates of birth control recognized and desired some or all of these changes. Most believed that an end to involuntary motherhood would improve women's social and economic position and the relationship between husband and wife. But since safe, legal abortions remained impossible for the majority of women and completely reliable methods of contraception were unavailable in the first half of the twentieth century, women's right to control their bodies could not be fully and freely exercised.

Document 46

The document below contains samples of responses given by working-class married women to questions about their birth control practices. The survey was done in Berlin just before World War I by Dr. Max Marcuse, a skin specialist and onetime secretary of the *Bund für Matterschutz und Sexualreform* (see document 39). Marcuse asked 100 of his patients between the ages of twenty and sixty (only five were over forty-five) how many living children they

*Sheila Rowbotham, *A New World for Women: Stella Browne—Socialist Feminist* (London, 1977), p. 58.

had, how many had died, how many times they had aborted, anα
what means of contraception and abortion they had employed.
The women reported 118 living children, 46 dead children, and
76 abortions or miscarriages. Their families were small; 30 had no
living children, 36 had one living child, 15 had two and none had
more than six. Sixty-four percent used some form of contraception
and 40 percent had had one or more abortions. Most of those who
reported inducing abortion admitted it freely, expressing the view
that abortion was "necessary," not immoral, and a common and
widespread occurrence. The doctor indicated that abortions were
probably underreported. Most of these women could not afford
expensive contraceptives. The majority relied on coitus interruptus
and douching, two very unreliable methods.

Survey of Abortion and Birth Control Methods
Germany, 1913

Number 21   Name: A.M.   Age: 33   Husband's Occupation:
chauffeur   Married: 15 years   Living Children: 3   Dead Children: 3   Aborted: 1
Methods of Abortion: Hot sitzbaths and took purgatives.
Methods of Contraception: —

Number 25   Name: J.S.   Age: 33   Husband's Occupation:
worker   Married: 9 years   Living Children: 2   Dead Children —
Aborted: 3
Methods of Abortion: When the period didn't occur, I've
                                always jumped off chairs and stools
                                and taken a very deep soapy water
                                douche; it always led to an abortion
                                in two months.
Methods of Contraception: Since last abortion (three years ago)
                                coitus interruptus without excep-
                                tion.

Number 27   Name: B.Z.   Age: 30   Husband's Occupation:
tailor   Married: 9 years   Living Children: 3   Dead Children: —

Max Marcuse, "Zur Frage der Verbreitung und Methodik der wilkürlichen
Gerburtenbeschränkung in Berliner Proletarierkreisen," *Sexual-Probleme* 9 (1913),
pp. 758–83.

Aborted: 1

Methods of Abortion: I sent for a [menstrual] period remedy that was advertised in the newspaper, it cost 5 Marks, it worked after 3 days. A child costs much more, to be sure.

Methods of Contraception: My husband always looks after it. How? I don't know, we don't talk about it; he only says that nothing more can happen.

Number 29 Name: A.S. Age: 33 Husband's Occupation: turner Married: 8 years Living Children: 1 Dead Children: — Aborted: 10

Methods of Abortion: I take hot baths and douches every time. Most of the time that was sufficient; otherwise you help it along. How? You know that yourself, Doctor.

Methods of Contraception: —

Number 40 Name: M.M. Age: 37 Husband's Occupation: locksmith Married: 13 years Living Children: — Dead Children: — Aborted: 1

Methods of Abortion: The midwife must have made a mistake during the examination because on the same evening it happened.

Methods of Contraception: —

Number 46 Name: M.L. Age: 20 Husband's Occupation: worker Married: 2 years Living Children: — Dead Children: — Aborted: 1

Methods of Abortion: A woman co-worker blew a powder into my womb for me.

Methods of Contraception: I always have a Lysol douche right after.

Number 58 Name: M.B. Age: 33 Husband's Occupation: mechanic Married: 6 years Living Children: 1 Dead Children: — Aborted: 1

Methods of Abortion: My husband got some medicine
                                from the druggist and I had to take
                                four bottles of it.

Methods of Contraception: I mostly wear a pessary; but it often
                                falls out with bowel movements
                                and so it has happened the two
                                times [I became pregnant].

Number 63 Name: O.B. Age: 28 Husband's Occupation: ele-
vator operator Married: 2 years Living Children: 1 Dead Children: — Aborted: 1

Methods of Abortion: I poked around with a quill a little
                                bit until blood came and then a
                                doctor scraped me out.

Methods of Contraception: Since the abortion, always coitus
                                interruptus.

Number 68 Name: W.P. Age: 47 Husband's Occupation: borer
Married: 24 years Living Children: 2 Dead Children: 1
Aborted: 2

Methods of Abortion: The wife of a co-worker of my
                                husbands mixed me a tea which
                                helped her every time. She aborted
                                5 times after using it. It also worked
                                splendidly with me. I don't know
                                what was in the tea. The woman
                                keeps her secret to herself and earns
                                a pretty sum of money. She has
                                helped the whole block.

Methods of Contraception: For the last 20 years, always coitus
                                interruptus.

Number 69 Name: M.G. Age: 45 Husband's Occupation:
plumber Married: 18 years Living Children: — Dead Children: — Aborted: —

Methods of Abortion: —

Methods of Contraception: Since the beginning of the mar-
                                riage always coitus interruptus;
                                just in the last 1–2 years since coitus
                                interruptus is not very good, a

prophylactic; nevertheless even with that I have a douche afterwards and no one knows.

Number 72   Name: F.L.   Age: 37   Husband's Occupation: worker   Married: 9 years   Living Children: 2   Dead Children: 1   Aborted: 2

Methods of Abortion: When the period did not come at the right time I went to the midwife and she took care of it for me.

Methods of Contraception: After the last abortion (four years ago) the midwife inserted a ring after each period of discomfort.

Number 77   Name: E.M.   Age: 32:   Husband's Occupation: nickel plater   Married: 7 years   Living Children: —   Dead Children: —   Aborted: 2

Methods of Abortion: Both times I had the druggist give me blood pills and blood tea. My husband must know nothing as he wants to have children very much.

Methods of Contraception: I have worn an aluminum obturator for the last five years without my husband knowing it.

Number 78   Name: K.R.   Age: 24   Husband's Occupation: worker   Married: 1 year   Living Children: 2   Dead Children: —   Aborted: —

Methods of Abortion: —
Methods of Contraception: —
Remarks: My husband can go to other women now; I don't want to have any more children.

Number 85   Name: R.D.   Age: 25   Husband's Occupation: worker   Married: 7 years   Living Children: 2   Dead Children: 1   Aborted: 1

Methods of Abortion: I drank a large pot of hot strong coffee and douched myself with soapy water.

Methods of Contraception: Since the last time (an abortion
                                   three years ago) coitus only in the
                                   rectum.

Number 100   Name: B.V.   Age: 30   Husband's Occupation:
blacksmith   Married: 8 years   Living Children: 3   Dead Children: 1   Aborted: 2

Methods of Abortion: Fetched pills from the druggist; the
                                   first time they worked wonderfully.
                                   The second time not so quickly but
                                   it happened anyway.

Methods of Contraception: My husband is against them (Contraceptives).

Document 47

The British Malthusian League was founded in 1877. Like neo-Malthusian organizations in other countries, its membership was composed of women and men who were primarily concerned with the problem of overpopulation and not with women's right to control their bodies. At first the League merely discussed family limitation from an economic standpoint and tried to convince people of the necessity of reducing family size. Then in 1913 it made a pamphlet of practical advice, *Hygienic Methods of Family Limitation*, available to working-class married men and women who filled out forms requesting it.

The League and other middle-class reformers have often been credited with instilling the need for birth control and causing the acceptance of artificial techniques among the working class. But the following letters, written to the League in 1919 and 1920, clearly show that working-class women already wanted to limit births when they turned to the League for advice on the means to do so (see document 45).

"Letters from Struggling Parents"
England, 1919 and 1920

I absolutely agree with the views of the society of which you are the Hon. Secty. regarding child birth. I am quite a young woman 31 years of age and have already had seven children, and being in

The Malthusian, September 15, 1919, p. 1, and March 15, 1920, p. 1.

very poor circumstances and quite ignorant of the methods of the upper classes have of preventing child birth I apply to you for your form of application for said advice regarding the above methods. Chelsea

Mrs. H.

I am in receipt of your Circular, and would be very glad if you would send me the Leaflet. We have 2 children and shall be shortly having a third, and I should be so very glad to know how to prevent having more as it is a constant struggle to keep them these hard times. Have filled up the form you enclosed. Birmingham

Mrs. R.

Will you please send my your leaflet, I have 8 children and still likely to have more and as I intend to emigrate to Canada it would prevent my going. I am very sorry indeed that I have not heard of a Malthusian League years ago. There are numbers of poor women around the neibourhood will have husbands coming home after the war cripples. I will do my best to make the League known. London, S.E.

Mrs. F.

Kindly forward me one of your Hygienic Methods of family limitation. As I have seven children and am only 34 years of age, and am strong and healthy and likely to have more. Attercliffe.

Mrs. W.

Document 48

F. W. Stella Browne (1883–1955) was a crusader for women's rights to birth control and abortion in England in the 1920s and 1930s. As early as 1915, when few others dared to mention the subject, she insisted that every woman had a right to have an abortion if she did not wish to bear a child. In 1936 she founded the Abortion Law Reform Association. Stella Browne believed that women's full emancipation could only come under socialism, but insisted that economic changes would not bring women self-determination and equality if they could not choose whether or not to bear children. In 1923 she left the Communist party over the birth control issue. The male-dominated British party, like communist and socialist parties elsewhere in Europe, viewed birth control at best as a humane but nonessential reform which would allow married women to devote more time to party work. Some parties were openly hostile to the practice of birth control because they believed it would decrease the number of future socialists. (See part two, chapter VI.)

Widening of the Scope of Human Freedom and Choice
F.W. Stella Browne, England, 1922

In my opinion as a Feminist and a Communist, the fundamental importance and value of birth control lie in its widening of the scope of human freedom and choice, its *self-determining* significance for women. For make no mistake about this: Birth Control, the diffusion of the knowledge and possibility of Birth Control, means freedom for women, social and sexual freedom, and that is why it is so intensely feared and disliked in many influential quarters to-day. For thousands of years births and the rearing—and often the losing—of unlimited broods of babies were considered to be women's business *par excellence*. But that women should *think* about this business, that they should judge and examine it, that they should look at their future and their children's future . . . this is, indeed, camouflage it as you may, the beginning of the end of a social system and a moral code.

Let me develop very briefly and sketchily my assertion that Birth Control means sexual freedom. The ostensible reasons for the established form of patriarchal marriage have always been (a) the inheritance of property, and (b) the protection ensured to the young children and to their mother during her child-bearing period. But when marriage no longer means the subjection of unlimited motherhood and the economic dependence of mothers, the main social reasons for its retention as a stereotyped monogamous formula will be at an end. Observe, I do not say that Birth Control will abolish or diminish real monogamy: there will probably always be as much, or rather as little, monogamy as there has always been. But it will no longer be *stereotyped* as the one

F. W. Stella Browne, "The Feminine Aspect of Birth Control," in *Report on the Fifth International Neo-Malthusian and Birth Control Conference* (London, 1922), pp. 40–43.

lifelong and unvarying form of legally recognised expression for anything so infinitely variable and individual as the sexual impulse.

Now the demand for Birth Control has long ago ceased to be academic. It is becoming very urgent and more widespread than many persons, even among those interested and sympathetic, quite realise. This demand touches the lives of the majority of women in this and every country very acutely. Any one who knows the lives and work of the wives and mothers of the working class—or, as I, a Communist, would prefer to style it, the exploited class—who has helped them and striven to teach them, not in the spirit of a schoolmistress, but as a fellow-woman and a friend—knows that these women are in no doubt as to the essential righteousness of their claim to control their own maternity. But how? Hardly any of these women, if she can speak to you fully and frankly as a friend, but will admit that—often more than once—she has, on finding herself, in the hideously significant phrase they use, "caught," had recourse either to drugs or to most violent internal operative methods in order to bring about a miscarriage. And these operative methods have, of course, been applied absolutely without antiseptic or aseptic precautions, and without any of the rest which is as essential after such an experiment as after a normal confinement at full term. Yet it ought not to be beyond the powers of medical and chemical science to invent an absolutely reliable contraceptive! Think of the marvels of destruction in the shape of asphyxiating and corrosive gases all ready for the next great war for liberty and civilization. Think of the knowledge we have already attained of the structure and functions of the endocrine glands, and the work which has been done in the direction of modifying, renewing or transforming sexuality and procreative power.... Surely a science which can perform such wonders, though the technique is obviously only in its first stages, should be able to prevent conception without injuring health or impairing natural pleasure!...

Now I am *not* concerned here to vindicate the moral right to abortion, though I am profoundly convinced that it is a woman's right, and have argued the case for that right in the Press, both in England and America. I am told, however, by one of the leaders of our movement, to whose penetrating judgment and wide nursing experience I give the highest honour, that abortion is *physiologi-*

cally injurious and to be deprecated. It is open, perhaps, to question whether the effects of abortion itself have been sufficiently separated from the appalling bad conditions of nervous terror, lack of rest and lack of surgical cleanliness in which it is generally performed. But *granted that it is injurious per se,* the demand for effective contraception is all the stronger. The ancient codes, the decaying superstitions and prejudices of an old theoretical morality which has never been thoroughly accepted in practice, are losing all the sanctity they ever had. For an increasing number of persons throughout the world, including all the most mentally capable and physically vigorous, *they mean just nothing at all.*

It is up to science to meet the demands of humanity; and one of the most urgent of those demands is that of true eugenics (not privilege and property defence) that life shall be given as Anna Wickham says, "frankly, gaily," or—not at all. Which shall it be?

Document 49

Aletta Jacobs (1854–1929) was the first woman admitted to a university in Holland and became the first woman doctor in her country. She was also the first woman in Holland to claim the right to vote (1883) and was a co-founder of the Dutch Women's Suffrage Society (1883) and the International Woman Suffrage Alliance (1902), (see documents 21 and 22). She was also active in the international campaign against state-regulated prostitution and was a leader of the international women's peace movement (see document 21). She did not start out as a feminist or birth control pioneer. Rather it was her direct experience as a physician and her contacts with feminists in other countries that led her to activism and to open the first birth control clinic in Europe.

The First Birth Control Clinic
Aletta Jacobs, Holland, 1928

In 1879 I finished my medical course and graduated as the first woman doctor in Holland. I started practice in Amsterdam, and soon came into close touch with poor women of the working

Norman Haire, ed., *Some More Medical Views on Birth Control* (New York, 1928), pp. 151–56.

classes. Before long I realized that these women needed teaching about hygiene and how to take care of their children.

With the help of the Trades Unions Council it was arranged that I should give a course of lectures on the hygiene and nursing of infants twice a week from 4 to 6 P.M. at the Council's headquarters. Very soon I found it necessary to extend the original scheme. I began to attend at the same place two mornings a week in addition, to give free medical advice and treatment to poor women and their babies.

From these women I learnt that they suffered a great deal from too many and too frequent pregnancies, which often, indeed, actually endangered their lives. Careful inquiry convinced me that if I could advise nothing but sexual abstinence as a means of avoiding pregnancy, my advice would be useless, for in the conditions under which they lived abstinence was impracticable. Many of the women became pregnant regularly every year, in spite of the fact that every fresh pregnancy meant a renewed fight against death, and many of the babies were born dead or with very deficient vitality. Others told me that they kept on having babies regularly every year, although they already had more children than they could provide and care for properly in the economic and social circumstances in which they were placed.

My experience with these poor women of the so-called "lower classes" of Amsterdam soon made me feel that one of the best and quickest ways to decrease individual suffering and unhappiness and to improve social welfare would be to provide harmless and reliable contraceptive knowledge for those who looked forward to the birth of additional children with anything but joy, and the increase of whose families was undesirable both in their own interest and in that of society.

But in 1880 no really reliable method of contraception was known. I began to make investigations, and in 1882 I read in a German periodical an article by Dr. Mensinga of Flensburg, recommending a method he had tried with success in just such cases as those I had in mind. I wrote to him, and a long correspondence ensued, in which he very kindly told me how to use the method.

After using this method in a number of women belonging to different classes of society, and keeping them under observation for several months to observe the results, I became convinced that at last I had found a really harmless and effective method of contraception. I let it be known that I was prepared to give contraceptive advice to patients who desired to avoid pregnancy for medical, economic, or ethical reasons. Poor women could see me without charge at my bi-weekly clinic, which by this time had become known as the "Dr. Jacobs Clinic," at the hours when I treated poor women and children. Soon I began to find from ten to twenty women waiting for contraceptive information every time I went to the Clinic, while in my private practice at least two patients a day came for the same sort of advice.

When I started my Birth Control work in 1882, I did so primarily to prevent illness, to decrease individual suffering, and to prevent the birth of children who would handicap both their parents and the community. At this time, of course, I could not know what effect the spread of contraceptive knowledge would have on public welfare, on sexual morality, on woman's position of economic dependence, or in other ways. In theory it seemed to me that it would be desirable in every way, but I had to ask myself if my theory was right, and if I should be able to convince my opponents, medical and clerical for the most part, that I was right and they were wrong.

At the time of writing (1927) almost half a century has passed. Many of the children of those parents whom I taught to limit their families and to have children only when they desired them are now grown up and have families of their own. Nowadays in Holland the knowledge of contraception has become so general that, except in orthodox religious circles, large families are very unusual. And actual experience has shown that forty-five years of Birth Control work has brought about the good results that I expected when I began my work.

From the beginning I realized the gravity of my undertaking. I was not only the only woman doctor in Holland, but none of my medical colleagues shared my view on the general status of women, and I realized that I must be prepared to receive, and able to rebut, all sorts of attacks from my opponents. So from the very first I took very full notes of all my cases. I kept a record of each woman's reason for asking me for contraceptive advice, of her previous history, and of her condition when I first saw her. I made a careful pelvic examination and recorded the findings. This careful examination served two purposes: it often brought to light some disorder which had hitherto been unsuspected and which could now be treated before it got any worse; and if a medical opponent of Birth Control attacked me at any time afterwards and pretended that my method had caused any disease, I had only to look up my records to see whether the disease had really begun after the use of the method, or whether it had already existed when the woman first came to consult me. In this way I was able to refute many false charges of harm resulting from the use of this method. If I found a woman suffering from any disease or deformity, I advised her to have it treated either by her own family doctor, or if necessary by a specialist; sometimes I used to give the treatment myself.

I want to make it quite clear that I never advised any contraceptive method other than this one, and that this is the method generally advised by other doctors in Holland who have followed me. Probably this is why it has become known in England and America as the "Dutch" method. Holland was the first country to practise scientific Birth Control on a large scale, and our experience of forty-five years enables us to answer the objections which have been, and still are, raised by opponents of the movement.

It is interesting to note that when Birth Control becomes the subject of discussion in any country, when the women of any nation begin to try to make maternity a real boon instead of the burden it so often is, the same old objections are raised that I had to meet forty years ago.

Document 50

In 1920 the government of the Soviet Union legalized abortion, citing as reasons for this step difficult economic conditions, the high incidence of unsafe, illegal operations to terminate pregnancy, and the government's desire to protect women's health. The new law provided for abortions to be performed on demand and without charge by doctors in hospitals. In the 1920s and 1930s many proponents of birth control in western Europe looked to the Soviet Union as a model of enlightened policy. But the Soviet leadership considered abortion on demand a necessary but temporary evil, and not a woman's right. They continued to proclaim the bearing of future builders of socialism to be every woman's duty. In 1936, as part of Stalin's program to promote a more conventional family life, establish a puritanical moral code, and increase the birth rate, the government drew up legislation which would once more make abortion illegal. In order to make the law more acceptable to women, the government included in it provisions for increasing the number of maternity homes, nurseries, and kindergartens, and for better collection of child-support payments from fathers if the parents were divorced. They also proposed to increase fees for divorce in order to discourage the practice. The government published the draft of the law and asked for public discussion. Two letters which appeared in *Pravda* and were written by women opposed to the law are reproduced here. Despite this opposition the law went into effect.

"I Object": Soviet Citizens on Abortion
U.S.S.R., 1936

Letter from a Student ("I Object")

I have read in the press the draft law on the prohibition of abortion, aid to expectant mothers, etc., and cannot remain silent on this matter.

There are thousands of women in the same position as myself. I am a student reading the first course of the second Moscow Medical Institute. My husband is also a student reading the same course at our Institute. Our scholarships amount jointly to 205 rubles. Neither he nor I have a room of our own. Next year we intend to apply for admission to a hostel, but I do not know whether our application will be granted. I love children and shall probably have some in four or five years' time. But can I have a child now? Having a child now would mean leaving the Institute, lagging behind my husband, forgetting everything I have learnt and probably leaving Moscow because there is nowhere to live.

There is another married couple in our Institute, Mitya and Galya, who live in a hostel. Yesterday Galya said to me: "If I become pregnant I shall have to leave the Institute; one cannot live in a hostel with children."

I consider that the projected law is premature because the housing problem in our town is a painful one. Very often it is the

Rudolf Schlesinger, ed., *The Family in the U.S.S.R.* (London, 1949), pp. 255-56, 265-66.

lack of living quarters that is the reason behind an abortion. If the draft included an article assuring married couples, who are expecting a baby, of a room—that would be a different matter.

In five years' time when I am a doctor and have a job and a room I shall have children. But at present I do not want and cannot undertake such a responsibility.

K.B.

Letter from "A Research Worker"

Doubts About Article I

The government's project of law reflects that constant care for the people's welfare which characterizes all its measures. It does so by the promise of developing still further the crèches, nurseries, maternity homes—all those institutions which are there to help us in our difficult task of bearing children and of bringing them up.

And yet the project's first article which speaks of the prohibition of abortion raises doubts. I want to express these doubts. Abortions are harmful to health. But there are a number of circumstances in everyday life which make it a heavy burden for a woman to have a large family. There are still many shortcomings in the work of the crèches, nurseries and communal restaurants. Our flats are often overcrowded and insufficiently equipped. Looking after the husband and even the grown-up children is hard toil for a woman. But we all want to be "working women." The tribe of "housewives" is dying out and should, I think, become extinct.

Our life in general is improving and becoming more organized. This has already led to an increase in the birth-rate despite the fact that abortions were legal. In the capitalist countries on the other hand abortions are prohibited and the birth-rate is declining. This speaks for itself.

I think that a happy Soviet woman, assisted by the solicitude of Party and government, will herself not want to evade the joys connected with motherhood.

I fear my letter may become too long; so I will not stop to examine the other questions which relate to the strengthening of the family. I shall say only this: I should not want to live with a husband who stays with me only because he lacks the 100 rubles necessary for the divorce. I should give him the money myself.

N.B.

XIV

Sexuality and Sexual Self-Definition

The dominant code of sexual morality in nineteenth-century Europe provided a highly repressive sexual ethic for women. This so-called Victorian morality sought to keep unmarried women chaste and married women passive and submissive to their husbands. Women were conditioned to repress their sexuality and view sex only as an obligation and a means of conceiving children. Men, on the other hand, were considered to be naturally lustful creatures whose sexual needs had to be gratified. In order to keep women of their own class virtuous and all women subordinate, upper- and middle-class men used working-class women for sexual gratification and "imposed" sex on their wives, who were supposed to receive no gratification from the sex act. The husband thereby asserted his sexual ownership and control of his wife. The belief that women were men's sexual property was not limited to the upper classes. Among the working class, too, sexual intercourse was widely viewed as a husband's right and a wife's duty.

This does not mean that all or even most women were sexless beings who found sexual relations distasteful. But cultural and religious strictures and economic and physical realities militated against women's ability to freely express and enjoy their sexuality. In addition, men and women had little understanding of each other's sexuality and how to meet each other's sexual needs. Most important, in the absence of completely effective means of contraception, sexuality was not separated from procreation. Sexual intercourse always involved the possibility of pregnancy, which could bring added physical and economic burdens and which posed dangers to women's health and life. Under these circumstances the right to control one's own body meant for many women the right to refuse to submit to sexual intercourse.*

*See Linda Gordon, "Voluntary Motherhood: The Beginnings of Feminist Birth Control Ideas in the United States," in Mary Hartman and Lois Banner, eds., *Clio's Consciousness Raised* (New York, 1974), pp. 54-74.

Of course, many women had active sex lives both outside and within the bounds of marriage. Indeed, to the horror of middle-class moralists, illegitimacy rates and ratios rose from the early part of the nineteenth century. This was interpreted as a sign of the breakdown of the family and a growing immorality in the working class. But the statistics may not reflect a "sexual revolution" as much as a continuation of traditional rural attitudes which condoned premarital intercourse but expected a couple to marry if the woman became pregnant. But urbanization and changes in family life and living patterns meant that many women who became pregnant out of wedlock could no longer count on marriage to the fathers of their children. The evidence on this matter is far from clear. Yet it is certain that many working-class mothers who had not married encountered little criticism from their working-class peers. Moreover, by the turn of the twentieth century some unwed mothers remained unmarried by choice (see document 33).

Yet illegitimacy was a grave problem for most women, since they usually had a very difficult time supporting themselves and their children. Many were forced to turn to prostitution. Indeed, the image of the "fallen" woman most often presented by social reformers in the nineteenth century was that of a seduced young woman who bore an illegitimate child and was then forced onto the streets to support it. In the second half of the nineteenth century women involved in rescue work among prostitutes recognized that the cause of prostitution lay in two areas; the lack of work opportunities for women and the double sexual standard, which insisted that men required a class of unchaste women upon whom they could exercise their lustful impulses. The reformers' solutions were increased education and job training for women and sexual restraint by men. They insisted that prostitution and its attendant evils would be eliminated only if middle- and upper-class men adhered to the same standards of moral purity as women. This demand was an important component of late-nineteenth-century campaigns to end state-regulated prostitution, which reformers believed legalized and institutionalized vice and the victimization of working-class women, and campaigns to stop white slavery, the buying and selling of women and young girls for sexual purposes.

The demand for more, not less, sexual restraint is understand-able in view of women's economic and social dependence in the nineteenth century. Greater sexual freedom would have meant more freedom only for men and the continued subordination of women. Even before the turn of the twentieth century, however, some women began to take a different view of sexual freedom and women's sexuality. By that time middle-class women had access to more effective contraceptive techniques. Moreover, gains women made in other areas led many women to expect to lead more independent and personally fulfilling lives. Some women openly advocated the recognition of women's sexuality and rights to sexual gratification.

As the twentieth century progressed, attitudes continued to change, and more and more women came to the conclusion that sexual freedom was an important part of women's emancipation and self-determination. By the 1920s and 1930s some women, mostly young and middle-class, were able to live more sexually emancipated lives within and outside of marriage. More open attitudes toward sexuality began to extend beyond heterosexual relations. The once tabooed topics of lesbianism and male homosexuality were discussed in some intellectual circles, and in some cities, most notably Berlin from the 1890s through the 1920s, homosexual subcultures, female and male, flourished.

But the majority of women were probably little touched by the new sexual freedom in the first half of the twentieth century, although old taboos and repressive attitudes continued to diminish. Women's sexual liberation and a woman's right to determine her own sexuality were not major feminist demands in this period. Those demands did not emerge until the 1960s when women had gained more social and economic independence and improved birth control techniques finally made possible the separation of sex from childbearing.

Document 51

Josephine Butler (1828–1906) was a member of a very respectable and prominent English family. She became involved in rescue work among prostitutes in the 1850s as an outlet for her energies and emotions after her young daughter died. She soon came to the conclusion that prostitutes were not merely sinners in need of redemption but were the victims of upper-class men's economic and sexual domination of women. She insisted that the double sexual standard was the root of prostitution and shocked Victorian society by openly discussing venereal disease, incest, and child selling and the responsibility of men of her own class for these evils.

Butler led the Ladies National Association and for seventeen years focused her attention on a campaign to repeal the Contagious Diseases Acts (1864, 1866, 1869). The official purpose of these laws was to stop the spread of venereal disease among soldiers and sailors stationed in certain towns in England and southern Ireland. Under the Acts women accused or suspected of being prostitutes were to be registered, placed under police supervision, subjected to periodic medical examinations, and, if found to be suffering from venereal disease, incarcerated in certified lock hospitals for a period of up to nine months. If a woman accused of being a prostitute refused to submit to an examination, she had to go before a magistrate and prove she was a "virtuous" woman.

Butler maintained that the true purpose of these laws was not to suppress vice but to ensure a clean class of prostitutes for soldiers and sailors. The following excerpt is from testimony she gave in 1871 to a Parliamentary inquiry into the Contagious Diseases Acts which were suspended in 1883.*

Men Will Have Their Victims
Josephine Butler, England, 1871

(Chairman.) I think you are the wife of the Rev. George Butler, Principal of Liverpool College? —I am.

You have taken great interest in the Acts which are the subject of inquiry by this Commission? —I have taken a great interest in the principle.

Before these Acts were passed had you turned your attention to the subject of these unhappy women? —Yes, for 15 years before 1869.

For 15 years before 1869 this had been the special subject of your attention? —In leisure moments which I could spare from my family.

*Eleanor Riemer is currently working on a study of Josephine Butler and the development of "women's networks" in the latter decades of the nineteenth century.

Josephine Butler testifying before the Royal Commission on the Contagious Diseases Acts, House of Lords, March 18, 1871, Twenty-eighth Day, Questions 12,841–12,850, 12,870–12,889, 12,893–12,896.

Had you been connected with any reformatory or refuge for women? —Not officially with anything of the kind, but I have received numberless women into my own home.

In what way, as domestic servants? —My husband and I have taken them in as friends, patients when ill, and keeping them until they died. We have had sometimes five living together in our house until I could find situations for them.

Then in fact your house itself was a small refuge for them? —It was, and is to this day.

How did you find the women you received into your house? —I visited them in the low parts of the town; I have gone to brothels occasionally, both at night and in the daytime; I see them in the streets and speak to them. I have gone to the workhouse, and to the Lock hospital. They get to know me, and then when they do, I seek them no longer, but they seek me.

Is this in Liverpool? —It is in Liverpool.

And have you numerous applications from women seeking refuge under your care? —Yes, I have, and also from gentlemen and ladies in different parts of the country; as lately there was a case of a young girl who was sent to me by train rescued from a first class brothel to which she had been sold. She is now in my house. I had yesterday two more applications. . . .

I gather . . . that you consider a law which requires women who are gaining their livelihood by prostitution to submit to a periodical examination in order to guard against their communicating a loathsome disease, is a withdrawal of moral restraint? —It is a regulating of vice for the facilitating of its practice. It is a lowering of the moral standard in the eyes of the people. When the moral standard is lowered the practice of vice will be increased.

You think the construction that people put on these Acts is, that prostitution is in some sense legalized? —Not only think so, but know it to be the fact, in Scotland and the whole of the north of England.

And you concur in that opinion? —Entirely.

And in your intercourse with various persons who have expressed the same opinion, you have expressed your concurrence? —Continually.

Then there would be no alteration of these Acts which could possibly reconcile you to them? —None whatever.

You would be satisfied with nothing but their entire repeal?— Nothing but their entire repeal. I am requested by 52 working men, many of them representative men, whose letters I have, to express that opinion for them to-day.

Then supposing these Acts were repealed, you would suggest no mode by which the State could interfere and regulate or check this evil? —Not to regulate, but we have abundant suggestions by which the State may check profligacy, not with the object of curing disease only, but to check the vice which is the cause of the disease.

Would you favor the Commission with one? —We have them drawn up in form, but it would be premature to lay them before the Commission just now. No doubt it will all come before you in due time; at present I will only give you a general idea of what we have to suggest, both in the way of enactments and other ways, reminding you that the great evil with its unpleasant physical consequences, must be met from a variety of sides at once. Legislation alone will not do it. Seduction must be punished. At present for the purpose of seduction, and of seduction only, our law declares every female child a woman at 12 years of age. I am ashamed to have to confess to such a shameful state of the law before you gentlemen, but a child is a woman, for that purpose alone, at 12 years of age. I know from my experience amongst this class of women, how many have become so from that cause. The law of bastardy must be altered. At present the responsibility of illegitimate children is thrown on the mothers only, the fathers are irresponsible. Better laws in this direction would aid in diminishing the causes of prostitution. A higher standard of public opinion as to the vice of men—that is a thing in which we women are most deeply interested; we have had enough to do with the reclamation of women, we know about that, but we know now that nothing can be done until the vices of men are attacked and checked. Above all things a higher standard with regard to the morality of men is needed, and we, thousands of us, are banded together to attain that if possible. The laws which we shall claim shall be constituted, they shall not be a breach of the Constitution, they shall be moral in their tendency, and above all they shall be just; that is, they shall be laws which shall tend to repress crimes which we abhor equally in both sexes and which shall deal with the vice itself, and not merely with its physical effects. Our measures will be directed against prostitution itself, and, with your permission, I will just call your attention to this, that whereas all legislation hitherto which is at all of the right kind has been directed against one sex only, we insist that it shall be directed against both sexes, and whereas it has been directed against the poor only, we insist, and the working men insist, that it shall also apply to the rich profligate. Partial laws, however excellent, will not effect the purification of society. It is quite the fashion, I find, in London, among the upper classes, to talk of this subject as if women were tempters, harpies, devils, while men are wholly innocent, and in every case the tempted, and legislation, following out this idea, has in almost all cases been protective for men and punitive for women. It cannot be said that men, in our own days, are entirely innocent and entirely the victims, while women are the sole assailants of purity. It cannot be said there is no such thing as seduction of young girls by gentlemen of the upper classes. It cannot be said there is no such thing as profuse patronage of houses of ill-fame by rich profligate men. I could tell you much of that from my own experience. Therefore we are profoundly convinced, and thousands among the working classes share our convictions in the matter, that legislation, however pure its aim, which is directed against the weaker sex only, will fail to accomplish any reduction in the amount of misery and sin there is amongst us. That is the general outline of a series of remedies, some of which it is intended to be proposed to the Legislature to adopt as legislative remedies. We have other remedies, especially with regard to increasing the number of industrial pursuits for women, which I should say is the most important, from the woman's side of the matter, but could hardly be touched, I suppose, by legislation.

To descend from the high views you have opened, from your extensive experience of these women, do you think they are tempted into a career of vice always by seduction? —Decidedly not. I will tell you my experience. I think perhaps persons, especially gentlemen, who are not conversant with the lives of these women, are too much apt to mass them into one class. Now we know something about pauperism. In Liverpool, and some other seaport towns I have some knowledge of, there is a mass of people, boys and girls, who begin to be unchaste and vicious from their earliest years. There is the commencement at once from the huddling together of poor people, like beasts. If you look at their lives you can scarcely wonder at it. I have opened a home for the reception of girls who have not fallen, but who wish to be saved from peril, and they have crowded to our home, and I can tell you of those girls, none of whom were prostitutes by any means, though they were not chaste, that it was a common thing that their own fathers, in a fit of intoxication, had violated them. They are obliged to sleep together, five or six of one family, and there is no difficulty in tracing the origin of their impurity, and it need not be charged to any wilful love of wickedness in poor children. Then I have some experience of a better class of fallen women, such as you find, for instance, in fashionable houses frequented by noblemen and gentlemen in London and elsewhere. They are people gifted with some degree of attractiveness, people who have generally lapsed from a higher class of life, tradesmen's daughters, and sometimes solicitors' and clergymen's daughters. I have traced the history of many of those, and a very large proportion of them have been brought down by seduction—a real passionate affection, or a fancied love affair, which has ended in this unhappy way.

Then the law against seduction, which is the only remedy I think you have mentioned, would reach, if effective only few of these cases? —It would reach a considerable number, I conceive, but I think I also mentioned the laws of bastardy.

But do not you think that, entirely apart from any legislation with reference to seduction or bastardy, a great many women go on the town, you say, from the deficiency of their domestic arrangements? —Decidedly.

That is one cause? —Yes.

From the negligence of their parents? —Yes; their parents sometimes sell them into vice.

Some from wantonness? —No doubt.

Some from love of dress? —I should never class the love of dress as one thing of itself; it may accompany other conditions. A girl who has no education has a vacant mind, ready to be engaged with trifles.

Some from starvation? —Positive starvation, that I know; and I have mentioned one most important cause of all, which is, the absolute want of industrial training and paid industries for women; then what is a friendless woman to do?

Then the state of this evil is much deeper than legislation has yet reached? —Much deeper, deeper than the law has yet reached, or can reach.

Then legislation must be aided by moral influences? —Decidedly; and we consider that this movement of ours, with all its drawbacks, is a very great blessing in having opened the minds of all classes to this question, and what is to be done with regard to it.

Then do you think this particular legislation, which is the subject of this inquiry, has not been in the interest of morality or otherwise? —We can never think it is in the interest of morality, because it is protective of vice. It also alleges that evil doctrine that prostitution is a necessity, which we deny....

Are you not aware that when a public woman comes under the operation of these Acts, not only is her body cured, but every effort is used to make her forsake her bad life? —I am aware that that is continually asserted by the supporters of the system.

But do you doubt the fact? —I doubt the fact to a very considerable degree. I believe fully the matrons of the hospitals are devotedly Christian women, and have done their best—because I have conversed with some of them—to save the souls of those who are under their care. I do not wish to enter upon those statistics, because I am neither able nor desirous to do so: but I grant you that you reclaim, how many would you say?

I will suppose 30 per cent? —I grant you then that you reclaim 90 per cent, of the women, if that will satisfy you, but it is not of the least consequence to my argument. Our position is not at all affected by the fact, because while you reclaim the women you are stimulating the vices of men. That is the point, and I insist on this Commission hearing it; and what is the use, I ask you, in the name of Heaven, to save women while you are stimulating the vices of men? For men will have their victims....

Yet you think notwithstanding these Acts may have had the effect of withdrawing a certain per-centage from the evil life, that which you admit to be a good has been more than overbalanced by the inducements which these Acts have held out to be sinful? —Far more than overbalanced. I should like to tell you the strong impression of the working men and other classes of the North as to the reclamations under these Acts. We do not wish to deny that you reclaim, but the common impression, take it for what it is worth, is that your vigorous work of reclamation will go on with great energy so long as the opponents of these Acts keep up their agitation, so long as we let in a flood of light on all your doing; but let our opposition languish, let our agitation cease, then will this reclamation be kept up? I doubt it and all those I have alluded to doubt it, for there is a double motive, there are two ends to be served by the Acts, and we cannot serve two masters. There are two motives, one the providing of clean harlots for the army and navy, the other the reclamation of women. Now, we cannot serve two masters, we shall either hate one and cleave to the other, or we shall cleave to the one and hate the other, and the reclamations will fall to nothing, as has been the case in Paris, Genoa, Vienna, and other places where they began vigorously, and now the results are nothing at all.

Document 52

By the 1890s a free-love movement advocated by men and women existed in many parts of Europe. Free love basically meant the right of people to engage in sexual relations outside of marriage. Unlike Josephine Butler, free-love advocates believed that the problem of prostitution would be solved if sexual restraints, especially restraints on middle-class women, were loosened, and legal marriage was abolished. Most proponents of free love were middle-class and the code of sexual behavior they proposed was realistic for only a very few women. Moreover, they failed to realize that the elimination of legal marriage could have disastrous consequences for many women unless it were accompanied by sweeping social and economic changes.

The British government sought to suppress free-love propaganda. The following two articles appeared in *The Adult: A Journal for the Free Discussion of Tabooed Topics* (later the subtitle was changed to *A Journal of Sex*). In 1898 the editor, George Bedborough, was indicted for printing "lewd," "scandalous," and "obscene" material. One of the passages cited in the indictment was the last paragraph of the first selection.

Challenges to Victorian Morality:
Selections from The Adult
England, 1897-1898

"Women Are Divided into Two Sets"

As a woman, I am often amazed that women should have allowed a sex which has from time immemorial claimed to be "morally inferior," and claimed it with pride, to arrange all moral, or so-called moral, laws between the sexes. In England, what voice has the female portion of the community in these sexual arrangements, which are arbitrarily managed by two large bodies

E. Wardlaw Best, "Our Troops in India," *The Adult*, vol. 1, 1897–1898, pp. 30, 32.

of men, calling themselves by the names of Church and State. Nowhere is this shown more outrageously than in the Indian Cantonment Acts (C.D. Acts, Women) which, in plain English, are Acts for serving up a certain number of women, ticketed and certified, for the sexual use of our soldiers, these women having to submit to the brutal embraces of as many men as desire them, at any time that may be convenient to these men, a private paying the sum of four annas and a sergeant one rupee. This infamous arrangement is the work of the State—an assemblage of men—a work that practically asserts that men must have intercourse with the opposite sex; whilst this same State upholds laws in direct contradiction for a sex not represented on its body, keeping thousands of women in enforced celibacy....

The whole subject is disgraceful in the extreme, and our marriage system is at the root of the whole matter. Women are divided into two sets, trained to detest each other; sets whose interests are diametrically opposed. The prostitute, the blackleg of the marriage system; while marriage, on the other hand, is held up as the market price of women. These sets are kept apart—by interest, and by the man who has created that interest. The one set used as a public harem by men, whilst the second set is starved of its natural sexual rights, excepting those chosen in marriage by the man for breeding purposes, to produce a family which is to belong primarily to him, and whose mother is to be kept handy for his sexual desires. This is the plain truth. Those not chosen, or who refuse to be used under this system, or to help to degrade their sex, are sexually starved, whilst their unfortunate sisters of the public harem are so disgusted and replete with the horrible life they lead, that suicide is common amongst them. Other women just manage to hang, like Mahomed's coffin, between the two principal sets, and lead, as best they can, something resembling a free life. The Church, meanwhile, continues to prate of "sin"; the State to oppress women; and the medical priesthood to reap a rich harvest.

"Free Thought and Free Love"

Much misery would be avoided and much positive happiness brought about by the earlier gratification of the sexual passion

Lucy Stewart, "Free Thought and Free Love," *The Adult*, vol. 1, no. 3 (October 1897), pp. 41–43.

which would take place if free love were in vogue. To healthy young adults, a certain amount of sexual intercourse is necessary in order to keep their bodies and minds in the best possible condition. The evil results of abstinence are especially noticeable in women, probably because abstinence is considerably less frequent among men. Undoubtedly it is unsatisfied sexual longing that is responsible for the greater part of the hysteria, chlorosis, and menstrual disorders which are so common among young unmarried women. So evident is this that we actually often find doctors prescribing marriage as a cure for these ailments, instead of some concoction of drugs—such a departure from the traditions of their conservative professions as can only be accounted for by supposing that it is clear to anyone who has studied the disorders mentioned, that their great cause is sexual abstinence. In men, the principal consequences of abstinence are the general weakening, and sometimes total decay, of the sexual powers. In both sexes there results a melancholy and irritable turn of mind, which incapacitates them for either business or pleasure.

Now, to attempt to restrain unmarried adults from the gratification of this passion, which only prompts them to do what is good for themselves and hurtful to no one, is certainly not Utilitarian, especially if it is borne in mind that when prompted by mutual affection the sexual act and the emotions connected with it are in themselves pleasures of the highest order. The case is particularly hard with women. A man may have connection with prostitutes without incurring any special disgrace if found out; and we consequently often see the melancholy spectacle of a young woman suffering in body and mind, as a consequence of unsatisfied desire, while *"her"* young man" is having regular intercourse with the women of the town.

Some will say that, though they are inclined to believe in free love, they do not think that society is yet ripe for it; they fear that if free sexual unions received sanction to-day, we should have numerous cases of men deserting their women and children on getting tired of them. The answer to this is that no one proposes that parents under free love should not be responsible for their offspring. A man would be as much bound to do his share towards the maintenance of his children as he now is. Again, there would certainly be very few cases of desertion of children by their father compared with what there are to-day; for, with a knowledge of Neo-Malthusianism, people would naturally not have children until they had good reason for thinking that they had found their life partners, and would then only have just that number they wished for. There can be little wonder that a man is tempted to leave his family when that family consists of a woman for whom he has little or no affection, and half a dozen, or more, children; and as such families would not exist in a society where free love and family limitation were popular, there would be a great falling off in the number of cases of paternal desertion. As for man's deserting his woman, surely women do not want any material reward for living with men as their wives. If they do, so much the worse for them; it is no argument against free love. I cannot see that much consideration is due to the woman who thinks she has any claim upon a man in return for having permitted intimacy, be she a common prostitute or a *respectable married woman*. Love, like virtue, is its own reward.

Document 53

The work of women like Josephine Butler and the free-love advocates gradually led to a loosening of taboos against the discussion of heterosexual relations. But lesbianism remained largely an unmentionable subject. Even in the twentieth century, when some individuals and women's groups took up the question of female sexuality, hardly anyone spoke of female homosexuality or lesbian rights. In 1907 the German government, probably in reaction against the women's movement and women's growing self-assertion, both admitted the existence of lesbianism and acknowledged it as a threat to male-dominated sexual culture. It proposed for the first time that homosexual acts between women be made illegal, as homosexual acts between men already were under paragraph 175 of the German legal code. Opponents of the legislation pointed out that this would not remove inequality between men and women, but would double injustice.

The following excerpt is from the autobiography of a German lesbian. It was published at the turn of the twentieth century by sex researcher Magnus Hirschfeld in his journal *Yearbook for Intersexual Variants [Jahrbuch für sexuelle Zwischenstufen]*. The journal's title and the material published in it reflect the view held by the editor and others at the time that homosexuals were neither male nor female but an intermediate sexual type. It is difficult to say whether the practice of male-female role playing, which the author of this selection and her lover practiced, was widespread among other lesbian couples in the period.

"The Truth About Myself": Autobiography of a Lesbian
Germany, 1901

Autobiography—self-purification. One should stay away from it and yet I can't do that. Why not? Well, because I've been challenged repeatedly to serve the cause of truth. But I'm alone and afraid, very afraid.

I am by no means one of those who considers herself unlucky or who is ashamed of her situation and says to everybody—"Oh, we poor lesbians. Forgive us for existing in this world." No, I'm proud of my exceptional orientation. I hold my head high, stamp my feet and say boldly: "See, that's what I am."

I was born in a small capital city, the daughter of a scholar, and I'm the oldest of eight children. Whether I was congenitally tainted or not will not be discussed here, for though I know something about the noble science of medicine, I am not inclined to write a scholarly treatise....

My childhood passed like that of many young boys who enjoy the advantages both of freedom in the countryside and the amenities of life in a large city, a situation that is only possible in a small capital. When I say I lived like the boys, this is what I mean. First, at that time I felt completely as though I were a boy and second, I had the good fortune to receive a thorough boy's education....

We had a small private school for boys in our city. Since it had been established through my father's efforts, primarily for my cousins (at that time my brothers were still too young) I was given permission to study everything taught there. That was really important to me since it reenforced my belief that I "really" was a boy and not a girl.

As part of my education I studied needlework and conversation in modern languages, etc. It is noteworthy that in the eyes of my male teachers I was such a good student, while to my women teachers I was insufferable, defiant and stubborn. I didn't want to

E. Krause, "Die Wahrheit über Mich," *Jahrbuch für sexuelle Zwischenstufen*, vol. 3 (1901), pp. 292–93, 298–300, 302–303, 305–307.

have a crush on any of them, yet I fell in love with my twenty-year-old French teacher. She had wonderfully large blue eyes, such beautiful black hair, and was so pretty. I soon learned that the military officers of the city shared my taste and I was not happy about that. As a result, when one of them took my idol as his wife, I wanted to challenge him to a duel. Nothing could make me attend their wedding even though I was invited. For over half a day I shut myself in my room and from time to time violently stamped my feet on the floor. I was fourteen years old then.

The next month our classroom education was completed. The boys, mostly older than I, received their certificates and went off to a Gymnasium in a larger city. And I, the one who had done the best on the exams? I was not accepted because I was a girl. That was the first real disappointment of my life. Crying was not my nature but I had to do something. I still wanted to take the university entrance examination and pass it before my male friends.

So I obtained a copy of the curriculum of their school and studied it with my father's help. I also studied music but to this day I am not good at it. One day I heard how the whole city was agitated by the fact that a young woman, who was well known to me, had passed the teacher's examination even though she was only eighteen years old. . . .

I eventually passed the examination—even before my former school chums were finished—but it took a great deal of work.

Then I went to Switzerland where I enrolled in a university. . . .

[After two years of practice teaching] the second part of the university program is hard [classroom] work. I decided on medicine as my major, along with astronomy and ancient languages, and was determined not to do any less well than my male colleagues. So I did very well on my examination and I chose to become a scholar. I settled in an idyllic region of our country; I have lived there with "her" until this day and we lead a life that cannot be any less divine or happy than Eden.

But that requires courage, a great deal of courage. You can have the same thing, my dear sisters, and it will show that you are justified in living a happy life and loving like the "normal" world. And in spite of the way you are, people will tolerate you, people will acknowledge you, people will envy you. Take up arms! We must and we will succeed. I've done it. Why shouldn't all of you? . . .

You poor, poor people! When will the hour of deliverance come? When will it come for our brothers who share our fate as we exceptions from the usual mold and the ancient, eternal law of nature. Should we make generalizations about us [homosexuals], our special talents and such things? Couldn't we be part of a design rather than an accident? There have been countless arguments about these questions and will continue to be, so I don't want to carry this discussion any further now. But throw down the gauntlet to me and I will pick it up and never be at a loss for an answer.

Take up arms until this legal clause [against homosexuality] is abolished. It has already caused so much misery and brought so much sorrow. Why should, why must the innocent suffer; they were created by the heavens with feelings, which when expressed in their own way, are not understood by the everyday world. That is taken for granted! I don't demand a code of morals just for homosexuals. What I demand is humane treatment, impartiality and equal rights for all....

Why, by the way, it there so much prejudice in our enlightened time against the "old maid," prejudice which causes so much mischief? One of the main reasons may be that people unfortunately know so little about the nature of homosexuality [*Konträr-sexualismus*—"contrary sexualism"] and understand nothing about the marriages of those who are apparently of the same sex. It is important for people to read literature on the subject. When I was studying medicine I had the good fortune to come across works by Krafft-Ebing.

Oh, how I reacted to them, and my eyes were opened. I felt so free and clear-sighted after reading these works. Now it was clear to me that I never, never had to marry a man. I never had to account for my past life and I understood my indifference to the opposite sex and why I had not fallen in love [with a man]. I understood why many a woman enchanted me through her beauty, grace, charm and natural understanding....

In speaking about my marriage I will make a deliberate attempt to characterize my relationship with my true friend. I hestitate to do it because our relationship is so sacred to me but it wouldn't be right to keep it a secret. I met "her" on an outing in the woods. Nature had enchanted me. I had wanted to reach out in order to soothe my inflamed soul. "She" was lying under an oak tree dressed entirely in pink.

I won't go any further. The whole thing is so hopelessly romantic that people will take it for a novel. She was married and I became very jealous and then despondent. I wanted to run away with her, kidnap her, but I had to admit I had no right to do that. After the sudden death of her husband in a hunting accident, I learned she was also in love with me. From that moment on we have lived together as a married couple. My lovely, confident little wife directs and guides our happy home like a genuine German housewife and I work and provide for us like an energetic, light-hearted man.

A Selected English-Language Bibliography for Further Reading

General Works

Atkinson, D., Dallin, A., and Lapidus, G. (eds.). *Women in Russia*. Stanford: Stanford University Press, 1977.

Banner, Lois W. "On Writing Women's History." *Journal of Interdisciplinary History* 2 (1971), pp. 347-58.

Beard, Mary R. *Woman as Force in History*. New York: Macmillan, 1946.

Branca, Patricia. *Women in Europe Since 1750*. London: Croom Helm, 1978.

———. "Women's History: Comments on Yesterday, Today and Tomorrow." *Journal of Social History* 11 (1978), pp. 375-59.

Bridenthal, Renate, and Koonz, Claudia (eds.). *Becoming Visible: Women in European History*. Boston: Houghton Mifflin, 1977.

Carroll, Berenice A. (ed.). *Liberating Women's History: Theoretical and Critical Essays*. Urbana: University of Illinois Press, 1976.

Davidoff, Leonore. *The Best Circles: Women and Society in Victorian England*. Totowa, N.J.: Rowman and Littlefield, 1973.

Davis, Natalie Z. "'Women's History' in Transition: The European Case." *Feminist Studies* 3 (3/4), 1975/76, pp. 83-103.

Dohm, Hedwig. *Women's Nature and Privilege*. Westport, Conn.: Hyperion, 1976 (1876).

Engels, Friedrich. *The Origin of the Family, Private Property and the State*. New York: International, 1942.

Griffiths, Naomi E. S. *Penelope's Web: Some Perceptions of Women in European and Canadian Society*. Toronto: Oxford University Press, 1976.

Hartman, Mary S., and Banner, Lois (eds.). *Clio's Consciousness Raised: New Perspectives on the History of Women*. New York: Harper & Row, 1974.

Kanner, S. Barbara. "The Women of England in a Century of Social Change, 1815-1914: A Selected Bibliography." In Vicinus, Martha (ed.), *Suffer and Be Still*. Bloomington: Indiana University Press, 1972.

———. "The Women of England in a Century of Social Change, 1815-1914: A Select Bibliography, Part II." In Vicinus, Martha (ed.), *A Widening Sphere*. Bloomington: Indiana University Press, 1977.

Kelly-Gadol, Joan. "The Social Relation of the Sexes: Methodological Implications of Women's History." *Signs* 1 (1975/76), pp. 809-23.

Lapidus, Gail Warhofsky. *Women in Soviet Society*. Berkeley: University of California Press, 1977.

Laslett, Peter. *The World We Have Lost*. New York: Scribner, 1965.

Lerner, Gerda. "Placing Women in History: Definitions and Challenges." *Feminist Studies* 3 (1/2), 1975/76, pp. 5-14.

Lougee, Carolyn C. "Modern European History." *Signs* 2 (1976/77), pp. 628-50.

MacCurtain, Margaret, and O Corráin, Donncha (eds.). *Women in Irish Society: The Historical Dimension*. Westport, Conn.: Greenwood, 1979.

Mill, John Stuart. *The Subjection of Women*. Cambridge, Mass.: M.I.T. Press, 1970.

Mitchell, Juliet. *Women's Estate*. Harmondsworth: Penguin, 1971.

Palmegiano, Eugenia M. "Women and British Periodicals, 1832-1867: A Bibliography." *Victorian Periodicals Newsletter*, March 1976.

Riemer, Eleanor S., and Fout, John C. "Women's History: Recent Journal Articles." *Trends in History* 1 (1979), pp. 3-22.

Rowbotham, Sheila. *Hidden from History*. New York: Vintage, 1974.

———. *Woman's Consciousness, Man's World*. Harmondsworth: Penguin, 1973.

———. *Women, Resistance and Revolution*. New York: Vintage, 1972.

Selivanova, Nina Nikolaevna. *Russia's Women*. Westport, Conn.: Hyperion, 1976 (1923).

Sharistanian, Janet, et al. "The (Dr. Aletta H. Jacobs) Gerritsen Collection, The University of Kansas." *Feminist Studies* 3 (3/4) 1975/76, pp. 200-206.

Smith-Rosenberg, Carroll. "The New Woman and the New History." *Feminist Studies* 3 (1/2), 1975/76, pp. 185-98.

Sullerot, Evelyne. *Woman, Society and Change*. New York: McGraw-Hill, 1971.

Van de Walle, Etienne. *The Female Population of France in the Nineteenth Century*. Princeton: Princeton University Press, 1974.

Vicinus, Martha (ed.). *Suffer and Be Still: Women in the Victorian Age*. Bloomington: Indiana University Press, 1972.

——— (ed.). *A Widening Sphere: Changing Roles of Victorian Women*. Bloomington: Indiana University Press, 1977.

Part One

Anderson, Adelaide Mary. *Women in the Factory: An Administrative Adventure, 1893 to 1921*. New York: Dutton, 1922.

Baker, Elizabeth. *Technology and Woman's Work*. New York: Columbia University Press, 1964.

Black, Clementina (ed.). *Married Women's Work*. London: Bell, 1915.

Blackburn, Helen, and Vynne, Nora. *Women Under the Factory Acts.* London: Williams & Norgate, 1903.

Bondfield, Margaret. *A Life's Work.* London: Hutchinson, 1948.

Boone, Gladys. *The Women's Trade Union Leagues in Great Britain and the U.S.* New York: Columbia University Press, 1942.

Boserup, Ester. *Women's Role in Economic Development.* London: St. Martin's Press, 1970.

Bridenthal, Renate. "Beyond *Kinder, Küche, Kirche:* Weimar Women at Work." *Central European History* 6 (1973), pp. 148–66.

———, and Koonz, Claudia. "Beyond *Kinder, Küche, Kirche:* Weimar Women in Politics and Work." In Carroll, Berenice A. (ed.), *Liberating Women's History.* Urbana: University of Illinois Press, 1976.

Burnett, John. *Annals of Labour Autobiographies of British Working-Class People 1820-1920.* Bloomington: Indiana University Press, 1974.

Butler, Josephine. *The Education and Employment of Women.* London: Macmillan, 1868.

Clark, Alice. *Working Life of Women in the Seventeenth Century.* London: Cass, 1968.

Davies, Margaret Llewelyn (ed.). *Life as We Have Known It* by Co-operative Working Women. New York: Norton, 1978 (1931).

———. *The Women's Co-operative Guild 1883-1904.* Westmoreland: Kirkby Lonsdale, 1904.

Dodge, Norton T. *Women in the Soviet Economy.* Baltimore: Johns Hopkins Press, 1966.

Drake, Barbara. *Women in Trade Unions.* London: Labour Research Department, 1924.

Hamilton, Mary Agnes. *Mary Macarthur, A Biographical Sketch.* Westport, Conn.: Hyperion, 1976 (1926).

Holcombe, Lee. *Victorian Ladies at Work: Middle Class Working Women in England and Wales 1850-1914.* Hamden, Conn.: Archon, 1973.

Horn, Pamela. *The Rise and Fall of the Victorian Servant.* New York: St. Martin's Press, 1975.

Hutchins, Elizabeth Leigh. *Women in Modern Industry.* London: Bell, 1915.

Jacoby, Robin Miller. "Feminism and Class Consciousness in the British and American Women's Trade Union Leagues 1890-1925." In Carroll, Berenice A. (ed.), *Liberating Women's History.* Urbana: University of Illinois Press, 1976.

Kent, Christopher. "Image and Reality: The Actress and Society." In Vicinus, Martha (ed.), *A Widening Sphere.* Bloomington: Indiana University Press, 1977.

Lewenhak, Sheila. *Women and Trade Unions: An Outline History of Women in the British Trade Union Movement.* New York: St. Martin's Press, 1977.

McBride, Theresa. *The Domestic Revolution: The Modernization of Household Service in England and France 1820-1920.* New York: Holmes & Meier, 1976.

————. "The Long Road Home: Women's Work and Industrialization." In Bridenthal, Renate, and Koonz, Claudia (eds.), *Becoming Visible: Women in European History.* Boston: Houghton Mifflin, 1977.

McIntyre, Jill R. "Women and the Professions in Germany, 1930-1940." In Nicholls, Anthony, and Matthias, Erich (eds.), *German Democracy and the Triumph of Hitler.* New York: St. Martin's Press, 1971.

McWilliams-Tullberg, Rita. "Women and Degrees at Cambridge University, 1862-1897." In Vicinus, Martha (ed.), *A Widening Sphere.* Bloomington: Indiana University Press, 1977.

Neff, Wanda F. *Victorian Working Women.* London: Allen and Unwin, 1927.

Parkes, Bessie Rayner. *Essays on Woman's Work.* 2nd ed. London: Strahan, 1865.

Peterson, M. Jeanne. "The Victorian Governess: Status Incongruence in Family and Society." In Vicinus, Martha (ed.), *Suffer and Be Still: Women in the Victorian Age.* Bloomington: Indiana University Press, 1972.

Pinchbeck, Ivy. *Women Workers and the Industrial Revolution.* New York: Crofts, 1932.

Schreiner, Olive. *Woman and Labour.* London: Fisher Unwin, 1911.

Shaffer, John W. "Family, Class, and Young Women: Occupational Expectations in Nineteenth Century Paris." *Journal of Family History* 3 (1978), pp. 63-77.

Silver, Catherine Bodard. "Salon, Foyer, Bureau: Women and the Professions in France." In Hartman, Mary S., and Banner, Lois (eds.), *Clio's Consciousness Raised.* New York: Harper & Row, 1974.

Smith, Harold. "The Issue of 'Equal Pay for Equal Work' in Great Britain, 1914-19." *Societas* 8 (1978), pp. 39-51.

Spring Rice, Margery. *Working Class Wives.* Harmondsworth: Penguin, 1939.

Stearns, Peter N. "Working-Class Women in Britain, 1890-1914." In Vicinus, Martha (ed.), *Suffer and Be Still.* Bloomington: Indiana University Press, 1972.

Strumingher, Laura S. *Women and the Making of the Working Class: Lyon 1830-1870.* St. Albans, Vt.: Eden Press, 1978.

Thane, Pat. "Women and the Poor Law in Victorian and Edwardian England." *History Workshop,* no. 6 (1978), pp. 29-51.

Thompson, E. P. *The Making of the English Working Class.* New York: Vintage, 1963.

Tilly, Louise A., Scott, Joan W., and Cohen, Miriam. "Women's Work and European Fertility Patterns." *Journal of Interdisciplinary History* 6 (1976), pp. 447-76.

Twining, Louisa. *Workhouses and Pauperism and Women's Work in the Administration of the Poor Law.* London: Methuen, 1898.

———. *Workhouses and Women's Work.* London: Longman, 1858.

Walkowitz, Judith. "The Making of an Outcast Group: Prostitutes and Working Women in Nineteenth-Century Plymouth and Southampton." In Vicinus, Martha (ed.), *A Widening Sphere.* Bloomington, Indiana Press, 1977.

Wiltsie, Daryl. "Women and Trade Unions in Nineteenth Century Britain." Senior Thesis, Bard College, 1979.

Part Two

Abray, Jane. "Feminism in the French Revolution." *American Historical Review* 80 (1975), pp. 43–62.

Anthony, Katharine. *Feminism in Germany and Scandinavia.* New York: Henry Holt, 1915.

Arendt, Hannah. *Rahel Varnhagen, the Life of a Jewish Woman.* New York: Harcourt Brace Jovanovich, 1974.

Balabanova, Anzhelika. *My Life as a Rebel.* New York: Harper, 1938.

Bebel, August. *Women Under Socialism.* New York: Schocken, 1971.

Becker, Lydia. *The Rights and Duties of Women in Local Government.* Manchester: Ireland, 1879.

Bidelman, Patrick Kay. "Maria Deraismes, Leon Richer, and the Founding of the French Feminist Movement 1866-1878." *Third Republic,* no. 3/4 (1977), pp. 20–73.

Blackburn, Helen. *A Handbook for Women Engaged in Social and Political Work.* Bristol: Arrowsmith, 1895.

Boxer, Marilyn J. "French Socialism, Feminism, and the Family." *Third Republic,* no. 3/4 (1977), pp. 128–67.

———, and Quataert, Jean (eds.). *Socialist Women.* New York: Elsevier, 1978.

Breshkovskaia, Katerina. *Hidden Springs of the Russian Revolution.* Stanford: Stanford University Press, 1931.

Broido, Vera. *Apostles into Terrorists: Women and the Revolutionary Movement in the Russia of Alexander II.* New York: Viking, 1977.

Browning, Hilda. *Women Under Fascism and Communism.* London: Lawrence, 1934.

Burdett-Coutts, Baroness Angela (ed.). *Woman's Mission: A Series of Congress Papers on the Philanthropic Work of Women by Eminent Writers.* London: Low, Marston, 1893.

Butler, Josephine. *An Autobiographical Memoir.* Bristol: Arrowsmith, 1909.

———. *Personal Reminiscences of a Great Crusade.* Westport, Conn.: Hyperion, 1976 (1911).

——— (ed.). *Woman's Work and Woman's Culture: A Series of Essays.* London: Macmillan, 1869.

Carroll, Berenice A. "'To Crush Him in Our Own Country': The Political Thought of Virginia Woolf." *Feminist Studies* 4 (1), 1978, pp. 99-131.

Clements, Barbara Evans. *Bolshevik Feminist: The Life of Aleksandra Kollontai.* Bloomington: Indiana University Press, 1979.

———. "Emancipation Through Communism: The Ideology of A. M. Kollontai." *Slavic Review* 32 (1973), pp. 323-38.

Deutsch, Regina. *The International Woman Suffrage Alliance: Its History from 1904-1929.* London: Board of the Alliance, 1929.

Du Bois, Ellen. "The Radicalism of the Woman Suffrage Movement: Notes Toward the Reconstruction of Nineteenth-Century Feminism." *Feminist Studies* 3 (1/2), 1975/76, pp. 63-71.

Ellsworth, Edward W. *Liberators of the Female Mind: The Shirreff Sisters, Educational Reform, and the Women's Movement.* Westport, Conn.: Greenwood Press, 1979.

Engel, Barbara A. "Women as Revolutionaries: The Case of the Russian Populists." In Bridenthal, Renate, and Koonz, Claudia (eds.), *Becoming Visible: Women in European History.* Boston: Houghton Mifflin, 1977.

———. "Women Medical Students in Russia, 1872-1882: Reformers or Rebels?" *Journal of Social History* 12 (1979), pp. 394-414.

Engel, Barbara Alpern, and Rosenthal, Clifford N. (eds.). *Five Sisters: Women Against the Tsar.* New York: Schocken, 1977.

Evans, Richard J. "Feminism and Female Emancipation in Germany 1870-1945: Sources, Methods and Problems of Research." *Central European History* 9 (1976), pp. 323-51.

———. *The Feminist Movement in Germany 1894-1933.* Beverly Hills: Sage, 1976.

———. *The Feminists: Women's Emancipation Movements in Europe, America and Australasia 1840-1920.* New York: Barnes & Noble, 1978.

———. "Liberalism and Society: The Feminist Movement and Social Change." In Evans, Richard J. (ed.), *Society and Politics in Wilhelmine Germany.* New York: Barnes & Noble, 1978.

Farnsworth, Beatrice Brodsky. "Bolshevism, the Woman Question, and Aleksandra Kollontai." *American Historical Review* 81 (1968), pp. 292-316.

Fawcett, Millicent Garrett. *What I Remember.* Westport, Conn.: Hyperion, 1976 (1924).

Figner, Vera. *Memoirs of a Revolutionist.* New York: International, 1927.

Flexner, Eleanor. *Mary Wollstonecraft.* Baltimore: Penguin, 1973.

Ford, Isabella. *Women as Factory Inspectors and Certifying Surgeons.* London: Women's Co-operative Guild, 1898.

Fulford, Roger. *Votes for Women.* London: Faber & Faber, 1957.

Hackett, Amy. "Feminism and Liberalism in Wilhelmine Germany, 1890-1918." In Carroll, Berenice A. (ed.), *Liberating Women's History.* Urbana: University of Illinois Press, 1976.

———. "The German Women's Movement and Suffrage, 1890-1914: A Study of National Feminism." In Bezucha, Robert J. (ed.), *Modern European Social History*. Lexington, Mass.: Heath, 1972.

———. "The Politics of Feminism in Wilhelmine Germany, 1890-1918." Ph.D. Dissertation, Columbia University, 1976.

Hammerton, A. James. "Feminism and Female Emigration, 1861-1866." In Vicinus, Martha (ed.), *A Widening Sphere*. Bloomington: Indiana University Press, 1977.

Hayden, Dolores. "Two Utopian Feminists and Their Campaign for Kitchenless Houses." *Signs* 4 (1978/79), pp. 274-90.

Hedman, Edwin R. "Early French Feminism from the Eighteenth Century to 1848." Ph.D. Dissertation, New York University, 1954.

Hollis, Patricia (ed.). *Women in Public, 1850-1900: Documents of the Victorian Women's Movement:* London: Allen & Unwin, 1979.

Honeycutt, Karen. "Clara Zetkin: A Left-Wing Socialist and Feminist in Wilhelmian Germany." Ph.D. Dissertation, Columbia University, 1975.

———. "Clara Zetkin: A Socialist Approach to the Problem of Woman's Oppression." *Feminist Studies*, 3 (3/4), 1975/76, pp. 131-41.

Hufton, Olwen. "Women in Revolution 1789-1796." *Past and Present* 53 (1971), pp. 90-108.

Hurwitz, Edith F. "The International Sisterhood." In Bridenthal, Renate, and Koonz, Claudia (eds.), *Becoming Visible*. Boston: Houghton Mifflin, 1977.

Kaplan, Marion A. "German-Jewish Feminism in the Twentieth Century." *Jewish Social Studies* 38 (1976), pp. 39-54.

———. *The Jewish Feminist Movement in Germany The Campaigns of the Jüdischer Frauenbund 1904-1938.* Westport, Conn.: Greenwood Press, 1979.

———. "Women's Strategies in the Jewish Community in Germany." *New German Critique* 5 (1978), 109-18.

Kaplan, Temma. "Other Scenarios: Women and Spanish Anarchism." In Bridenthal, Renate, and Koonz, Claudia (eds.), *Becoming Visible*. Boston: Houghton Mifflin, 1977.

Key Ellen. *Rahel Varnhagen*. Westport, Conn.: Hyperion, 1976 (1913).

———. *The Woman Movement*. Westport, Conn.: Hyperion, 1976 (1912).

Knight, Amy. "The Fritschi: A Study of Female Radicals in the Russian Populist Movement." *Canadian-American Slavic Studies* 9 (1975), pp. 1-17.

Koonz, Claudia. "Conflicting Alliances: Political Ideology and Women Legislators in Weimar Germany." *Signs* 1 (1975/76), pp. 663-83.

———. "Mothers in the Fatherland: Women in Nazi Germany." In Bridenthal, Renate, and Koonz, Claudia (eds.), *Becoming Visible*. Boston: Houghton Mifflin, 1977.

Kraditor, Aileen Selma. *The Ideas of the Woman Suffrage Movement 1890-1920*. New York: Columbia University Press, 1965.

Madison, Bernice. *Social Welfare in the Soviet Union.* Stanford: Stanford University Press, 1968.

Mason, Tim. "Women in Germany, 1925-1940: Family, Welfare and Work." *History Workshop,* no. 2 (1976), pp. 5-32.

———. "Women in Nazi Germany." *History Workshop,* no. 1 (1976), pp. 74-113.

McNeal, Robert H. "Women in the Russian Radical Movement." *Journal of Social History* 5 (1971/72), pp. 143-63.

Mitchell, Hanna. *The Hard Way Up: The Autobiography of Hanna Mitchell, Suffragette and Rebel.* London: Faber, 1968.

Muggeridge, Kitty, and Adam, Ruth. *Beatrice Webb: A Life 1858-1943.* London: Secker & Warburg, 1967.

Offen, Karen M. "Introduction: Aspects of the Woman Question during the Third Republic." *Third Republic,* no. 3/4 (1977), pp. 1-19.

———. "The 'Woman Question' as a Social Issue in Nineteenth Century France: A Bibliographical Essay." *Third Republic* no. 3/4 (1977), pp. 238-99.

Pankhurst, Emmeline. *My Own Story.* New York: Hearst's, 1914.

Pankhurst, Estelle Sylvia. *The Suffragette Movement.* New York: Longmans, 1931.

Peck, Mary Gray. *Carrie Chapman Catt.* Westport, Conn.: Hyperion, 1976 (1944).

Peterson, Brian. "The Politics of Working-Class Women in the Weimar Republic." *Central European History* 10 (1977), pp. 87-111.

Pethick-Lawrence, Emmeline. *My Part in a Changing World.* Westport, Conn.: Hyperion, 1976 (1938).

Phillips, Roderick. "Women's Emancipation, the Family and Social Change in Eighteenth-Century France." *Journal of Social History* 12 (1979), pp. 553-67.

Pope, Barbara Corrado. "Angels in the Devil's Workshop: Leisured and Charitable Women in Nineteenth-Century England and France." In Bridenthal, Renate, and Koonz, Claudia (eds.), *Becoming Visible.* Boston: Houghton Mifflin, 1977.

Puckett, Hugh Wiley. *Germany's Women Go Forward.* New York: Columbia University Press, 1930.

Quataert, Jean. "Feminist Tactics in German Social Democracy: A Dilemma." *Internationale Wissenschaftliche Korrespondenz zur Geschichte der deutschen Arbeiterbewegung* (IWK) 13 (1977), pp. 48-65.

———. "The German Socialist Women's Movement 1890-1918: Issues, Internal Conflicts and the Main Personages." Ph.D. Dissertation, University of California, 1974.

———. *Reluctant Feminists in German Social Democracy, 1885-1917.* Princeton: Princeton University Press, 1979.

Racz, Elizabeth. "The Women's Rights Movement in the French Revolution." *Science and Society* 16 (1951/52), pp. 151-74.

Raeburn, Antonia. *The Militant Suffragettes.* London: Joseph, 1973.

Rosenthal, Bernice Glatzer. "Love on the Tractor: Women in the Russian Revolution and After." In Bridenthal, Renate, and Koonz, Claudia (eds.), *Becoming Visible.* Boston: Houghton Mifflin, 1977.

Rover, Constance. *Women's Suffrage and Party Politics in Britain 1866-1914.* London: Routledge & Kegan Paul, 1967.

Rupp, Leila J. *Mobilizing Women for War: German and American Propaganda, 1939-1945.* Princeton: Princeton University Press, 1978.

———. "Mother of the *Volk:* The Image of Women in Nazi Ideology." *Signs* 3 (1977/78), pp. 362-79.

Sanford, Jutta Schroers. "The Origins of German Feminism: German Women 1789-1870." Ph.D. Dissertation, Ohio State University, 1976.

Schirmacher, Kaethe. *The Modern Woman's Rights Movements.* Westport, Conn.: Hyperion, 1976 (1912).

Schoenbaum, David. *Hitler's Social Revolution: Class and Status in Nazi Germany 1933-39.* Garden City, N.Y.: Anchor, 1966, chap. VI, "The Third Reich and Women."

Schuster, A. "Women's Role in the Soviet Union: Ideology and Reality." *Russian Review* 30 (1971), pp. 260-67.

Sowerwine, Charles. "Women and the Origins of the French Socialist Party: A Neglected Contribution." *Third Republic* no. 3/4 (1977), pp. 104-27.

———. "Women, Socialism, and Feminism, 1872-1922: A Bibliography." *Third Republic* no. 3/4 (1977), pp. 300-66.

Stephens, Winifred. *Women of the French Revolution.* London: Chapman & Hall, 1922.

Stephenson, Jill. *Women in Nazi Society.* New York: Barnes & Noble, 1975.

Stites, Richard. *The Women's Liberation Movement in Russia: Feminism, Nihilism and Bolshevism, 1860-1930.* Princeton: Princeton University Press, 1978.

Strain, Jacqueline. "Feminism and Political Radicalism in the German Social Democratic Movement 1890-1914." Ph.D. Dissertation, University of California, 1974.

Thönnessen, Werner. *The Emancipation of Women: The Rise and Decline of the Women's Movement in German Social Democracy 1863-1933.* London: Pluto Press, 1973.

Thomas, Edith. *The Women Incendiaries.* New York: Braziller, 1966.

Thomas, Katherine. *Women in Nazi Germany.* London: Gollancz, 1943.

Tillion, Germaine. *Ravensbruck: An Eyewitness Account of a Women's Concentration Camp.* Garden City, N.Y.: Anchor, 1975.

Weintraub, Rodelle (ed.). *Fabian Feminist: Bernard Shaw and Women.* University Park: Pennsylvania State University Press, 1977.

Whittaker, Cynthia. "The Women's Movement During the Reign of Alexander II." *Journal of Modern History* 43 (1976) (microfiche).

Wollstonecraft, Mary. *A Vindication of the Rights of Women*. New York: Norton, 1967 (1792).

Part Three

Ariès, Philippe. *Centuries of Childhood: A Social History of Family Life*. New York: Vintage, 1962.

Austin, Sarah Taylor. *Two Letters on Girls' Schools, and on the Training of Working Women*. London: Chapman & Hall, 1857.

Branca, Patricia. "Image and Reality: The Myth of the Idle Victorian Woman." In Hartman, Mary S., and Banner, Lois (eds.), *Clio's Consciousness Raised*. New York: Harper & Row, 1974.

———. *Silent Sisterhood: Middle Class Women in the Victorian Home*. Pittsburgh: Carnegie-Mellon University Press, 1975.

Brenzel, Barbara. "Lancaster Industrial School for Girls: A Social Portrait of a Nineteenth-Century Reform School for Girls." *Feminist Studies* 3 (1/2), 1975/76, pp. 40-53.

Bridenthal, Renate. "Something Old, Something New: Women Between the Two World Wars." In Bridenthal, Renate, and Koonz, Claudia (eds.), *Becoming Visible*. Boston: Houghton Mifflin, 1977.

Calder, Jenni. *Women and Marriage in Victorian Fiction*. London: Oxford University Press, 1976.

Cowan, Ruth Schwartz. "A Case Study of Technological and Social Change: The Washing Machine and the Working Wife." In Hartman, Mary S., and Banner, Lois (eds.), *Clio's Consciousness Raised*. New York: Harper & Row, 1974.

Davies, Emily. *The Higher Education of Women*. London: Strahan, 1866.

Davin, Anna. "Imperialism and Motherhood." *History Workshop*, no. 5 (1978), pp.9-65.

Dunbar, Janet. *The Early Victorian Woman: 1837-1857*. London: Harrap, 1953.

Hartman, Mary S. "Crime and the Respectable Woman: Toward a Pattern of Middle-Class Female Criminality in Nineteenth-Century France and England." *Feminist Studies* 1 (1), 1974/75, pp. 38-56.

———. *Victorian Murderesses*. New York: Schocken, 1978.

Hertz, Deborah. "Salonières and Literary Women in Late Eighteenth Century Berlin." *New German Critique* 5 (1978), pp. 97-108.

Hewitt, Margaret. *Wives and Mothers in Victorian Industry*. London: Rockliff, 1958.

Holcombe, Lee. "Victorian Wives and Property: Reform of the Married Woman's Property Act." In Vicinus, Martha (ed.), *A Widening Sphere*. Bloomington, Indiana University Press, 1977.

Hufton, Olwen. "Women and the Family Economy in Eighteenth-Century France." *French Historical Studies* 9 (1975), pp. 1-22.

Kahne, Hilda. "Economic Research on Women and Families." *Signs* 3 (1977/78), pp. 652-65.

Key, Ellen. *The Century of the Child.* New York: Putnam, 1909.

Kirkpatrick, Clifford. *Nazi Germany: Its Women and Family Life.* New York: Bobbs-Merrill, 1938.

Kovalevskaya, Sofya. *A Russian Childhood.* New York: Springer, 1978 (1895).

Kunzle, David. "Dress Reform as Antifeminism: A Response to Helene E. Roberts' 'The Exquisite Slave: The Role of Clothes in the Making of the Victorian Woman.'" *Signs* 2 (1976/77), pp. 570–79.

Lange, Helene. *Higher Education of Women in Europe.* New York: Appleton, 1901.

Laslet, Peter, and Wall, R. (eds.). *Household and Family in Past Time.* New York: Cambridge University Press, 1972.

Medick, Hans. "The Proto-industrial Family Economy: The Structural Function of Household and Family During the Transition from Peasant Society to Industrial Capitalism." *Social History* 1 (1976), pp. 291–315.

Michel, Andrée. "Family Models of the Future." In Bridenthal, Renate, and Koonz, Claudia (eds.), *Becoming Visible.* Boston: Houghton Mifflin, 1977.

Mitchell, Sally. "The Forgotten Woman of the Period: Penny Weekly Family Magazines of the 1840's and 1850's." In Vicinus, Martha (ed.), *A Widening Sphere.* Bloomington: Indiana University Press, 1977.

———. "Sentiment and Suffering: Women's Recreational Reading in the 1860's." *Victorian Studies* 21 (1977), pp. 29–45.

Nyström-Hamilton, Louise. *Ellen Key: Her Life and Her Work.* New York: Putnam, 1913.

Oren, Laura. "The Welfare of Women in Laboring Families: England, 1860–1950." In Hartman, Mary S., and Banner, Lois (eds.), *Clio's Consciousness Raised.* New York: Harper & Row, 1974.

Phillips, Roderick. "Women and Family Breakdown in Eighteenth Century France; Rouen 1780–1800." *Social History* 1 (1976), pp. 197–218.

Pinchbeck, Ivy, and Hewitt, Margaret. *Children in English Society.* 2 vols. Toronto: University of Toronto Press, 1970/1973.

Richardson, Joanna. "The Great Revolution: Women's Education in Victorian Times." *History Today* 24 (1974), pp. 420–27.

Roberts, Helene E. "The Exquisite Slave: The Role of Clothes in the Making of the Victorian Woman." *Signs* 2 (1976/77), pp. 554–69.

Rosenberg, Charles E. (ed.). *The Family in History.* Philadelphia: University of Pennsylvania Press, 1975.

Satina, Sophie. *Education of Women in Pre-revolutionary Russia.* New York, 1966.

Shorter Edward. *The Making of the Modern Family.* New York; Basic, 1975.

Stock, Phyllis. *Better Than Rubies: A History of Women's Education.* New York: Putnam, 1978.

Stone, Lawrence. *The Family, Sex and Marriage in England 1500-1800.* New York: Harper & Row, 1977.

Tilly, Louise A., and Scott, Joan W. *Women, Work, and Family.* New York: Holt, Rinehart & Winston, 1978.

Tomes, Nancy. "A 'Torrent of Abuse': Crimes of Violence Between Working Men and Women in London, 1840-1875." *Journal of Social History* 11 (1978), 328-45.

Trumbach, Randolph. *The Rise of the Egalitarian Family: Aristocratic Kinship and Domestic Relations in Eighteenth Century England.* New York: Academic Press, 1978.

Vicinus, Martha. "The Perfect Victorian Lady." In Vicinus, Martha (ed.), *Suffer and Be Still.* Bloomington: Indiana University Press, 1972.

Vodovozova, Elizaveta. *A Russian Childhood.* London: Faber & Faber, 1961.

Part Four

Banks, Joseph. *Prosperity and Parenthood: A Study of Family Planning Among the Victorian Middle Classes.* London: Routledge & Kegan Paul, 1954.

Banks, Joseph, and Banks, Olive. *Feminism and Family Planning in Victorian England.* New York: Schocken, 1964.

Besant, Annie. *The Law of Population.* London: Butts, 1878.

Bloch, Ruth H. "Untangling the Roots of Modern Sex Roles: A Survey of Four Centuries of Change." *Signs* 4 (1978/79), pp. 237-52.

Burnet, John. *Plenty and Want: A Social History of Diet in England from 1815 to the Present Day.* London: Penguin, 1966.

Christ, Carol. "Victorian Masculinity and the Angel in the House." In Vicinus, Martha (ed.), *A Widening Sphere.* Bloomington: Indiana University Press, 1977.

Cominos, Peter T. "Innocent Femina Sensualis in Unconscious Conflict." In Vicinus, Martha (ed.), *Suffer and Be Still.* Bloomington: Indiana University Press, 1972.

———. "Sexual Respectability and the Social System." *International Review of Social History* 8 (1963), pp. 18-48, 216-50.

Conway, Jill. "Stereotypes of Femininity in a Theory of Sexual Evolution." In Vicinus, Martha (ed.), *Suffer and Be Still.* Bloomington: Indiana University Press, 1972.

Cook, Blanche Wiesen. "Women Alone Stir My Imagination: Lesbianism and the Cultural Tradition." *Signs* 4 (1978/79), pp. 718-39.

Cott, Nancy F. "Passionlessness: An Interpretation of Victorian Sexual Ideology, 1790-1850." *Signs* 4 (1978/79), pp. 219-36.

Degler, Carl. "What Ought to Be and What Was: Women's Sexuality in the Nineteenth Century." *American Historical Review* 79 (1974), pp. 1467-90.

Dunham, Vera. "Sex: From Free Love to Puritanism." In Inkeles, A., and Geiger, K. (eds.), *Soviet Society*. Boston: Houghton Mifflin, 1961.

Dyhouse, Carol. "Working-Class Mothers and Infant Mortality in England, 1895-1914." *Journal of Social History* 12 (1978), pp. 248-62.

Fee, Elizabeth. "The Sexual Politics of Victorian Social Anthropology." *Feminist Studies* 1 (3/4) 1972/73, pp. 23-39.

Fryer, Peter. *The Birth Controllers*. New York: Stein & Day, 1965.

Gittins, Diana. "Married Life and Birth Control During the Wars." *Oral History* 3 (1975), pp. 53-64.

Gordon, Linda. *Woman's Body, Woman's Right: A Social History of Birth Control*. New York: Grossman/Viking, 1976.

Grossman, Atina. "Abortion and Economic Crisis: The 1931 Campaign Against ¶218 in Germany." *New German Critique* 5 (1978), pp. 119-37.

Himes, Norman E. *Medical History of Contraception*. New York: Schocken, 1970 (1936).

How-Martyn, Edith, and Breed, Mary. *The Birth Control Movement in England*. London: Bale & Danielsson, 1930.

Johansson, Sheila Ryan. "Sex and Death in Victorian England: An Examination of Age- and Sex-Specific Death Rates, 1840-1900." In Vicinus, Martha (ed.), *A Widening Sphere*. Bloomington: Indiana University Press, 1977.

Knight, Patricia. "Women and Abortion in Victorian England." *History Workshop*, no. 4 (1977), pp. 57-69.

Knodel, John E. *The Decline of Fertility in Germany 1871-1939*. Princeton: Princeton University Press, 1974.

Kollontai, Aleksandra. *The Autobiography of a Sexually Emancipated Communist Woman*. New York: Herder and Herder, 1971.

————. *Love of Worker Bees*. Chicago: Academy Chicago Limited, 1978.

Leadbetter, Rosanna. *History of the Malthusian League, 1877-1927*. Columbus: Ohio State University Press, 1976.

Mclaren, Angus. "Abortion in France: Women and the Regulation of Family Size 1800-1914." *French Historical Studies* 10 (1978), pp. 461-85.

————. *Birth Control in Nineteenth Century England*. New York: Holmes & Meier, 1978.

————. "Doctor in the House: Medicine and Private Morality in France, 1800-1850." *Feminist Studies* 2 (2/3), 1974/75, pp. 39-54.

————. "Sex and Socialism: The Opposition of the French Left to Birth Control in the Nineteenth Century." *Journal of the History of Ideas* 37 (1976), pp. 475-92.

————. "Women's Work and Regulation of Family Size." *History Workshop* no. 4 (1977), pp. 70-81.

Neuman, Robert P. "Industrialization and Sexual Behavior: Some Aspects of Working Class Life in Imperial Germany." In Bezucha, Robert J.

(ed.), *Modern European Social History.* Lexington, Mass.: Heath, 1972.

———. "Working Class Birth Control in Wilhelmine Germany." *Comparative Studies in Society and History* 20 (1978), pp. 408-28.

Peel, J., and Dowse, R. E. "The Politics of Birth Control." *Political Studies* 13 (1965), pp. 181-97.

Rover, Constance. *Love Morals and the Feminists.* London: Routledge & Kegan Paul, 1970.

Rowbotham, Sheila. *A New World for Women: Stella Browne, Socialist Feminist.* London: Pluto, 1977.

Showalter, Elaine, and Showalter, English. "Victorian Women and Menstruation." In Vicinus, Martha (ed.), *Suffer and Be Still.* Bloomington: Indiana University Press, 1972.

Sigsworth, E. M., and Wyke, T. J. "A Study of Victorian Prostitution and Venereal Disease." In Vicinus, Martha (ed.), *Suffer and Be Still.* Bloomington: Indiana University Press, 1972.

Smith, F. Barry. "Sexuality in Britain, 1800-1900: Some Suggested Revisions." In Vicinus, Martha (ed.), *A Widening Sphere.* Bloomington: Indiana University Press, 1977.

Smith, Hilda. "Gynecology and Ideology in Seventeenth Century England." In Carroll, Berenice (ed.), *Liberating Women's History.* Urbana: University of Illinois Press, 1976.

Smith-Rosenberg, Carroll. "Puberty to Menopause: The Cycle of Femininity in Nineteenth-Century America." *Feminist Studies* 1 (3/4), 1972/73, pp. 58-72.

Stella Browne, F. W. "Women and Birth Control." In Paul, Eden, and Paul, Cedar (eds.), *Population and Birth Control.* New York: Critic and Guide, 1917.

Stopes, Marie. *Married Love.* New York: Putnam, 1939.

———. *Wise Parenthood.* London: Fifield, 1919.

Sussman, George. "The Wet-Nursing Business in Nineteenth Century France." *French Historical Studies* 9 (1975), pp. 304-23.

Tilly, Louise; Scott, Joan; and Cohen, Miriam. "Women's Work and European Fertility Patterns." *Journal of Interdisciplinary History* 6 (1976), pp. 447-76.

Trudgill, Eric. *Madonnas and Magdalens: The Orgins and Development of Victorian Sexual Ideas.* New York: Holmes & Meier, 1976.

Walkowitz, Judith R. "Notes on the History of Victorian Prostitution." *Feminist Studies* 1 (1/2), 1972/73, pp. 105-14.

Walkowitz, Judith, and Walkowitz, Daniel J. "We Are Not Beasts of the Field: Prostitution and the Poor in Plymouth and Southampton Under the Contagious Diseases Acts." In Hartman, Mary S., and Banner, Lois (eds.), *Clio's Consciousness Raised.* New York: Harper & Row, 1974.

Wertz, Richard W., and Wertz, Dorothy C. *Lying-In: A History of Childbirth in America.* New York: Schocken, 1977.

Wood, Ann. "Fashionable Diseases: Women's Complaints and Their Treatment in 19th Century America." In Hartman, Mary S., and Banner, Lois (eds.), *Clio's Consciousness Raised.* New York: Harper & Row, 1974.

Index

Abortion, 88, 90, 91, 106, 181, 202-14, 218-19
Abortion Law Reform Association (Great Britain), 211
Adler, Dr. Victor, 97
Agriculture. See Work
Alcoholism, 60, 69, 80, 124, 126, 128. See also Temperance
Arbeiter-Zeitung (Workers' Newspaper, Austria), 96
Arbeiterinnen-Zeitung (Women Workers' Newspaper, Austria), 22, 94, 96, 98, 126
Artificial feeding, 157-61, 170
Aryan race, 105-10. See also Nazism
Attitudes toward women, xiii, xviii
Austria, 20-23, 88, 91-99, 118, 126-31, 165-68

Baader, Ottilie, 88
Baby-farming, 78
Baby feeding, 157-61
Becker, Lydia, 57
Bedborough, George, 229
Belgium, 190-93
Birth control, 88-89, 106, 201, 202-17, 220-22
Birth control clinics, 106, 203-05, 214-17
Birth Control News (Great Britain), 205
Birth rate, 105, 169, 182, 194, 202, 205, 218, 219
Bolsheviks, 90, 110, 176
Boschek, Anna, 22, 97
Breast feeding, 157-58, 160-61
Browne, F.W. Stella, 181, 211-14
Brunhilde, 107
Budgets. See Working-class women
Bund Deutscher Frauenvereine (Federation of German Women's Associations), 107
Bund für Mutterschutz und Sexualreform (Society for the Protection of Motherhood and Sexual Reform, Germany), 168-69, 171, 205

Butler, Josephine E., 1, 222-29, 232
Cahier Féministes (Belgium), 190
Capitalism, 56, 89, 91, 115, 176-77
Cauer, Minna, 98
Chaperones. See Single women
Charitable activities, xviii, 2, 8, 33, 36, 47, 51, 60
"Charter of Reforms," 23-26. See also Women's Co-operative Guild
Childbed (puerperal) fever. See Pregnancy
Childbirth. See Pregnancy
Childhood, 117-31; child care, 90-91, 165-68, 176-80; child labor, 4, 14, 16, 117-19, 129-30; child rearing, 157-61, 163-80; child rescue, 60, 81, 122-26; day care centers (nurseries, crèches), 90, 164, 168, 174, 176, 218, 219; employment, 4, 14, 16, 117-19, 129-30; middle- and upper-class, 118-22; minimum age for work, 118; moral endangerment, 122-24, 221-29; physical and sexual abuse, 122-31, 221-29; working class, 117-18, 122-31, 142-43, 226-27. See also Education; Nutrition
Child selling, 223, 227
Civil service jobs. See Work, clerical
Clothes, 15, 55-56, 126, 129, 130, 133, 148, 227. See also Health
Coitus interruptus. See Birth control
Communism and the Family. See Kollontai, Alexandra
Communist Party of the Soviet Union, 99-103, 176-80
Concentration camps (Nazi Germany), 92, 107, 111, 113
Contagious Diseases Acts (Great Britain), 222-29
Contraception. See Birth control
Contraceptive devices. See Birth control
Co-operatives, 19, 23-26, 38-39, 162
Courtship and marriage. See Single women
Cult of domesticity, 163. See also Motherhood

Day care centers. *See* Childhood
"The Declaration of the Rights of
Women." *See* Gouges, Olympe de
Deutsche Textilarbeiter-Verband
(German Textile Workers' Union),
161, 199
Diaphragm. *See* Birth control
Diehl, Guida (Newland Movement),
106–07
Diet. *See* Nutrition
Divorce, 80, 90, 91, 135, 151
*Dokumente der Frauen (Women's
Documents*, Austria), 165
Domestic service. *See* Work
Double sexual standard, 220–221,
222–23, 225–26
Downright, Dora, 67–71
Dowry, 133
Dress reform. *See* Health
Drug abuse, 185, 213
Duncan, Isadora, 188
"Dutch" method of birth control. *See*
Birth control
Dutch Women's Suffrage Society, 214

Economic rights of women, 85–86
Education, 59, 60, 67, 84, 129, 134,
176–77, 179, 190; compulsory,
117–18, 126, 129, 130; elementary,
80, 94, 118, 130, 142–43; for work,
29–30, 31, 34–36, 37–40, 44, 46,
47–49, 51, 90, 221, 227; home
education, 119–23, 190; parental
attitudes toward, 118, 129, 130;
school boards, 60, 67; secondary, 80,
134; university, 30, 96, 134–35, 234
Employment. *See* Work
Engels, Friedrich, 89
English Woman's Journal (Great
Britain), 1, 2, 31, 32–34, 51, 53, 151,
187
Equal pay for equal work. *See* Work
Equal rights for women, 32, 63–67,
100
The Ethical Society (Austria), 97

Factories. *See* Work
Family law, 60
Feminism (first feminist movement),
xv, xix-xxi, 30, 40, 50–51, 58, 59–86,
104–05, 107, 111, 151, 163, 164–65,
171, 190, 212, 214, 222; woman
movement (women's movement),
168, 174. *See* also Socialist feminists

*La Femme de L'Avenir (The Woman
of the Future*, France), 10
Fertilization, 190, 191–92
Fickert, Auguste, 96
Fighting Women's Union for
National Socialism (Nazi
Germany), 107
First International Conference of
Socialist Women (*1907*), 88
Food. *See* Nutrition
Forced feeding, 72–75
France, 9–12, 43–45, 62–67, 79–81, 87,
118–26, 134, 141–45, 164, 169,
183–84, 204
Frauendienst ("Nazi" Women's
Service, Germany), 112
Free love, 220–22, 229–32
French Association for Child Rescue
(Union Française pour le Sauvetage
de L'Enfance), 122–26
French Revolution, 59, 62–67, 95

General Austrian Women's
Association, 96–98
General German Women's
Association, 38, 53, 107
German Evangelical Women's
Federation, 47, 48
Germany, 18–19, 31, 37–42, 47–49,
53–56, 67, 84, 85, 91–92, 104–15,
134–35, 139–41, 161–62, 167, 168–71,
181, 183–84, 199–201, 204, 205–10,
232–36
Goebbles, Josef, 111
Gouges, Olympe de, 62–63
Governesses, 9, 30, 34
Great Britain, xvi, 5–8, 18, 23–26,
30–37, 42–43, 45–46, 51–52, 57,
67–78, 115, 135–38, 151–55, 157–61,
164, 169, 181, 187–90, 193–99,
203–05, 210–14, 222–32

Health, 182–201, 222–29; dress reform,
184–85; in workplace and
sanitation, 4–8, 23–26, 27, 112,
199–201; obstetrics and gynecology,
182, 185–87, 194–99; physical
education, 187–90. *See also*
Nutrition; Pregnancy
Heller factory (Austria), 22
Heynrichs, Jenny, 53
Hirschfeld, Magnus, 232
Hitler, Adolf, 104–07, 110
Holland, 57, 81–82, 190, 204, 214–17

Home education. *See* Education
Home industry. *See* Work
Housework, 89–91, 102, 115, 146–57, 184, 194, 196, 197, 198–99
Housing. *See* Middle- and upper-class women; Working-class women

Illegitimacy, 77–78, 142–44, 221
Incest, 223, 227
Industrialization and modernization, xvi, xvii–xviii, 2, 4, 105, 117, 132, 146–47, 150
Infant mortality, 118, 157, 159, 169, 170
International Alliance of Women (IAW, formerly the International Woman Suffrage Alliance, later the International Alliance of Women for Suffrage and Equal Citizenship), 71–72, 84, 85, 86, 214
International Congress of Women (The Hague, *1915*), 57, 81–84
International Congress of Women's Work and Institutions (Paris, *1890*), 123
International Council of Women (ICW), 71–72, 81
International Socialist Workers' Congress (Zurich, *1893*), 91, 92
International Women's League for Peace and Freedom, 111, 112
Italy, 27, 147

Jacobs, Dr. Aletta H., 57, 81, 204, 214–17
Jameson, Anna, 35, 50–52, 53
Jews in Nazi Germany, 106, 107, 110
Jüdischer Frauenbund (League of Jewish Women, Germany), 107
Jus Suffragii The International Woman Suffrage News, 13–17, 81–84

Kautsky, Karl, 91
Kautsky, Louise, 91–92
Kergomard, Pauline, 121
Key, Ellen, 171, 172
Kienle, Dr. Else, 181
King, Gertrude J., 37
Kollontai, Alexandra, 89–90, 115, 176
Krause, E., 233–36
Krol, Mrs. "Nellie" van, 190

Labor unions. *See* Work
Lactation. *See* Breast feeding

Ladies National Association (Great Britain), 187, 223
Lang, Marie, 96–98
Lenin, N. (Vladimir Ilyich Ulianov), 100–01
Lesbianism, 222, 232–36
Liddle, Helen Gordon, 72
Living alone. *See* Single Women
Living conditions. *See* Middle- and upper-class women; Working-class women
Lloyd George, David, 76
Local government, women in, 57, 60, 67, 75–78
London Society for Returning Women as Guardians (Great Britain), 70

Maier, Anna, 93–95
Malthusian League (Great Britain), 210
Manchester Education Committee (Great Britain), 78
Manchester Women's Suffrage Society (Great Britain), 75
Marcuse, Dr. Max, 204, 205–06
Marriage, 146–51, 163–65, 229–32; changing patterns of, 163–65; expectations about, 54, 163–65; middle-class, 146–51; rates of, 146–51, 163–65; working-class, 146–51. *See also* Single women
Married women, 2, 146–51, 161–63; family, 79–80, 146–62, 176–80; multiple home and work responsibilities, 4–8, 19, 91, 104, 115, 146–48, 150, 161–62; parttime work, 146–48; "perfect" wife, 29, 115, 155; property rights, 66, 79, 86; rights within marriage, 86, 90, 99; right to their own name, 90; right to their own residence, 90; servants, 141, 149, 151–55, 166–67; wife-beating, 127; work, 4–8, 20, 34, 112–13, 146–48, 161–62. *See also* Childhood; Housework; Motherhood
Martineau, Harriet, 135–37
Marx, Karl, 97
Marxism, 87–89, 91–92, 93–103
Marxist feminists. *See* Socialist feminists
Maternity leave. *See* Pregnancy

Mayreder, Rosa, 97, 98, 165
Menarche, 184
Mensinga, Dr., 215
Menstruation (and menstrual cycle),
  185, 231
Middle- and upper-class women,
  xvii–xix; family, 79, 80, 146–62,
  176–80; housing, 41–42, 183–84;
  meaning of work, 50–54; politics,
  57–86; servants, 141, 149, 151–55,
  166–67; work, 29–55. See also
  Abortion; Birth control; Charitable
  activities; Education; Marriage
Midwives. See Pregnancy
Migration, 130–31, 132–33, 142, 143
Miscarriages. See Pregnancy
Modernization. See Industrialization
  and modernization
Morality, higher standard of women's,
  xviii, 37
Morgenstern, Lina, 98
Motherhood, cult of (motherliness),
  157–61, 163–80. See also Married
  women; Pregnancy
Mueller, Paula, 47

National Congress of Russian
  Women, 14
National Socialist Women's
  Association (NS Frauenschaft,
  Germany), 107
Nazism (National Socialism,
  Germany), 104–14
Nazism and women (Germany), xv,
  104–14
Neue Bahnen (New Paths, Germany),
  53, 139
Die neue Zeit (The New Time,
  Germany), 96–97
Nightingale, Florence, 35
Nurina, Fanni, 99
Nurseries (crèches). See Childhood
Nutrition, 5–8, 15–16, 24, 157–61, 164,
  170, 194, 196, 198

Obstetrics and gynecology. See Health
Otto, Louise, 139
Our Sisters (Great Britain), 42–43, 157

Paid employment. See Work
Pankhurst, Christabel, 75
Pankhurst, Emmeline, 72, 75–78
Pankhurst, Dr. Richard, 75
Pankhurst, Sylvia, 75

Paquet-Mille, A., 43
Parkes, Bessie Rayner, 31
Paternity suits, 80
Peace movement, 60, 81–85, 214
Perlen, Frieda, 111
Physical education. See Health
Pokzovskaia, Dr. M.I., 13
Poor law guardians (Great Britain),
  60, 67–71, 75–78
Popp, Adelheid Dworschak, 21, 93,
  97–98, 126–31
Pregnancy, 69, 168–71, 182–87,
  190–201, 215; abdominal injuries,
  168–71, 193–201; childbed
  (puerperal) fever, 95, 186–87;
  childbirth, 142, 182, 184, 185–87,
  192–99, 201; difficulties during,
  185–87, 194–201; lying in, 170, 182,
  185–87, 194–201; maternity benefits,
  4, 88, 168–71, 176–80, 187, 193–201;
  midwives, 185–86, 196, 203, 207,
  209; miscarriages, 194–98, 202–04,
  205–11; numbers of, 194–99, 202–04,
  205–11, 215; placenta, 186, 192;
  post-natal period, 168–71; prenatal
  care, 168–71; still births, 194, 206;
  varicose veins, 199, 200, 201;
  womb, 185–86, 191–92; work, 77,
  194–201. See also Work
Principles of the National Socialist
  Women's Organizations (Nazi
  Germany), 109–10
Prostitution, 9, 17, 60, 81, 86, 96, 98,
  122, 133, 214, 221, 222–28, 230, 231,
  232
Protective legislation. See Work

Race-hygiene, 109, 175
Racial deterioration, 71
Russia, xiii, xvi, 12–17, 88–91;
  U.S.S.R., 90–91, 99–103, 176–80,
  217–19
Russian Revolution of 1917, 89, 90
Russian Social Democratic Labor
  Party, 176–80. See also Bolsheviks

Sales work. See Work, clerical
Sauget, Juliette, 141–45
Schlesinger-Eckstein, Therese, 93,
  95–99
Schmidt, Hannah, 111
Seduction, 77–78, 221–22, 224–27
Seidl, Amalie, 20–23
Sex education, 190–93, 195, 197

Sexual exploitation, 4, 16-17, 133, 225-26, 228, 230
Sexual freedom, 105, 212-13, 222, 229-31
Sexual intercourse, 190, 220-21, 231
Sexual morality, 133-34, 216, 218, 220-32
Sexuality, 133-34, 169, 212-13, 221-22, 229, 230-236
Shop Assistants' Trade Union (Great Britain), 23, 25
Single women, 2, 132, 45; chaperones, 137-38; courtship and marriage, 132-35; entertainment, 10, 15, 133-35; family, 132-45; living alone, 138-41; parental authority, 133; personal independence, 43, 132-35; work, 4-5, 8-12, 14-15, 20, 29, 34, 53-54, 76, 114, 132-35, 141-45. *See also* Widowhood
Social reform and social welfare, 58, 59-61, 122-26, 222-29
Social work, 47-49
Socialism (Social Democracy), 19, 22, 23, 27, 56, 87-89, 91-92, 93-103, 126, 168, 211-13
Socialist feminists, xv, 88, 91, 93, 211-12
Society for Promoting the Employment of Women (Great Britain), 31-37, 51
Society of Bookbinders (Great Britain), 18
Society of Dressmakers, Milliners and Mantlemakers (Great Britain), 18
Society of Upholstresses (Great Britain), 18
Song of Gudrun, 107-08
Stalin, Josef, 90, 217
Sterilization, 113
Sterilized milk, 164
Stopes, Dr. Marie, 203-04, 205
Strikes. *See* Work
Suffrage, 57-86, 95-96
Sweden, 171-72
Switzerland, 62, 91-92, 155

Technology and mass production, 4, 40, 43, 117, 133
Temperance, 7-8, 60
Textile industry, 3-4, 12-17, 20-23, 55-56, 117, 131, 161-62
Tobacco Workers' Union (Austria), 95

Unemployment (and unemployment insurance), 8-10
Union Française pour le Suffrage des Femmes (French Women's Suffrage Association), 79
Union of Tailoresses, Dressmakers and Allied Trades (Italy), 27
Urbanization, xvi, 132, 133, 138, 149, 150
U.S.S.R. *See* Russia

Venereal disease, 223, 224
Victorian morality, 220, 223

Wages. *See* Work
Well-baby clinics, 164
Wet nurse, 142-45
Widowhood, 29, 77, 95, 135, 139, 141
Wife-beating. *See* Married women
Wollstonecraft, Mary (*Vindication of the Rights of Women*), 59
Woman movement. *See* Feminism
Woman's Penny Paper (Great Britain), 136
Women-centered history, xiii-xiv
Women's Co-operative Guild (Great Britain), 23-26, 193-94, 203, 205
Women's Disabilities Removal Bill (Great Britain), 75
Women's Educational Association of Leipzig (Germany), 37-40
Women's life cycle, xv, 116
Women's movement. *See* Feminism
Women's politics, definition of, 58
Women's Protective Union (Russia), 16
Women's Social and Political Union (W.S.P.U., Great Britain), 72, 75
Women's sources for historical research, xiii-xiv
Work: agricultural, 3-8, 92, 101-03, 142-43; attitudes toward, 29-30, 43-46, 50-55; clerical, 10-12, 23-26, 31-37, 40-42, 133; domestic service, 3-5, 22, 76, 118, 132-33, 142, 143-44, 166-68; employment bureaus for women, 30-37, 48; equal pay for equal work, 14, 86, 90, 93; factories: employment for women in, 12-17, 20-23, 199-201; fines and punishments, 4, 15-16, 24-25; hours, 4, 13, 16; inspectors, 12, 13, 17, 60, 67, 92; working conditions in, 4, 12-17, 20-23, 55-56, 112, 114,

199–201; home industries, 5, 19, 27, 93–94, 130–31, 170; increasing opportunities for, 10–11, 31; labor unions, 18–28, 80, 87–99; numbers of women employed, 2, 13–14, 18–19, 20, 29, 79–80; prejudice against working women, 5, 19, 29–30, 40–43, 104, 112, 114, 200; promoting the employment of women, 29–54, 64, 86, 96, 224, 226–27; protective legislation, 26–27, 81, 88, 90, 91–93; shorter working hours, 20–23, 25, 26–27; skilled work, 3; strikes, 20–23; sweat shops, 4; unskilled work, 12–17, 19–23, 31, 91, 104; varieties of occupations, 3–56; wages, 3, 5–8, 10, 12–17, 20–28, 37, 41–42, 45, 80, 112, 114, 130, 143–44; women's traditional work, xviii, 3–4, 30, 43, 47–49, 51; women's work and

motherhood, 47, 163–65, 168–71. *See also* Pregnancy
Workhouses, 8–10, 67–71, 76–78
Working-class women, xix–xx; family, 161–65, 168–71, 176–80; family budgets, 14–15, 148, 198; housing (living conditions), 5, 10, 17, 24, 127, 131, 183, 196; meaning of work, 50, 55–56; single, 8–17, 132–35, 142–45; work, 3–28, 31, 55–56, 193–201; working conditions, 3–23, 26–28, 55–56, 193–201. *See also* Abortion; Birth control; Childhood; Education; Pregnancy; Work
World War I, 81–84, 105, 145, 187, 193, 205
World War II, 91, 187

Zhenotdel (Women's Bureau, U.S.S.R.), 90, 100, 176